Learning iPhone Programming

Learning iPhone Programming

Alasdair Allan

Beijing · Cambridge · Farnham · Köln · Sebastopol · Taipei · Tokyo

Learning iPhone Programming
by Alasdair Allan

Published by O'Reilly Media, Inc., 1005 Gravenstein Highway North, Sebastopol, CA 95472.

O'Reilly books may be purchased for educational, business, or sales promotional use. Online editions are also available for most titles (*http://my.safaribooksonline.com*). For more information, contact our corporate/institutional sales department: 800-998-9938 or *corporate@oreilly.com*.

Editor: Brian Jepson
Production Editor: Sarah Schneider
Copyeditor: Audrey Doyle
Proofreader: Kiel Van Horn

Indexer: Seth Maislin
Cover Designer: Karen Montgomery
Interior Designer: David Futato
Illustrator: Robert Romano

Printing History:

| March 2010: | First Edition. |

RepKover™

This book uses RepKover™, a durable and flexible lay-flat binding.

ISBN: 978-0-596-80643-9

[M]

1267220348

Table of Contents

Preface

The arrival of the iPhone changed everything. Or, at the very least, it changed the direction of software development for mobile platforms, which is a pretty big thing. It spawned an entire generation of copycat devices and shook an entire multibillion-dollar industry to its knees. Despite this, it still fits in your pocket.

Who Should Read This Book?

This book gives a rapid introduction to programming for the iPhone and iPod touch for those with some programming experience. If you are developing on the Mac for the first time, drawn to the platform because of the iPhone, or alternatively you are an experienced Mac programmer making the transition to the iPhone, this book is for you.

What Should You Already Know?

The book assumes some knowledge of C, or at least passing knowledge of a C-derived language. Additionally, while I do give a crash course, some familiarity with object-oriented programming concepts would be helpful.

What Will You Learn?

This book will guide you through developing your first application for the iPhone, from opening Xcode for the first time to submitting your application to the App Store. You'll learn about Objective-C and the core frameworks needed to develop for the iPhone by writing applications that use them, giving you a basic framework for building your own applications independently.

What's in This Book?

Here's a short summary of the chapters in this book and what you'll find inside:

Chapter 1, *Why Go Native?*
> This chapter discusses the need for native applications and compares building native applications to building web applications.

Chapter 2, *Becoming a Developer*
> This chapter walks you through the process of registering as an iPhone developer and setting up your work environment, from installing Xcode and the iPhone SDK to generating the developer certificates you'll need to build your applications and deploy them onto your own iPhone or iPod touch.

Chapter 3, *Your First iPhone App*
> This chapter allows you to get hands-on as quickly as possible and walks you through building your first Hello World application, including how to deploy and run the application on your iPhone or iPod touch.

Chapter 4, *Coding in Objective-C*
> This chapter provides a crash course in the basics of the Objective-C language, and if you're familiar with another C-derived language (and perhaps with object-oriented programming), it should be enough to get you up and running with Objective-C and the Cocoa Touch frameworks.

Chapter 5, *Table-View-Based Applications*
> The `UITableView` and associated classes are perhaps the most commonly used classes when building user interfaces for iPhone or iPod touch applications. Due to the nature of the applications, these classes can be used to solve a large cross section of problems, and as a result they appear almost everywhere. In this chapter, we dive fairly deeply into the table view classes.

Chapter 6, *Other View Controllers*
> After discussing the table view controller in detail, we discuss some of the other view controllers and classes that will become useful when building your applications: simple two-screen views, single-screen tabbed views, modal view controllers, and a view controller for selecting video and images.

Chapter 7, *Connecting to the Network*
> This chapter discusses connecting to the Internet, browsing the Web, sending email, and retrieving information.

Chapter 8, *Handling Data*
> This chapter discusses how to handle data input, both from the application user and programmatically, and how to parse XML and JSON documents. The chapter also covers storing data in flat files and storing data with the SQLite database engine.

Chapter 9, *Distributing Your Application*

This chapter talks about how to add some final polish to your application and walks you through the process of building your application for distribution, either via ad hoc distribution or for the App Store.

Chapter 10, *Using Sensors*

This chapter discusses how to determine what hardware is available and illustrates how to deal with the major sensors on the iPhone and iPod touch: the accelerometer, magnetometer, camera, and GPS.

Chapter 11, *Geolocation and Mapping*

This chapter walks you through the process of building applications that make use of the Core Location and MapKit frameworks.

Chapter 12, *Integrating Your Application*

This chapter shows you some of the tricks to integrate your application with the iPhone's software ecosystem, how to present user preferences with Settings Bundles, and how to use custom URL schemes to launch your application. It also discusses how to make use of the Media Player and Address Book.

Chapter 13, *Other Native Platforms*

This chapter deals with the PhoneGap and MonoTouch platforms for building native applications for the iPhone and iPod touch that can be sold on the App Store. The chapter then walks you through the installation process and building your first Hello World application for both platforms.

Chapter 14, *Going Further*

This chapter provides a collection of pointers to more advanced material on the topics we covered in the book, and material covering some of those topics that we didn't manage to talk about in the book.

Conventions Used in This Book

The following typographical conventions are used in this book:

Italic

Indicates new terms, URLs, email addresses, filenames, and file extensions

`Constant width`

Used for program listings, as well as within paragraphs to refer to program elements such as variable or function names, databases, data types, environment variables, statements, and keywords

`Constant width bold`

Shows commands or other text that should be typed literally by the user

`Constant width italic`

Shows text that should be replaced with user-supplied values or by values determined by context

This icon signifies a tip, suggestion, or general note.

 This icon signifies a warning or caution.

Using Code Examples

This book is here to help you get your job done. In general, you may use the code in this book in your programs and documentation. You do not need to contact us for permission unless you're reproducing a significant portion of the code. For example, writing a program that uses several chunks of code from this book does not require permission. Selling or distributing a CD-ROM of examples from O'Reilly books does require permission. Answering a question by citing this book and quoting example code does not require permission. Incorporating a significant amount of example code from this book into your product's documentation does require permission.

We appreciate, but do not require, attribution. An attribution usually includes the title, author, publisher, and ISBN. For example: "*Learning iPhone Programming*, by Alasdair Allan. Copyright 2010 Alasdair Allan, 978-0-596-80643-9."

If you feel your use of code examples falls outside fair use or the permission given here, feel free to contact us at *permissions@oreilly.com*.

How to Contact Us

Please address comments and questions concerning this book to the publisher:

O'Reilly Media, Inc.
1005 Gravenstein Highway North
Sebastopol, CA 95472
800-998-9938 (in the United States or Canada)
707-829-0515 (international or local)
707-829-0104 (fax)

We have a web page for this book, where we list errata, examples, and any additional information. You can access this page at:

http://oreilly.com/catalog/9780596806439

Supplementary materials are also available at:

http://www.learningiphoneprogramming.com/

To comment or ask technical questions about this book, send email to:

bookquestions@oreilly.com

For more information about our books, conferences, Resource Centers, and the O'Reilly Network, see our website at:

http://www.oreilly.com

Safari® Books Online

Safari Books Online is an on-demand digital library that lets you easily search over 7,500 technology and creative reference books and videos to find the answers you need quickly.

With a subscription, you can read any page and watch any video from our library online. Read books on your cell phone and mobile devices. Access new titles before they are available for print, and get exclusive access to manuscripts in development and post feedback for the authors. Copy and paste code samples, organize your favorites, download chapters, bookmark key sections, create notes, print out pages, and benefit from tons of other time-saving features.

O'Reilly Media has uploaded this book to the Safari Books Online service. To have full digital access to this book and others on similar topics from O'Reilly and other publishers, sign up for free at *http://my.safaribooksonline.com*.

Acknowledgments

Books do not write themselves, but a book is also not the work of just a single person, despite what it may say on the front cover. I'd like to thank my editor, Brian Jepson. His hard work and constant prodding made the book better than it might otherwise have been. I'd also like to offer more than thanks to my long-suffering wife, Gemma Hobson. Without her support, encouragement, and willingness to make those small (and sometimes larger) sacrifices that an author's spouse has to make, this book wouldn't be in your hands today. Thank you. Finally to my son, Alex, who is as yet too young to do more than chew on the cover, daddy's home. I can only hope for your sake that O'Reilly uses tasty paper.

CHAPTER 1

Why Go Native?

When the iPhone was introduced, there was no native SDK. Apple claimed that one wasn't needed and that applications for the device should be built as web applications using JavaScript, CSS, and HTML. This didn't go down well with the developer community; they wanted direct access to the hardware and integration with Apple's own applications.

Only a few months after the iPhone's release, the open source community had accomplished something that many thought impossible. Despite Apple locking the device down, developers had gained access, reverse-engineered the SDK, and gone on to build a free open source tool chain that allowed them to build native applications for the device. At one point, it was estimated that more than one-third of the iPhones on the market had been "jail broken" by their users, allowing them to run these unsanctioned third-party applications.

This open source development effort is ongoing today, and if you want to know more, I recommend *iPhone Open Application Development*, Second Edition (*http://oreilly .com/catalog/9780596155209/*) by Jonathan Zdziarski (O'Reilly). However, the book you hold in your hands isn't about the open source "hacker" SDK, because in March 2008 Apple publicly changed its mind and released the first version of the native SDK to a waiting developer community. Whether this release was in response to this effort, or perhaps because it was (the notoriously secretive) Apple's plan all along, we'll probably never know.

The Pros and Cons

When the native SDK was introduced, a number of people in the industry argued that it was actually a step backward for developers. They felt that web-based applications, especially once home screen icons for these applications arrived on the 1.1.3 firmware, were good enough. By writing code specifically for the iPhone in Objective-C, you were making it more difficult to port your applications, and porting a web application more or less consisted of simply restyling it using a new CSS template.

It seemed that the users of the applications disagreed. It's arguable why this is the case, but it's very hard to make native-looking web applications that can be reused across many different platforms, though it is possible. Just as applications on the Mac desktop that have been ported from Windows tend to stand out like a sore thumb by not quite working as the user expects, web applications, especially those that are intended to be used across different platforms, tend to do the same.

If you integrate your application into the iPhone ecosphere, make use of the possibilities that the phone offers, and optimize your user interface (UI) for the device, the user experience is much improved. It's also really hard to write web applications that work well when you need to design for a smaller screen, implying as it does a simpler UI and less exposed functionality, without using native controls.

Why Write Native Applications?

The obvious reason to use the native SDK is to do things that you can't do on the Web. The first generation of augmented reality applications is a case in point; these needed close integration with the iPhone's onboard sensors (e.g., GPS, accelerometer, digital compass, and camera) and wouldn't have been possible without that access. Although the iPhone's Safari browser supports the new geolocation capabilities HTML 5 provides (*http://www.w3.org/TR/geolocation-API/*), this doesn't alleviate the problem entirely. It's doubtful that all platform-specific hardware is going to get the same sort of treatment, so it's unlikely that you will see the arrival of augmented reality web applications.

> If you are coming from a web development background, you may be interested in the cross-platform PhoneGap framework (*http://phonegap .com/*). This framework provides native wrapper classes and allows you to build native applications in HTML/JavaScript on a range of mobile platforms. One of the platforms it targets is the iPhone. I talk about PhoneGap, and the other alternative native development platforms for the iPhone, in Chapter 13.

Sometimes it's not about doing things that can't be done; it's about doing things faster, and doing client-side error handling. For instance, the Apple iTunes and App Store applications that are provided with the iPhone are actually web applications wrapped inside native applications. Just like the iTunes Store on the Mac, the main display you see is a web page, but the surrounding infrastructure is a native application. This means that while the application can't do a lot without an Internet connection, it can at least start up.

But those are extreme examples. A lot of the applications in the App Store combine remote data and native interfaces. Without access to the network, some of the UI is generally disabled. However, native applications can be built to degrade gracefully when the device's network connection disappears or if it was never present in the first place. The user can still use the bits of the application that don't need a network connection to work.

Sometimes it's also about what an application doesn't need. If it doesn't need a network connection, the idea that your phone needs to be connected to the network to use it, sucking extra battery power in the process, is wasteful. Even when it is connected, the device isn't always connected to a fast Internet connection. Anything you can do to minimize the amount of data you need to suck down the data connection will improve users' interaction with your application. That means generating your UI locally, and populating it with data pulled from the Internet.

Network performance will affect the user's perception of speed; rendering your UI while a web request is made to populate it allows your application to remain responsive to user interaction even while it's waiting for the network. That can only be a good thing.

I haven't even mentioned game development yet, and with Apple pitching the iPod touch as "the funnest iPod ever," that's important. You cannot develop the sorts of games now starting to appear on the App Store using web-based technologies. While this book covers the basics of how to program for the iPhone or iPod touch, if you want to delve deeply into game programming on the platform, I recommend *iPhone Game Development (http://oreilly.com/catalog/9780596159863/)* by Paul Zirkle and Joe Hogue (O'Reilly).

The Release Cycle

Paul Graham, one of my favorite dispensers of wisdom, argues that the arrival of web-based software has changed not just the user experience, but the developer experience as well:

> One of the most important changes in this new world is the way you do releases. In the desktop software business, doing a release is a huge trauma, in which the whole company sweats and strains to push out a single, giant piece of code. Obvious comparisons suggest themselves, both to the process and the resulting product.
>
> —From "The Other Road Ahead" by Paul Graham

He is exactly right. Working in the cloud, you rarely make a software release in the old sense of the word. Despite the benefits, I must admit I actually somewhat miss the "big push" where, usually with a great deal of trepidation, you roll out a new, improved version of a piece of software. However, one problem with writing native applications is that we've made a return to the release cycle.

With web-based software you can make incremental releases, fixing bugs when and if they occur. Native applications are far more like desktop software.

I cover the details of how to submit applications to the App Store in Chapter 10. However, you should prepare yourself now for some amount of pain. The review process is notoriously opaque, and it can (and does) take time. Plus, each of your applications must go through it, not just when you initially submit it to the store, but also for each new version you release. Typically, it can take up to 14 days from submitting your application for it to be approved (or rejected) by the review team, although it can take much longer. Based on my experience, although some of my applications have sailed through the submission process in only a couple of days, I have had applications in the review process for up to four months before receiving approval.

Build It and They Will Come

Of course, the big advantage, even with today's crowded App Store, is exposure. If nobody can find your application, nobody can pay for it, and the Web is a big place. One big advantage a native application has over a web application is that it's easier for potential users to find, and much easier to pay for when they find it. That is, if you can get people to pay for web applications at all. People don't impulse-subscribe to a web service; they impulse-buy from the App Store.

However, don't assume that if you build it, users will appear. Unless you're really lucky and your application goes viral, you still need to market your application. The App Store may be a lot smaller than the Web, but it's still a pretty big place.

Marketing your application is like marketing any product; you need to make use of the tools available and your contacts to get news of your software to your target market. Apple provides promotional codes for your application (although at the time of this writing, these work only on the U.S. App Store) that will give free downloads of your applications. Many developers reach out to high-profile blogs or the many application catalog sites and offer them review copies in hopes that they will publicize the application. If it's well designed and useful, they might well be interested in reviewing it.

Produce a screencast showing how your application works and how to use it. Also, applications with good support resources (such as forums and trouble-ticket systems) sell more copies. Applications with good design stand out in the store and sell more copies.

Good design often means that you do things "the Apple way." Integrate your application well with the other applications on the phone. Don't reinvent the wheel: use the standard widgets and UI elements familiar to iPhone users.

CHAPTER 2

Becoming a Developer

Before you start writing code, you need to do some housekeeping. First, you'll need to install Xcode, Apple's development environment, as well as the iPhone SDK. Both of these are available directly from Apple, although you may already have Xcode on your Mac OS X install DVD. However, before you can install the iPhone SDK, you'll have to register with Apple as a developer. If you enroll in one of the developer programs, you'll also need to create, download, and install a number of certificates and profiles to allow you to deploy your applications onto your iPhone or iPod touch. Let's get these housekeeping tasks out of the way now so that you can get to the interesting bit—the code—as quickly as you can.

 Developing applications for the iPhone requires an Intel Mac running Mac OS X 10.5 (Leopard) or later.

Registering As an iPhone Developer

Before you can develop for the iPhone, you need to become a registered iPhone developer so that you can download and install the iPhone SDK. This will give you access to the SDK and allow you to build and test your applications in iPhone Simulator.

If you take it a step further and enroll in the iPhone Developer Standard or Enterprise Program (both of these have a yearly fee), you'll be able to test applications on your own iPhone or iPod touch. We will discuss how to enroll in these programs in the next section.

If you choose the free account, you won't be able to install your applications onto your own iPhone or iPod touch, nor will you be able to sell applications on Apple's App Store (Standard Program) or distribute them to people within your own company (Enterprise Program). If you stick with a free account, you also won't have access to prerelease versions of the iPhone SDK or the iPhone OS.

You can sign up at *http://developer.apple.com/iphone/*.

If you are an existing Apple Developer Connection (ADC) member, or if you have an iTunes or MobileMe account, you can use your existing Apple ID to register as an iPhone developer. However, if you intend to sell software commercially, you may want to create a new identity for use with the program to keep it separate from your existing Apple ID.

You'll initially be asked to either choose an existing Apple ID or create a new one. If you create a new one, you'll be asked for some details (e.g., email and physical addresses); if you choose an existing Apple ID, you'll still need to confirm some of these details, although they should be filled in with the most recent information Apple has.

You'll also be asked to provide a professional profile, indicating what sort of applications you'll be developing and whether you also develop for other mobile platforms.

Finally, you'll need to agree to the developer license. After you do, a verification code may be sent to the email address you registered with Apple, although this doesn't happen in all cases. However, if this happens to you, the final step of registering as an iPhone developer will be to verify your email address.

Apple Websites

You'll use four main websites as part of the iPhone development process:

The iPhone Dev Center (http://developer.apple.com/iphone/)
> This site is where you can get access to the latest versions of the iPhone SDK, along with background technical information, API documentation, sample code, and instructional videos. You need to be a registered iPhone developer to access the site.

The Developer Program Portal (http://developer.apple.com/iphone/manage/overview/index.action)
> This site is where you can generate and manage the certificates, provisioning profiles, approved devices, and other housekeeping tasks necessary to test your applications on the iPhone and iPod touch and prepare them for distribution. You'll need to be both a registered iPhone developer and enrolled in one of the iPhone Developer Programs to access this site.

The App Store Resource Center (http://developer.apple.com/iphone/appstore/)
> This site provides help and advice on how to distribute your application on the App Store, including preparing your app for submission, understanding the App Store approval process, and learning how to manage your apps on the App Store. You'll need to be both a registered iPhone developer and enrolled in the iPhone Developer Standard Program to access this site.

iTunes Connect (https://itunesconnect.apple.com/)
> This site provides you with the tools to manage your applications on the iTunes App Store and your contracts with Apple. You'll need to be both a registered iPhone developer and enrolled in the iPhone Developer Standard Program to access this site.

Enrolling in the iPhone Developer Program

If you intend to sell your applications on the App Store, or you just want to be able to deploy them onto your own iPhone or iPod touch, you'll also need to enroll in the iPhone Developer Program. If you've not already registered as an iPhone developer, you can do that during this process.

 Your iPhone Developer Program membership lasts for 1 year and can be renewed starting 60 days before the expiration date of your existing membership. If you do not renew your membership, your ability to distribute your applications will be curtailed. In addition, your developer and distribution certificates will be revoked. Finally, any applications you have on the iTunes App Store will be removed.

You have two options when enrolling in the iPhone Developer Program. Most people will want to register for the Standard Program, which costs $99 per year. This will allow you to create free—or, once you've filled out some paperwork, commercial—applications for the iPhone and iPod touch, and distribute them either via the App Store or via the ad hoc distribution channel where you provide both the application binary and a provisioning certificate to the end user.

 Ad hoc distribution allows you to distribute your application directly to your users, bypassing the App Store. However, distribution is limited to just 100 devices during the course of your one-year membership and, at least for the end user, is more complicated than distributing your application via the App Store. It's mainly intended for beta testing programs, and it isn't a substitute for publishing your application to the store. If you need to conduct large-scale rollouts to a specific group of users and you want to avoid the App Store, you should probably look at the Enterprise Program.

The more expensive Enterprise Program, at $299, is intended for companies with more than 500 employees that wish to create applications for in-house distribution. While this program allows you to distribute your applications inside your own company, it does not allow you to publish them for sale on the App Store. If you're thinking about selling your applications to the public, you need the Standard Program.

An iPhone Developer University Program is also available (*http://developer.apple.com/iphone/program/university.html*), but this is designed specifically for higher education institutes looking to introduce iPhone development into their curricula. Unless you're an academic at such an institute, it's unlikely that this program will be applicable to you.

The Apple Developer Connection

As well as enrolling as a member of the iPhone Developer Program, you may also wish to register as a member of the Apple Developer Connection. Doing so is a good idea if you're serious about developing with the Mac, and all but the free membership tiers will give you access to the Software Seeding Program, which provides prerelease copies of both the Mac OS X operating system and Apple's developer tools. You can sign up for ADC at either *http://developer.apple.com* or *https://connect.apple.com*.

Three membership plans are available: a free online membership, the $500 Select membership, and the Premier membership that costs several thousand dollars (although it also includes a ticket to the Apple Worldwide Developers Conference).

Installing the iPhone SDK

Once you have registered as an iPhone developer, you can log in to the iPhone Dev Center and download the iPhone SDK.

 At the time of this writing, Apple combined the iPhone SDK and Xcode into a single download. It is possible that in future releases you may need to install Xcode first, and then install the iPhone SDK from a separate installer.

Newer prerelease beta versions of the SDK may be available to those enrolled in the iPhone Developer Program; however, the current stable version will be available even if you choose not to pay to enroll in the program.

The combined download of the Xcode development tools and the iPhone SDK is around 2.5 GB in size. The combined bundle will be downloaded as a disk image file. After it downloads, the image should automatically mount; double-click on the iPhone SDK and Tools package file to install the SDK, as shown in Figure 2-1.

The installer will ask you to agree to the terms of the software license agreement before prompting you to install the software. You should install it in the suggested location, and the default installation options will include everything you need to develop applications for the iPhone or iPod touch. However, you'll need at least 5.9 GB of free space on your disk to install the Xcode developer tools and the iPhone SDK.

After installation, you can check that everything has gone OK by starting Xcode, which will have been installed in the */Developer/Application* folder on your machine. Project templates should be available for the iPhone OS, as shown in Figure 2-2.

You now have everything you need to write applications and test them in the simulator.

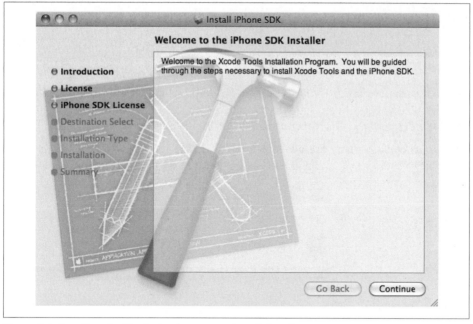

Figure 2-1. Installing the Xcode development tools and the iPhone SDK

If you want to test your code on an actual iPhone, you will need to enroll in either the Standard or Enterprise iPhone Developer Program. However, the amount of time it takes to be accepted into the program varies, so after you enroll and have been accepted, you should bookmark this page and finish the steps in this chapter. You can use iPhone Simulator for the examples in this book while you wait to be accepted.

While the simulator is very good, it's not perfect. Code runs much faster on the simulator than it does on the device. If you're dealing with applications that have a complicated UI or consume a great deal of processor power, the difference in performance between the simulator and the device could become important. On several occasions I've had to go back and rewrite my code and refactor the way in which my UI functions; when I tested my application on the simulator it worked fine, but on real hardware it just ran too slowly. You can also allocate much more memory in the simulator than is available on the real hardware.

Additionally, some frameworks are available to you in the simulator—notably the `NSPredicate` and `NSXMLDocument` classes—that just don't exist on the device. Code that uses these missing classes will compile and run on the simulator, but not on the device. As well as regularly building your application in iPhone Simulator, it's therefore a good idea to do regular device builds. If you accidentally use one of these "missing" classes, it will show up as a link error at compile time for such a build. After all, you don't want to get too far down the road of developing your application only to discover (hours, or

Figure 2-2. The Xcode New Project window

worse yet, days later) that you're using classes or frameworks that aren't actually present on the device.

 Both NSPredicate and NSXMLDocument are commonly used classes. For instance, NSXMLDocument is the class most people programming in Objective-C on the Mac (rather than the iPhone) would use to perform an XQuery on an XML document. The lack of NSXMLDocument is something that most developers notice quite quickly.

While I've seen some complaints that the simulator can sometimes be slightly off on pixel alignment of UIKit elements, I've not yet come across this myself. However, when using lower-level graphics libraries, such as OpenGL ES, the renderer used on the iPhone and iPod touch is slightly different from the one used in the simulator, so when a scene is displayed on the simulator it may not be identical to the actual device at the pixel level.

Additionally, the simulator has some built-in limitations. For instance, if your application's UI is designed to respond to touch events with more than two fingers, you can't test it in the simulator.

While it doesn't allow you to simulate gestures requiring many fingers, iPhone Simulator does allow you to test applications that require two-finger (multitouch) touch gestures. You can use Option-click (for pinch) or Option-Shift-click (for drag) while using the mouse to get two "fingers."

Furthermore, you will not have access to the accelerometer, GPS, Bluetooth, or digital compass when running your application in the simulator. If your application relies on these hardware features, you have no choice but to test it on your device.

Preparing Your iPhone or iPod touch

Before you can install applications onto your iPhone or iPod touch, you must follow a number of steps, and you'll need to do so in the order shown in Figure 2-3.

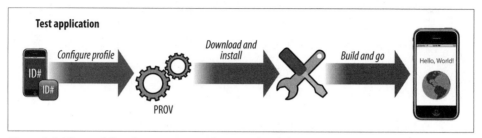

Figure 2-3. The workflow for creating certificates and mobile provisioning profiles

So, if you have enrolled in either the Standard or Enterprise iPhone Developer Program, now is the time to generate the appropriate certificates and provisioning profiles so that you will be able to deploy the test application from the next chapter onto your device.

Certificates and Provisioning Profiles

You must have a development certificate for Xcode to sign your application binaries. This certificate also identifies you as a developer. When you build your iPhone application, Xcode will look in your Mac OS X keychain for this certificate and the corresponding certificate from Apple, called the WWDR Intermediate certificate, which you'll also need to download from the Developer Portal.

Provisioning profiles associate a development certificate, and hence a developer, with a hardware device and an iPhone application ID, which is a unique identifier for your application. To install an application that you've signed with your development certificate onto your iPhone or iPod touch, you need to install the associated provisioning profile onto your device.

Creating a Development Certificate

The first thing you need is a development certificate and Apple's WWDR Intermediate certificate. To request a development certificate from the Developer Portal, you need to generate a certificate-signing request (CSR) using the Keychain Access application.

You can find the Keychain Access application in the */Applications/Utilities* folder. Launch the application and select Keychain Access→Preferences from the menu. Go to the Certificates Preferences pane to confirm that the Online Certificate Status Protocol (OCSP) and Certificate Revocation List (CRL) options are turned off, as shown in Figure 2-4.

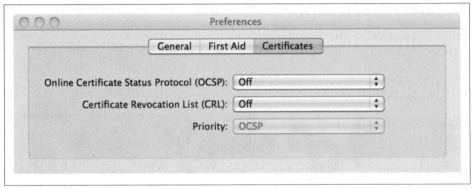

Figure 2-4. The Certificates tab of the Keychain Access application's Preferences pane

Next, select Certificate Assistant→Request a Certificate from a Certificate Authority from the Keychain Access menu, and enter the email address that you selected as your Apple ID during the sign-up process along with your name, as shown in Figure 2-5. Click the "Saved to disk" and the "Let me specify key pair information" radio buttons and then click Continue. You'll be prompted for a filename for your certificate request.

Accept the defaults (a key size of 2,048 bits using the RSA algorithm) and click Continue. The application will proceed to generate a CSR file and save it to disk. The file will be saved to the location you specified when you were prompted to choose a filename (the default is usually your desktop).

Next, log in to the iPhone Dev Center (*http://developer.apple.com/iphone/*) and click on the link to the iPhone Developer Program Portal. This will take you to the main portal used to manage certificates and devices associated with your developer program account.

Click the Certificates link, then go to the Development tab and click Request Certificate. Follow the instructions to upload your CSR file to the portal.

If you joined the iPhone Developer Program as an individual, you now need to approve your own certificate request, again in the Development tab in the Certificates section

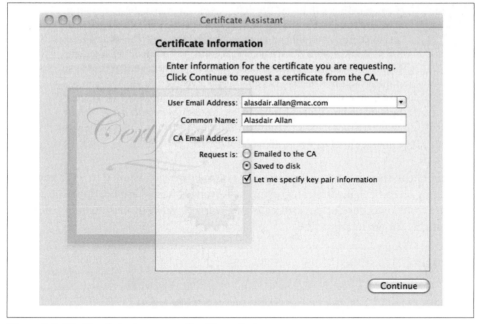

Figure 2-5. The Keychain Access.app Certificate Assistant

of the portal (simply click Approve). If you are part of a development team, your nominated team admin must do this for you.

 If you don't see the Download option appear after you click Approve, click the Development tab link to refresh the page, and it should appear.

Once you do this, you need to download your personal certificate and the WWDR Intermediate certificate and install them in your Mac OS X keychain.

Still in the Development tab, click the Download button to download your personal certificate. Next, right-click on the link to the WWDR Intermediate certificate and save the linked file to disk.

Once both of these certificates have downloaded to your local machine, you need to install them in your Mac OS X keychain. Double-click on the certificate files to install them into your keychain. This will activate the Keychain Access application and ask you to confirm that you want to add the certificates to your Mac OS X keychain.

If you have more than one keychain, you need to make sure the certificates are installed in the default keychain, normally called *login*. The default keychain is highlighted in bold in the list of keychains at the top left of the *Keychain Access.app* application. It's normally best to keep the *login* keychain the default, but if this is not the case you can make it the default by selecting the File→Make Keychain "login" Default option from the menu bar. If the certificates are not installed into the default keychain, Xcode will be unable to find them, and hence will be unable to sign binaries with them. This means you will not be able to install your applications onto your iPhone or iPod touch.

You can check that the two certificates have been correctly installed in your keychain by clicking on the Certificates category in the Keychain Access application. You should see both your own developer certificate and Apple's WWDR certificate in the *login* keychain, as shown in Figure 2-6.

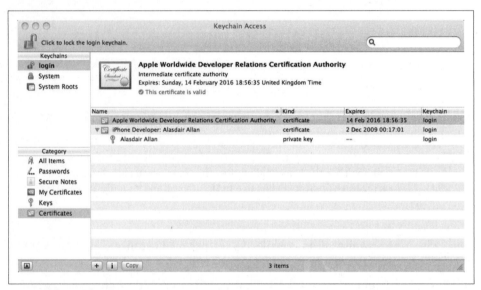

Figure 2-6. The Keychain Access application showing the newly installed certificates necessary for Xcode to sign your binaries and deploy them onto your iPhone

Getting the UDID of Your Development Device

Plug the iPhone or iPod touch you intend to use for development into your Mac. Open Xcode and select the Window→Organizer item from the menu bar. The Organizer window will open, showing the list of connected devices (see Figure 2-7).

You'll need the unique device identifier (UDID) of your development device so that you can create a mobile provisioning profile for this device. Right-click or Ctrl-click on the 40-character string labeled Identifier (see Figure 2-7) and select Copy.

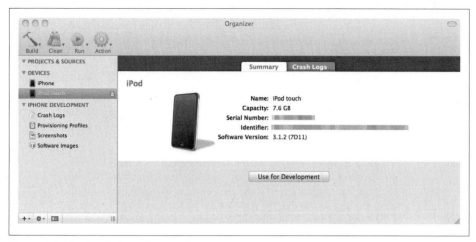

Figure 2-7. The Xcode Organizer window

Return to the iPhone Developer Program Portal, click Devices, and select the Manage tab. Next, click Add Devices. Enter the device name in the appropriate box and the UDID in the box labeled Device ID, and click Submit. You have now registered your device.

Creating an App ID

To install your application onto your iPhone or iPod touch, you will need to create an App ID. This is a unique identifier that the iPhone uses to grant your application access to its section of the keychain, limiting the application's access to usernames, passwords, and certificates used by other applications.

The App ID is also used as part of the mobile provisioning profile. The mobile provisioning profile is different from the certificate you generated earlier. Certificates stay in the keychain on your Mac and are used by Xcode to digitally sign the iPhone application binaries. The mobile provisioning profile you're about to generate is tied to one or more devices and is transferred by Xcode onto your iPhone or iPod touch. This allows the applications you create to run on that device.

Go to the App IDs section of the iPhone Developer Program Portal, select the Manage tab, and click on New App ID. Enter a name for your App ID; this should be a human-readable name used to refer to this particular App ID. It's entirely arbitrary what you use as the name for the App ID. Since this is your first App ID, for the Bundle Seed ID select Generate New.

Finally, enter a Bundle Identifier. This must be unique, and most developers use a reversed version of their domain name so that this is the case. For instance, my domain name is *babilim.co.uk*, so I entered **uk.co.babilim.*** as my Bundle Identifier.

The asterisk (*) that appears at the end of my Bundle Identifier is the *wildcard* symbol. Using a * in the Bundle Identifier means you will be able to use this App ID for multiple applications. If you did not use a wildcard here, you'd have to generate a new App ID for each of your applications, and a new provisioning profile for each of these applications, before you could deploy your application onto your iPhone or iPod touch. Using a wildcard means you can generate a single mobile provisioning profile that will allow you to deploy multiple applications onto your developer device.

Technically, this means that all the applications created using this Bundle Identifier will share the same portion of the keychain on your iPhone. I discuss the implications of this later. Using a wildcard in the Bundle Identifier also means that the applications you create using this App ID, and the mobile provisioning profile(s) associated with it, will not be able to use the Apple Push Notification and in-app purchase services.

Click Submit. The portal will now generate a new 10-character Bundle Seed ID and prepend it to the Bundle Identifier you provided. This is your App ID.

You need to make a note of your Bundle Identifier as you'll need to supply it to Xcode, as described near the end of Chapter 3, to allow you to deploy the application you are developing onto your iPhone or iPod touch.

Creating a Mobile Provisioning Profile

Now you're ready to create a mobile provisioning profile. Go to the Provisioning section of the iPhone Developer Program Portal, select the Development tab, and click on New Profile.

Enter a profile name. While it's more or less arbitrary what you put here, I recommend using "Developer Profile" somewhere in the name. You may be generating a number of provisioning profiles, including ones later on for distribution (both ad hoc and to the App Store), so it's helpful to know that this profile is to be used for development.

Check the relevant certificate box: if you're an independent developer, you'll have only one choice here, the certificate you generated earlier using the Keychain Access application.

Select the App ID you generated in the previous section, and then select the development device (or devices if you have more than one available) for which this profile will be valid. As I mentioned before, Xcode will transfer the provisioning profile onto your iPhone or iPod touch, and application binaries built by Xcode using a provisioning profile will run successfully only on devices for which this profile is valid. If you don't select the correct device here, your code will not run on it. Don't worry, though: you can add additional devices to the profile at any time, but you'll need to regenerate a provisioning profile inside the Program Portal.

Click Submit to generate the new mobile provisioning profile that you'll use during development. I discuss provisioning profiles needed for distributing your applications later in the book. The status will appear as pending; click the Development tab to reload it until it is no longer pending.

When the profile is ready, click Download and download the provisioning profile to your Mac. You can install it in a number of ways, but the easiest way is to drag the *.mobileprovision* file you downloaded onto the Xcode icon in the dock. This will install it in Xcode and make it available for development.

Making Your Device Available for Development

The final step before you can start coding is to make your device available for development. Return to Xcode and click Window→Organizer from the menu. Select your development device from the lefthand pane and click Use for Development. If Xcode doesn't manage to correctly register your device, you may have to disconnect and reconnect your iPhone or iPod touch so that Xcode can find it correctly. If that fails to work, you should try turning your device off and then on again. Depending on the version of the SDK you installed and the version of the OS currently on your device, you may have to restore your device from the Organizer window inside Xcode. In the process, you'll lose any data you have on it. If this is necessary, you can back up your data by syncing with iTunes as normal before restoring the OS using Xcode. After the restore, return to iTunes and restore your data.

If you can afford the extra cost, I recommend using a separate device for development than you use as your day-to-day iPod or phone. In the future, you may wish to install prerelease versions of the iPhone operating system onto your development device, and by definition, these are always unstable. If you're relying on your iPhone to keep you in touch, you may not want to use it for development.

Once you've installed the profiles, you can verify that Xcode has correctly stored them by opening the *Library* folder in your home directory and looking in *MobileDevice/ Provisioning Profiles*. The next time you sync your development device with iTunes (and you should probably do that now), the mobile provisioning profile will be installed onto it.

You can verify that the profile has been installed by going to Settings→General→Profile on your iPhone and iPod touch and checking that the profile has been correctly installed and verified, as shown in Figure 2-8.

You can now confirm that everything has worked correctly by noting the status light next to your device in the Xcode Organizer window. If Xcode has managed to connect to the device, and it is correctly enabled for development, the status light next to the listing on the lefthand pane will be green. You'll also see your mobile provisioning profile listed in the center box in the main pane, as shown in Figure 2-9.

Figure 2-8. The development provisioning profile installed on my iPod touch

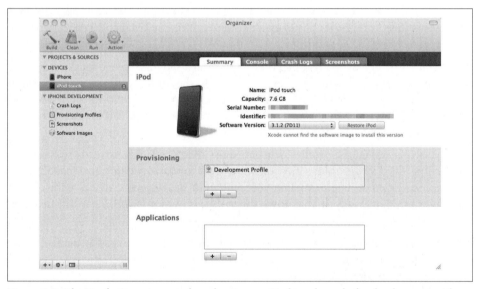

Figure 2-9. The Xcode Organizer window showing my iPod touch ready for development with my development provisioning profile installed

Congratulations, you now have all the certificates and profiles in place to allow you to start running code on your iPhone or iPod touch.

CHAPTER 3

Your First iPhone App

In this chapter, you'll build a small Hello World application and run it in iPhone Simulator. If you're enrolled in the iPhone Developer Program, you'll even get to run the application on your iPhone or iPod touch. I'm going to take you through this step by step, just to give you an idea of how Xcode and Interface Builder work together.

Enrolling in the iPhone Developer Program is separate from registering as an iPhone developer. Enrollment ($99 or $299 per year, depending on which program you join) provides you with the software certificates and online provisioning tools needed to run your own apps on your own iPhone and submit them for approval to the App Store.

However, even if you don't plan to enroll in a Developer Program, you will need to register so that you can download the iPhone SDK needed to create apps. See Chapter 2 for more information on registering and enrolling.

Objective-C Basics

I talk in detail about how Objective-C applications are normally structured in Chapter 4. However, in this chapter, although I do get into Objective-C's sometimes quirky syntax, I'm going to give you a higher-level overview of the language to get you going quickly.

Object-Oriented Programming

If you've heard someone explain object orientation before, the distinction between the terms *class* and *object* may not be totally clear. However, there is a difference. A class is the blueprint for objects; each time you create an object, the class definition determines its structure. An object is a collection of operations (*methods*) and information (*data*) that occupies space in memory and can be instructed to perform operations (*invoke methods*) on that information.

For those of you who are new to programming, the following list defines some of the terms you'll come across frequently:

Objects and classes

A class consists primarily of two things: variables that can store data and methods that can perform operations. The methods are used to retrieve, set, and manipulate the variables. Objects—sometimes referred to as *instances* of a class—have specific values associated with these variables. For example, you might use Apple's UIView Controller class to manage the view (i.e., UI) you present to the user of your application. You also might create an instance of that class named myViewController to actually carry out the work of managing the view presented to the user. This would then be referred to as the myViewController object. An *instance* of a class should not be confused with its *implementation*, which is the realization of the class in code.

Subclasses

Classes can also inherit functionality from an existing class (the parent or base classes, commonly known as the *superclass*); classes that inherit functionality in this way are referred to as subclasses. This means you can invoke a method of the parent class on an object that is an instance of a subclass of the parent. Subclassing is normally done so that you can extend the functionality of that class with additional methods or data. For example, when writing applications for the iPhone you commonly define a subclass of the UIViewController class to manage your views, instead of using the class directly. The subclass of the standard view controller inherits all of the properties of its parent class, but in addition it allows you to implement code to handle the specific view presented to the user, such as data entry and validation.

Instance and class variables

Both instance and class variables are defined as part of the class declaration. However, every object (instance of the class) holds a separate copy of an instance variable. In other words, if a class defines a variable foo, the value of foo can be different for objects for the same class. Changing the value of an instance variable in one object will not affect the value of the same variable in all the other objects of that class. Conversely, only a single copy of a class variable exists. If you change the value of a class variable from one object, the value of that variable will change for all the objects of that class.

Accessor methods

Accessor methods, sometimes called *getters* and *setters*, are usually fairly simple methods used to get and set instance variables in a class. They are used to provide an abstraction layer between variables and the outside world so that the implementation of the class can change without having to change any code outside of the class itself. In Objective-C, the compiler can generate these commonly used functions for you.

Class methods

Class methods (also known as *static methods*) are similar in nature to class varia-bles. These are methods that are associated directly with the class rather than the object instance; they therefore will not have access to object instance variables.

Events and messages

An event is a message generated by the user interacting with your application's controls. For instance, if you tap the screen of your iPhone or iPod touch, this generates a UI event in your application that is passed via a message from the application to an object that has been delegated to deal with that specific type of event.

Protocols

A protocol definition declares methods that any class can implement. If your class declares that it abides by a particular protocol definition, you are announcing that you have implemented the minimum mandatory methods declared in the protocol definition, and may optionally have implemented some nonmandatory methods.

Delegate classes

A delegate class is a class that implements a protocol for handling events. Each delegate protocol specifies a number of methods that must be implemented, and additionally methods that may optionally be implemented. Declaring your class a delegate implies that it (at least) implements the mandatory methods. For instance, if your UI has a button, you can declare your class a delegate to handle events generated by the button.

Event loop

The main event loop is the principal control loop for your application. This loop is the process that receives and then passes external events, such as the user tapping the iPhone's screen or changes in the device's orientation, to the appropriate del-egate classes that you've included in your application.

Frameworks and libraries

A framework is a collection of related classes, protocols, and functions collected together within a cohesive architecture. When you make use of a framework many of the design decisions about how you as a developer will use the code it includes have been taken out of your hands. However, by using the standard frameworks, you inherit standard behavior. For example, when Apple introduced Copy & Paste to the iPhone with the release of version 3.0 of the firmware, it was enabled by default in most third-party applications because the developers made use of the standard UIKit framework to build those applications.

The Objective-C Object Model

For those of you coming from an object-oriented background, there are a number of differences between the Objective-C model of object orientation and the one imple-mented by Simula-derived languages such as C++, Java, and C#.

While its nonobject operations are identical to C, Objective-C derives its object syntax almost directly from the Smalltalk language. Its object model is based on sending messages to object instances; in Objective-C you do not invoke a method, but instead send a message. What's the difference? Invoking a method implies that you know something about that method. Sending a message leaves it up to the receiver of the message to figure out what to do with it.

This kind of loosely coupled chain of command means that Objective-C is much more dynamic at runtime than the Simula-derived languages, but it also means it might appear to be insubordinate.

That's because in Simula-derived languages, you must know the type of an object before you can call a method on it. In Objective-C this is not the case. You simply send the object a message. The receiving object then attempts to interpret the message, but there is no guarantee of a response. If it doesn't understand the message, it will ignore it and return `nil`. Among other things, this kind of model does away with the need to continually cast objects between types to ensure that you are sending a message that will be understood.

 Casting is the process whereby you represent one variable as a variable of another type. This is done both for primitive types (suppose you want to change a float to an integer as part of an integer arithmetic operation), as well as for objects. An object can be cast to another object type if it is a subclass of that type. In Objective-C, objects can be represented by the generic `id` type, and you can cast objects to this type without regard for their parent class.

The other main difference is in the way memory is managed. While languages such as Java use garbage collection to handle memory management, in Objective-C memory is managed using reference counting (the alloc-retain-release cycle, as discussed in Chapter 4).

Garbage Collection and Reference Counting

In the simplest case, memory management must provide a way to allocate a portion of memory and then free that memory when it is no longer needed. Garbage collection is a form of memory management that automatically attempts to free memory that is no longer in use. While garbage collection frees the developer from having to worry about manually managing memory, the point where memory is automatically freed can be unpredictable, and the garbage collection routines consume additional computing resources.

Reference counting is a form of garbage collection, which counts the number of references to an object (or portion of memory) and frees the associated memory when the number of references reaches zero. The main advantage of reference counting over "classic" garbage collection is that memory is freed as soon as it is no longer in use.

Although most programmers wouldn't necessarily class it as such, reference counting is among the simplest garbage collection algorithms, as it frees the developer from having to manually manage memory at a low level.

Finally, the applications are almost invariably based on the Model-View-Controller (MVC) (design) pattern, which is pervasive in the Cocoa Touch and other frameworks that you'll use to build iPhone applications. Rather than encouraging you to create subclasses, the MVC pattern makes use of *delegate classes*. A pattern is a reusable solution to a commonly occurring problem; in object-oriented programming, patterns usually describe how the developer should model the application in terms of the classes that are used, and how the developer should structure the interactions and relationships between these classes.

For example, the root `UIApplication` class implements the behavior necessary for an application, but instead of forcing you to subclass the `UIApplication` class for your own application and add your own code to the subclass, it delivers notification messages of events to an assigned delegate class that implements the `UIApplicationDelegate` protocol. The `UIApplication` class asks the delegate class to respond to events when they occur.

The Basics of Objective-C Syntax

I'll dive a bit deeper into Objective-C as we go through the book, but to make it through this chapter all you really need to know is that while variable declarations look much the same as variable declarations do in other languages, method calls are surrounded by square brackets. So, for example, both of the following lines of code are method calls:

```
[anObject someMethod];❶
[anObject someMethod: anotherObject];❷
```

❶ The `someMethod` message is sent to the `anObject` object.

❷ The `someMethod` message is sent to the `anObject` object and passes `anotherObject` as an argument.

Despite the sometimes quirky syntax (including the square brackets and colon shown in the preceding code) that Objective-C has inherited from Smalltalk, the logic of what is going on should be clear, and we'll discuss the syntax in much greater detail in the next chapter.

Creating a Project

Now let's create our first application in Xcode. Launch Xcode by double-clicking its icon (it's located in the */Developer/Applications* folder on your hard drive). Click "Create a new Xcode project" in the Xcode welcome window, and then click Application under the iPhone OS section on the left side of the screen. Next, click the View-based

Application template and click Choose. When prompted, name your new project *HelloWorld*. Make sure you don't put a space between *Hello* and *World*, as this can sometimes confuse Xcode.

If you don't see a welcome window when you start up Xcode, you can create a new project by choosing File→New Project.

Xcode will now open a project window. The left pane shows the classes and other files associated with the project, organized into groups. If you double-click on each group icon, the group will expand to show you the files it contains, as shown in Figure 3-1. The application template you choose determines how the groups are arranged, but you can move the files around and create your own groups if you prefer to organize things differently. The two main groups you'll be working with are Classes, which contain all the classes that make up the application, and Resources, which contain other supporting files, including the *.xib* files that the Interface Builder application uses to describe your application's UI. By default, the project will open to the top level of the project hierarchy, and the top-right pane will show a list of all the files associated with the project. The bottom-right pane (blank at first) will show you the source code of whichever file you have clicked on.

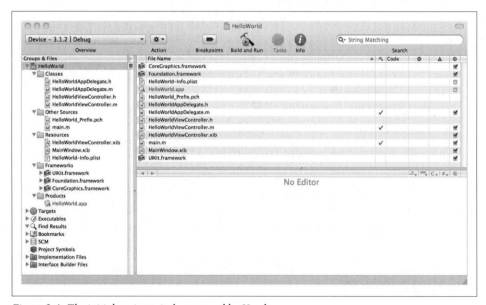

Figure 3-1. The initial project window opened by Xcode

Exploring the Project in Xcode

When you created the project, Xcode generated a number of files and, along with them, a lot of the boilerplate code you'd otherwise have to laboriously type in. In fact, the project that Xcode generates for you is a complete (if boring) iPhone application. You know those flashlight applications that have proliferated on the App Store? You've just written one....

If you click the Build and Run button in the Xcode toolbar (see Figure 3-1), Xcode will compile the application, deploy it in iPhone Simulator, and then run it. After the application opens, what you see in the simulator should look very similar to Figure 3-2, a simple, blank, gray view.

Figure 3-2. Our Xcode template compiled and running inside iPhone Simulator

Let's look at the files Xcode has generated as part of the template and how it has divided them into separate groups in the Groups & Files pane of the interface:

Classes

The Classes group contains the classes and header files we're most interested in and will be working with in this chapter. These are *HelloWorldAppDelegate.h*, *HelloWorldAppDelegate.m*, *HelloWorldViewController.h*, and *HelloWorldView-Controller.m*. These are the classes that do most of the heavy lifting in our application, in particular managing the view (the UI) that the application's user sees.

Other Sources

The Other Sources group contains just two files: the prefix header for the project, *HelloWorld_Prefix.pch*, and *main.m*. The prefix header file is implicitly included by each of your source files when they're built; if you need to include a header file in all of the classes in your project, you can add it here. However, it's unlikely that you'll need to do this, so you can safely ignore it for the time being. The *main.m* file contains the `main()` routine; this is the place where your program begins. In this project, the *main.m* file handles some memory management duties (discussed in Chapter 4) and then calls the `UIApplicationMain` function, which is the main controller, responsible for handling the event loop. You'll almost never have to change anything in the Other Sources group, as the boilerplate code the template generated should serve you fairly well.

Resources

The Resources group contains the *.xib* files Interface Builder uses to describe your application's UI.

The *HelloWorld-Info.plist* (property list) file also plays a role in defining the UI. This property list is an XML file that describes basic information about your application for Xcode and the compiler. You'll look inside the *HelloWorld-Info.plist* file later in the chapter when you deploy your application onto your iPhone or iPod touch.

Frameworks

The Frameworks group contains a list of external frameworks that your application links to. These frameworks provide the headers and libraries you need to write software for the iPhone OS.

Products

The Products group contains the application binary that is generated when you compile your application. At first the *HelloWorld.app* file is shown in red. Xcode knows this file should exist, but since you haven't yet compiled the application, the file currently doesn't exist.

If you open the Mac OS X Finder and navigate to where you saved the project, you'll be able to see how the project files are organized on disk.

Overview of an iPhone application

Figure 3-3 shows a high-level overview of an iPhone application life cycle. This illustrates the main elements of a typical iPhone application. Most iPhone applications make use of the MVC pattern (see Chapter 4 for more details).

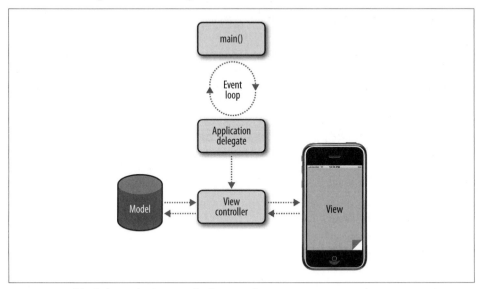

Figure 3-3. A block diagram of a typical iPhone application

When the user launches your application by tapping its icon on the home screen, the application's `main()` function is called. The `main()` routine calls the `UIApplication Main` function, which is the main application controller responsible for handling the event loop. From this point, the heavy lifting is done by the UIKit framework, which loads the UI and starts the main event loop. During this loop, UIKit dispatches events, such as notification of touches and orientation changes, to your objects and responds to commands issued by your application. When the user performs an action that would cause your application to quit, UIKit notifies your application and begins the termination process.

The application delegate is the core class in your application and receives messages from the main event loop. It is responsible for handling critical system messages. For example, the application delegate handles both the `applicationDidFinishLaunching:` and the `applicationWillTerminate:` messages. Every iPhone application must contain an application delegate object.

The view controller class is responsible for providing views, or a set of views, and presenting them to the user. The class also acts as a delegate and manages your application's response to some of the standard system behaviors (e.g., a change in device orientation), rearranging and resizing the views it manages in response to these system events.

Declarations, Interfaces, and Implementation

The declaration of a class announces its existence to the compiler, while the implementation of a class consists of the actual code that is the realization of the declaration. Just like the UI the application presents to the world, the class declaration presents an interface to the developer. The declaration declares an interface to your code, and the implementation carries out the task the code has been written to perform.

It's a common practice to separate the declaration of the class and the implementation into separate header and implementation files. The reason this is done is because header files can be, and usually are, included in multiple source files. Therefore, if we separate the class declaration from its implementation, we make the resultant code more flexible and increase reusability. We can change the underlying implementation of the class without having to recompile the (possibly many) source files that make use of that class.

The application delegate

Let's begin at the beginning, with the definition of the application delegate class. Click on the *HelloWorldAppDelegate.h* file, which contains the declaration of the class:

```
#import <UIKit/UIKit.h>

@class HelloWorldViewController;

@interface HelloWorldAppDelegate : NSObject <UIApplicationDelegate> {
    UIWindow *window;
    HelloWorldViewController *viewController;
}

@property (nonatomic, retain) IBOutlet UIWindow *window;
@property (nonatomic, retain) IBOutlet
    HelloWorldViewController *viewController;

@end
```

Here we see the app delegate class declaration, beginning with the `@interface` directive and ending with the `@end` directive. This is the delegate class that implements the `UIApplicationDelegate` protocol and receives messages from the `UIApplication` class. Breaking down this interface directive, we see that our class is called `HelloWorldAppDe legate`, it's a subclass of the main object superclass `NSObject`, and it implements the `UIApplicationDelegate` protocol.

Let's look at the corresponding implementation. Click on the *HelloWorldAppDelegate.m* file to open it in the Xcode editor:

```
#import "HelloWorldAppDelegate.h"❶
#import "HelloWorldViewController.h"

@implementation HelloWorldAppDelegate❷
```

```
@synthesize window;
@synthesize viewController;

- (void)applicationDidFinishLaunching:(UIApplication *)application {

    // Override point for customization after app launch
    [window addSubview:viewController.view];❸
    [window makeKeyAndVisible];❹
}

- (void)dealloc {
    [viewController release];
    [window release];
    [super dealloc];
}


@end❺
```

❶ The header files are imported with the class declarations for both the `HelloWorldApp Delegate` and the `HelloWorldViewController` classes.

❷ This is the beginning of the declaration of the Hello World application delegate class.

❸ Here, I add the view managed by the `viewController` object as a subview of the main window.

❹ This makes the window visible using the `makeKeyAndVisible` method.

❺ This is the end of the declaration of the Hello World application delegate class.

Quick Access to Class and Method Documentation

In Xcode 3.2 (which comes with Mac OS X 10.6 Snow Leopard), if you Option-double-click on a class or method name, information about that class or method will appear in a small pop-up window. (On most Apple keyboards, the Option key is also labeled as the Alt key, is positioned between the Control and Command keys, and may have the ⌥ symbol on it.) Click the book icon in the top right of the pop up, and you'll get to see the full documentation. Click on the small *.h* icon to go to the header file where that class or method is declared. The trick still works in previous versions of Xcode, but instead of a little pop-up window appearing, you're taken directly to the class documentation.

Option-double-click on the `UIApplicationDelegate` in the app delegate header file, then click on the book icon to go to the full documentation, and you'll see the protocol reference. This shows you the methods the app delegate must implement as well as the optional methods (which are marked as such in the protocol documentation). These represent the messages the `UIApplication` class sends to the application delegate.

In the app delegate declaration file (which is also known as a header file), you'll see that we declare a `UIWindow` object as part of the class, and after telling the compiler that `HelloWorldViewController` is a class using the `@class` directive, we also declare a `Hello WorldViewController` object. The `UIWindow` class defines an object that coordinates the views (the UI) that we see on the iPhone's screen. Both of these objects are then declared as class properties using the `@property name` directive.

Properties are a generic way of declaring the data a class provides. In the app delegate implementation, we see that accessor methods for both of our properties are "synthesized" using the `@synthesize` directive. The synthesis directive tells Objective-C to automatically generate accessor methods for us, and vastly reduces the amount of code we need to write ourselves.

If you return to the declaration (*HelloWorldAppDelegate.h*) shown earlier, you'll see that these properties were declared with the symbol `IBOutlet`. This symbol doesn't affect how our code is compiled, but it is a place marker to tell Xcode that this object in our code can be connected to a UI component in Interface Builder. This allows the UI constructed in Interface Builder to receive messages from our code. The corresponding `IBAction` declaration on method declarations, which we'll meet later, is yet another place marker for Interface Builder, allowing us to connect calling actions in response to events happening in the UI to a method. In many instances, a UI element will also have an associated delegate protocol, and we can declare classes to act as delegates to specific UI elements. Our class will then receive messages when the UI element generates events. For instance, in Chapter 5 you'll see the `UITableView` class and associated delegate protocols in action.

Now let's examine the `applicationDidFinishLaunching` method. This is where we can insert our own code to customize the application after it launches. See Chapter 5 and the City Guide application for an example of this sort of customization. At the moment, it contains the following:

```
[window addSubview:viewController.view];
[window makeKeyAndVisible];
```

You make an object perform an operation by sending a message to the object. Messages are enclosed in square brackets. Inside the brackets, the object receiving the message is on the left side and the message (along with any parameters the message requires) is on the right. The parameters follow the colon (see "The Basics of Objective-C Syntax" on page 23 for another example).

The view controller

Next, let's look inside the `HelloWorldViewController` class. The interface file for this class is called *HelloWorldViewController.h*; the implementation file is called *HelloWorldViewController.m*.

Let's start with the interface file. Click on the *HelloWorldViewController.h* file in the Classes group to open the file in the Xcode editor.

Back in *HelloWorldAppDelegate.h*, the application delegate declared a `viewControl` `ler` object of the class `HelloWorldViewController`, which right now doesn't contain any methods or properties of its own:

```
#import <UIKit/UIKit.h>

@interface HelloWorldViewController : UIViewController {

}

@end
```

However, looking at the header file you'll see that our `HelloWorldViewController` class is a subclass of the `UIViewController` class. This is the class that provides the fundamental view-management model for iPhone applications, and this class is associated in Interface Builder with a NIB file (when you create a view-based project, Xcode automatically creates the associated NIB file). That NIB file contains the UI that will be displayed when we make this view visible.

 Although the Interface Builder files end with the *.xib* extension, Cocoa programmers still refer to them by their old name, NIBs.

Next, click on the *HelloWorldViewController.m* file in the Classes group and look at the implementation of the class. You'll see here that the template has provided quite a bit of commented out *stub code* (code that you need to fill for it to be functional). We'll return to this stub code later; for now, bear in mind that this subclass relies on its parent class to handle the messages that are left undefined by virtue of being commented out:

```
#import "HelloWorldViewController.h"

@implementation HelloWorldViewController

/*
// The designated initializer. Override to perform setup that is required
// before the view is loaded.
- (id)initWithNibName:(NSString *)nibNameOrNil
            bundle:(NSBundle *)nibBundleOrNil {
    if (self = [super initWithNibName:nibNameOrNil bundle:nibBundleOrNil]) {
        // Custom initialization
    }
    return self;
}
*/

/*
// Implement loadView to create a view hierarchy programmatically,
// without using a nib.
- (void)loadView {
}
```

```
*/


/*
// Implement viewDidLoad to do additional setup after loading the view,
// typically from a nib.
- (void)viewDidLoad {
    [super viewDidLoad];
}
*/


/*
// Override to allow orientations other than the default portrait orientation.
- (BOOL)shouldAutorotateToInterfaceOrientation:
                              (UIInterfaceOrientation)interfaceOrientation {
    // Return YES for supported orientations
    return (interfaceOrientation == UIInterfaceOrientationPortrait);
}
*/

- (void)didReceiveMemoryWarning {
    // Releases the view if it doesn't have a superview.
    [super didReceiveMemoryWarning];

    // Release any cached data, images, etc that aren't in use.
}

- (void)viewDidUnload {
    // Release any retained subviews of the main view.
    // e.g. self.myOutlet = nil;
}


- (void)dealloc {
    [super dealloc];
}

@end
```

Our Project in Interface Builder

I've talked about Interface Builder quite a bit so far, but we haven't looked at it. Let's do that now. Interface Builder allows you to create and lay out the UI for your iPhone application visually; it stores your application's interface in a bundle (an XML file that, for historic reasons, is generally referred to as a NIB file) containing the interface objects and their relationship with your own code. However, unlike almost all other similar design systems that generate code, NIB files are *serialized* (also known as *freeze-dried*) objects. In other words, the files contain the read-to-run object instances, rather than code to generate these objects at compile time.

We can use Interface Builder to associate the laid out UI elements with our own code by connecting outlets, actions, and delegates to the UI elements inside the Interface Builder application. However, to do so we must first declare the objects and methods in our code as either an `IBOutlet` or an `IBAction` where appropriate, and the classes as delegates.

Open the Resources group and double-click on the *HelloWorldViewController.xib* file. This will open Interface Builder and display the NIB file, as shown in Figure 3-4.

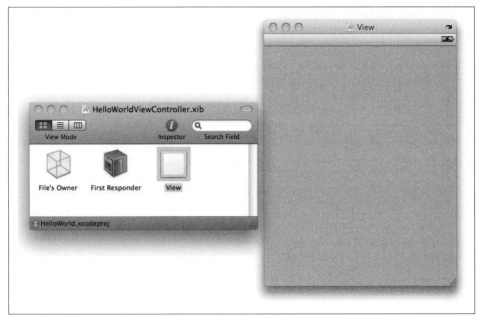

Figure 3-4. The basic HelloWorldViewController.xib in Interface Builder

You'll see four windows: the main Interface Builder window showing the contents of the NIB file; the View window which shows the contents of the NIB's view; the Library window; and the Attributes window (commonly known as the Inspector window). The Library window contains all the UI elements you can use to build your UI, while the Inspector window allows you to inspect the connections and other properties of a specific UI element.

We'll discuss the details of what's going on inside Interface Builder in later chapters; for now, we're just going to add a button and a label to our view. Then we'll modify our code so that it knows about those UI elements, and then go back into Interface Builder to connect the UI elements to the objects in our code. At that point, we'll have a working Hello World application.

Click on the View window and make sure the leftmost tab (the Attributes tab) of the Inspector window is selected. Let's start by changing the rather dull gray background of the view to white. Click on the Background Color box to bring up the standard Mac OS X color picker. Push the opacity slider to 100% and change the color to something more interesting. In my case, I picked white, which is, I suppose, only marginally more interesting than gray. Close the color picker; the background of your View window should now be a more interesting color.

Now go to the Library and click and drag a label (UILabel) and a round rect button (UIButton) onto your view and drop them in a sensible place. (Make sure Library→Cocoa Touch→Inputs & Values is currently selected in the top pane first.) Delete the placeholder text in the label by double-clicking on the label text to select it and then pressing the Backspace key, and then type some appropriate replacement text for the button—"Push me!" perhaps. Now save your NIB file and return to Xcode; as you can in most Mac applications, you can save your changes by using the keyboard shortcut ⌘-S.

Adding Code

At this point, we need to tell our code about the UI elements we added to our view so that we can return to Interface Builder and make the connections between our new label and button and our code. Open the *HelloWorldViewController.h* file and add a UILabel and a UIButton declaration inside the HelloWorldViewController interface directive:

```
#import <UIKit/UIKit.h>

@interface HelloWorldViewController : UIViewController {
    UILabel    *label;
    UIButton   *button;
}

@property (nonatomic, retain) IBOutlet UILabel *label;

-(IBAction)sayHello:(id) sender;

@end
```

We also need to declare our UILabel as a property and an IBOutlet. Finally, we need to declare a sayHello method to be called when our button is clicked. We'll use this to change the text associated with our label and tell the world "Hello!" For now, just duplicate the preceding code; we'll discuss the layout of Objective-C methods in the next chapter.

Debugging Using NSLog

If you have problems developing this application, or any of the other applications we talk about in the rest of the book, you may want to make use of the NSLog function. You can use this function to print debugging statements to the Console, which you can bring up by clicking on Run→Console in the Xcode menu. Here's how an NSLog is used in your code:

```
NSLog( @"Prints this string to the console." );
```

The NSLog function understands the conventions used by the standard C library printf function, including %f for floats and %d for integers, but in addition uses %@ for objects:

```
NSLog( @"Prints the UILabel object %@ to the console.", label);
```

This works by asking the object to describe itself and produces sensible output for many standard objects. This is done by calling the description: method in the object, which returns a string describing the receiving class. The default implementation gives the name of the class, although many objects override this implementation. For example, with the NSArray object, it prints out a list of values.

Next, we need to open the *HelloWorldViewController.m* file. We need to synthesize our label accessors, which will automatically generate accessor methods for us, and write the implementation of the sayHello method. If you look at the documentation for the UILabel class, you'll see that all you need to do is to set the text property to change the text displayed by the label:

```
#import "HelloWorldViewController.h"

@implementation HelloWorldViewController

@synthesize label;


-(IBAction) sayHello:(id) sender {
    label.text = @"Hello World";
}

- (void)didReceiveMemoryWarning {
    [super didReceiveMemoryWarning];
}

- (void)viewDidUnload {
}


- (void)dealloc {
    [label release];
    [button release];
    [super dealloc];
}

@end
```

Here @"Hello World" is a constant NSString object.

Connecting the Outlets in Interface Builder

Save both the header and implementation files and return to the *HelloWorldViewCon-troller.xib* file in Interface Builder. We've made all the code changes we need to make inside Xcode. In Interface Builder, click on File's Owner and select the Connections tab (the second from the left, or press ⌘-2) in the Inspector window.

You'll see that a `label` outlet and a `sayHello:` received action are listed. If you briefly visit the Identity tab (the one farthest to the right), you'll see that the Class Identity of this NIB file is that of a `HelloWorldViewController`; this class owns the NIB.

By adding code to the `HelloWorldViewController` class and marking the label object as an `IBOutlet` and our method as an `IBAction`, we've made these available inside Interface Builder.

Return to the Connections Inspector (⌘-2) and click and drag from the small circle next to your label outlet to the label in the View window. See Figure 3-5 for what this should look like when you do that. Release the mouse button and you should see a new outlet forming in the Connection window. The `label` outlet is now linked to the `Label` (`label`) UI element.

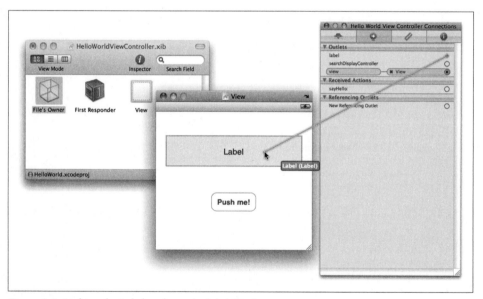

Figure 3-5. Linking the Label outlet to the label UI element

Now click and drag from the `sayHello:` received action to your button, as shown in Figure 3-6. When you release the mouse button you'll be presented with a pop-up menu showing you all of the different types of events that a `UIButton` can generate. For now, we're just interested in a simple button push, so select the `Touch Up Inside` event from the pop-up menu. You should now see a connection formed between the `sayHello:`

received action and the `Round Rect Button (Push me!) Touch down` event. Whenever this event occurs, our `sayHello:` method will be called.

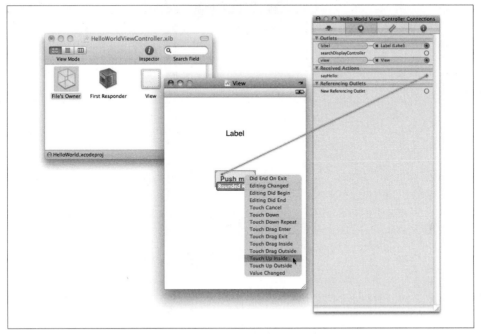

Figure 3-6. Connecting the sayHello action to the button

We're done, so save the NIB file and return to Xcode. Make sure Simulator – 3.0 | Debug is selected in the Overview drop down, and click on the Build and Run button in the menu bar. This will start iPhone Simulator and run our code. Click on the "Push me!" button and our initially blank label should now read "Hello World" (see Figure 3-7).

Congratulations, you've written your first iPhone application. Now let's get it to work on your iPhone and iPod touch.

Putting the Application on Your iPhone

Open the *HelloWorld-Info.plist* file, as shown in Figure 3-8, and edit the "Bundle identifier" line to be the same as the wildcard Bundle Identifier you supplied to Apple in Chapter 2. For instance, I entered `uk.co.babilim` as my Bundle Identifier, so I would replace the string `com.yourcompany` with `uk.co.babilim` in the property list file.

Figure 3-7. iPhone Simulator running our Hello World application

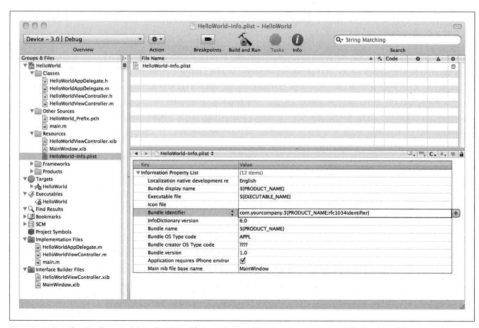

Figure 3-8. The HelloWorld-Info.plist file; replace com.yourcompany with the Bundle Identifier you gave to Apple in Chapter 2

Remember the following for future reference as you try to run the examples in this book on your device:

If you ever see the error "Code Sign error: a valid provisioning profile matching the application's Identifier 'com.yourcompany.Application-Name' could not be found," return to this section and follow these instructions to put your Bundle Identifier in the app's *Info.plist* file.

Now double-click on the HelloWorld project icon at the top of the Groups & Files pane of the Xcode interface; this will open the Project Info window. Click on the Build tab and use the search box, or just scroll down the list of project properties and find the Code Signing Identity associated with this project. Click on the drop-down menu next to the "Any iPhone OS Device" entry and select iPhone Developer, as shown in Figure 3-9.

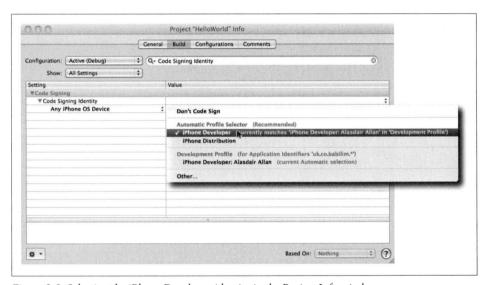

Figure 3-9. Selecting the iPhone Developer identity in the Project Info window

Make sure you have completed all the steps needed to use your iPhone or iPod touch for development that we talked about in the preceding chapter, and make sure your device is plugged in and Xcode is aware of it by opening the Organizer window. You should see a green light next to the name of your device in the lefthand pane.

Now change the Active SDK in the Overview drop down in Xcode's toolbar from "iPhone Simulator 3.0" to "iPhone Device *X.Y* (Base SDK)", where *X.Y* is the version of the most recent iPhone SDK you've installed (unless you have some need to compile for an older SDK, you should always use the most recently supported SDK from Apple). If everything seems OK at this point, click the Build and Run button on the toolbar.

Xcode should compile the application and transfer it onto your device. You can monitor this process using the Organizer window.

Congratulations, you've written and deployed your first iPhone application.

 When you become more experienced at developing iPhone applications, and your applications become more complex, you might want to think about using a wireframing application such as Briefs (*http://give abrief.com/*). This allows you to experience how your concept feels without investing the expense and time needed to fully develop the concept into a working application. Since Briefs is image-based, it allows you to mock up your application using anything from scanned paper sketches to full-blown image mockups created by your graphic design team.

CHAPTER 4

Coding in Objective-C

Thus far, you've built a simple iPhone application and discovered that it's not that hard to build apps for the iPhone or iPod touch. Let's step back and take a broader look at the Objective-C language.

Objective-C is an object-oriented language that adds Smalltalk-style messaging to C. The language is a superset of the C language, providing constructs to allow you to define classes and objects. Once you get the hang of the Smalltalk-style syntax, if you've programmed in an object-oriented language before, things should look fairly familiar. However, there are some differences, and I discuss them in this chapter. One of the bigger differences, especially for those who are coming from a Java background, is in how Objective-C deals with memory management.

Declaring and Defining Classes

As is the case in almost all other object-oriented languages, in Objective-C classes provide the building blocks to allow encapsulation of data and methods that act on that data. Objects are specific instances of a class, and they contain their own instance data and pointers to the methods implemented by the class. Classes are specified in two pieces: the *interface* and the *implementation*. The interface contains the declaration of the class and is normally contained in a *.h* file. The implementation contains your actual code (the definition) and is normally contained in a *.m* file. We briefly discussed this in Chapter 3, but let's take some time to look at it in more detail here.

Declaring a Class with the Interface

Let's return to the declaration of the `HelloWorldViewController` class from Chapter 3, which illustrates a typical class interface. The interface begins with the `@interface` keyword, followed by the name of the class being declared and ending with a colon followed by the name of the base (or parent) class:

```
@interface HelloWorldViewController : UIViewController
```

An Objective-C class cannot inherit from multiple classes; however, the class it inherits from may in turn inherit from another class. In the case of `HelloWorldViewController`, its base class is `UIViewController`, which itself inherits from `UIResponder`, which inherits from `NSObject`, the root class of most Objective-C class hierarchies.

 Objective-C allows objects to descend from any root class. Although `NSObject` is the most common root class, it is not the only one. For instance, `NSProxy` is also a root class. So, you cannot always assume that a given class is derived from `NSObject`.

After that first line, the instance variable declarations appear within curly braces. Following that, we have the declaration of properties and methods associated with the class. The class declaration is wrapped up with the `@end` keyword:

```
#import <UIKit/UIKit.h>❶

@interface HelloWorldViewController : UIViewController {
    UIButton *button;
    UILabel *label;
}

@property (nonatomic, retain) IBOutlet UILabel *label;

-(IBAction)sayHello:(id) sender;

@end
```

❶ The `#import` statement is not technically part of the class declaration. Instead, this is a C preprocessor directive that avoids multiple inclusions of the same header file and is effectively equivalent to the C preprocessor directive `#include <UIKit/UIKit.h>`.

Defining a Class with the Implementation

The `HelloWorldViewController` implementation from Chapter 3 begins by importing the class interface in the *.h* file. The implementation begins with the `@implementation` declaration and ends with the `@end` declaration:

```
@implementation HelloWorldViewController

    ...

@end
```

After the implementation begins, we must synthesize the accessor for the properties we declared in our interface file and implement the declared methods:

```
#import "HelloWorldViewController.h"

@implementation HelloWorldViewController
```

```
@synthesize label;


-(IBAction) sayHello:(id) sender {
    label.text = @"Hello World";
}

- (void)didReceiveMemoryWarning {
    [super didReceiveMemoryWarning];
}

- (void)viewDidUnload {
}


- (void)dealloc {
    [label release];
    [button release]
    [super dealloc];
}

@end
```

Now that you've taken a quick look at the structure of an interface and implementation, let's take a detailed look at the individual parts.

Object Typing

When instance variables are themselves objects—for instance, when the HelloWorld ViewController class declares UIButton and UILabel variables—you should always use a pointer type. However, Objective-C adds an interesting twist: it supports both strongly typed and weakly typed declarations. Here's a strongly typed declaration:

```
UIButton *button;
```

Here we declare anObject. In the first instance we use strong typing, declaring it as an object of the class SomeClass.

Here's a weakly typed version of the declaration, where it is declared as an object of class id:

```
id button;
```

The id class is a generic C type that Objective-C uses to represent an arbitrary object; it's a general type representing any type of object regardless of class and can be used as a placeholder for both a class and a reference to an object instance. All objects therefore are of type id. This can prove very useful; you can imagine that if you wanted to build a generic class implementing a linked list, the type of object held in each node would be of type id, since you'd then be able to store any type of object.

Properties

The declaration of properties using the `@property` compiler directive is a convenience to avoid the declaration and, usually, the implementation of accessor methods for member variables. You can think of a property declaration as the equivalent of declaring accessor methods. You can also dictate how the automatically generated accessor methods behave by declaring custom attributes (see the sidebar "Declaring Custom Attributes for Properties"). In the `HelloWorldViewController` class, we declare the property to be (`nonatomic, retain`):

```
@property (nonatomic, retain) IBOutlet UILabel *label;
```

We can also declare both of our properties to be an `IBOutlet`. While not formally part of the list of attributes for an `@property` declaration, `IBOutlet` denotes that this property is an Interface Builder outlet. I talked about outlets briefly in Chapter 3 and will discuss them in more detail later.

Declaring Custom Attributes for Properties

Accessor Methods

By default, the automatically generated accessor methods created when you `@synthe size` a property are `propertyName:` and `setPropertyName:`. You can change this by using the `getter=getterName` and `setter=setterName` custom attributes. Bear in mind that changing the default names will invariably break the *dot syntax* syntactic sugar (see "The Dot Syntax" on page 45) that Objective-C normally provides.

Writability

You can choose whether the property has an associated setter accessor method by specifying the `readonly` custom attribute. If this is set, only a getter method is generated when you `@synthesize` the property in your implementation.

Setter Semantics

The `assign`, `retain`, and `copy` custom attributes govern the setter accessor method and are mutually exclusive. The `assign` attribute is the default and implies that the generated setter uses simple assignment. The `retain` attribute specifies that a `retain` should be invoked on the object when it is assigned, and the previous value should be sent a `release` message. See "Memory Management" on page 47 for the implications of this constraint. Finally, the `copy` attribute implies that a copy of the object should be used when the object is assigned, rather than a straight assignment. This attribute is valid only for objects that implement the `NSCopying` protocol.

Atomicity

The `nonatomic` custom attribute specifies that the accessor method is nonatomic. Properties are atomic by default so that the accessor methods are robust in multithreaded environments. Note that while the accessor is robust, it is not necessarily thread-safe. Specifying `nonatomic` implies that the accessor is conversely not robust in such environments, and that the generated accessor method returns the object directly. However,

---

it does result in considerably faster code and is generally recommended for iPhone applications.

Synthesizing Properties

When you declare an `@property` in the class interface, you must also synthesize the property (unless you wish to implement the getter and setter methods yourself) using the `@synthesize` declaration, as we do for the `label` property in the `HelloWorldViewCon troller` class:

```
@synthesize label;
```

This asks the compiler to generate the accessor methods according to the specification in the property declaration, and much reduces the amount of boilerplate code that you have to write yourself.

The Dot Syntax

When you declare a member variable as a property and synthesize the declared accessors using the `@synthesize` declaration in the `@implementation` of the class, you can (entirely optionally) make use of some syntactic sugar that Objective-C provides, called the *dot syntax*, as an alternative to using the automatically generated accessor methods directly. For instance, this lets us do the following:

```
label.text = @"Hello World";
```

instead of doing this (note that Objective-C capitalized the *t* in *text* when it generated the accessor method):

```
[label setText:@"Hello World"];
```

The dot syntax is arguably somewhat neater and easier to read.

Declaring Methods

We declare one method in the `HelloWorldViewController` class, called `sayHello:`.

```
#import <UIKit/UIKit.h>

@interface HelloWorldViewController : UIViewController {
    UILabel     *label;
    UIButton    *button;
}

@property (nonatomic, retain) IBOutlet UILabel *label;

-(IBAction)sayHello:(id) sender;

@end
```

The minus sign in front of the method indicates the method type, in this case an instance method. A plus sign would indicate a class method. For example:

```
+(void)aMethod:(id) anObject;
```

The `sayHello:` method takes an `id` object as an argument and is flagged as an `IBAction` for Interface Builder. When compiled, `IBAction` is replaced with `void` and `IBOutlet` is removed; these compiler directives are simply used to flag methods and variables to Interface Builder. This method is passed a generic `id` object as an argument since we intended it to be triggered by a UI event, and we want to leave it open as to what sort of UI element will be used. Under our UI, it's triggered when the user clicks the "Push me!" button in the UI, and this `id` object will be the `UIButton` that the user clicked to trigger the `HelloWorld` event application. We can recover the `UIButton` object by casting the `sender` object to a `UIButton`:

```
UIButton * theButton = (UIButton *)sender;
```

It's a standard practice in Objective-C to call such objects `sender`. If we were unsure of the underlying type of an `id` object, we could check the type using the `isKindOfClass` method:

```
if([thisObject isKindOfClass:[anotherObject class]]) { ... }
```

Calling Methods

If you want to call a method exposed by an object, you do so by sending that object a message. The message consists of the method signature, along with the parameter information. Messages are enclosed in square brackets; the object receiving the message is on the left and the parameters are on the right, with the parameter following a colon. If the method accepts more than one argument, this is explicitly named, and the second parameter follows a second colon. This allows multiple methods with the same name and argument types to be defined.

```
[anObject someMethod];
[anObject someMethod: anotherObject];
[anObject someMethod: anotherObject withAnotherArgument: yetAnotherObject];
```

The name of the method is the concatenation of the method name and any additional named arguments. Hence in the preceding code we have `someMethod:` and `someMethod:withAnotherArgument:`. This may seem odd to people coming in from other languages, which usually have much terser naming conventions, but in general Objective-C method names are substantially more self-documenting than in other languages. Method names contain prepositions and are made to read like sentences. The language also has a fairly entrenched naming convention, which means that method names are fairly regular.

While Objective-C method names are long, Xcode will perform code completion as you type. Press Return to accept its suggestion, or F5 to present a pop-up list of matching methods. Pressing Ctrl-/ will step you through the parameters of the method.

Methods can return output, as shown here:

```
output = [anObject someMethodWithOutput: anotherObject];
```

And they can be nested, as in the following:

```
output = [anObject someMethodWithOutput: [anotherObject someOtherMethod]];
```

When I originally started writing in Objective-C, one of the main problems I had with the language was the way it dealt with method calls. For those of us who are coming from more utilitarian languages, the behavior of Objective-C in this regard does seem rather strange. Although Objective-C code can be valid and not follow the rules I've described here, modern Objective-C is not really separable from the Cocoa framework, and Cocoa rules and conventions have become Objective-C's rules and conventions.

Calling Methods on nil

In Objective-C, the nil object is functionally equivalent to the NULL pointer found in many other C-derived languages. However, unlike most of these languages, it is permissible to call methods on nil without causing your application to crash. If you call a method on (although in Objective-C we are actually passing a message to) the nil object type, you will get nil returned.

Memory Management

The way memory is managed in Objective-C on the iPhone is probably not what you're used to if you're coming in from a language such as Java. If you're writing an application in Objective-C for the Mac, you have the option of enabling garbage collection; however, on the iPhone you are restricted to using reference counting. This isn't as bad as it seems, and sticking to a few simple rules means that you can manage the memory that is allocated.

Creating Objects

You can create an object in two ways. As shown in the following code, you can manually allocate the memory for the object with alloc and initialize it using init or an appropriate initWith method (e.g., NSString has an initWithString method):

```
NSString *string = [[NSString alloc] init];
NSString *string = [[NSString alloc] initWithString:@"This is a string"];
```

Alternatively, you can use a convenience constructor method. For instance, the NSString class has a stringWithString class method that returns an NSString object:

```
NSString *string = [NSString stringWithString:@"This is a string"];
```

In the preceding two cases, you are responsible for releasing the memory you allocated with alloc. If you create an object with alloc, you need to release it later. However, in the second case, the object will be *autoreleased*. You should never manually release an autoreleased object, as this will cause your application to crash. An autoreleased object will, in most cases, be released at the end of the current function unless it has been explicitly retained.

The Autorelease Pool

The autorelease pool is a convenience that defers sending an explicit release message to an object until "later," with the responsibility of freeing the memory allocated to objects added to an autorelease pool devolved onto the Cocoa framework. All iPhone applications require a default autorelease pool, and the Xcode template inside the *main.m* file creates it for us:

```
int main(int argc, char *argv[]) {

    NSAutoreleasePool * pool = [[NSAutoreleasePool alloc] init];❶
    int retVal = UIApplicationMain(argc, argv, nil, nil);
    [pool release];❷
    return retVal;
}
```

❶ The default autorelease pool is set up prior to entering the main event loop.

❷ The default autorelease pool is drained after exiting the loop.

An additional inner autorelease pool is created at the beginning of each event cycle (i.e., iteration through your application's event loop), and is released at the end.

The need for and existence of autorelease makes more sense once you appreciate why it was invented, which is to transfer control of the object life cycle from one owning object to another without immediately deallocating the object.

The alloc, retain, copy, and release Cycle

Although the autorelease pool is handy, you should be careful when using it because you unnecessarily extend the time over which the object is instantiated, thereby growing your application's memory footprint. Sometimes it makes a lot of sense to use autoreleased objects. However, beginning Cocoa programmers often overuse convenience constructors and autoreleased objects.

Apple, writing in its Cocoa Fundamentals guide, officially discourages the use of autorelease objects on the iPhone due to the memory-constrained environment on the device, stating that "Because on iPhone OS an application executes in a more memory-constrained environment, the use of autorelease pools is discouraged in methods or blocks of code (for example, loops) where an application creates many objects. Instead, you should explicitly release objects whenever possible."

When handling memory management manually using the retain count and the `alloc`, `retain`, and `release` cycle (see Figure 4-1), you should not release objects you do not own. You should always make sure your calls to `retain` are balanced by your calls to `release`. You own objects that you have explicitly created using `alloc` or `copy`, or that you have added to the retain count of the object using `retain`. However, you do not own objects you have created using convenience constructors such as `stringWith String`.

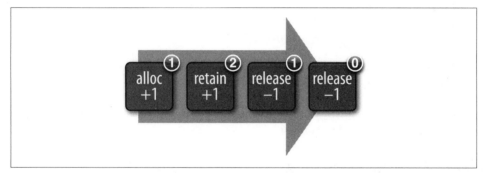

Figure 4-1. The alloc-retain-release cycle; an object is allocated, retained, and then released twice, bringing the reference count back to zero and freeing the memory

When releasing the object, you have the option of sending it either a `release` message or an `autorelease` message:

```
[anObject release];
[anObject autorelease];
```

Sending a `release` message will immediately free the memory the object uses if that `release` takes the object's retain count to zero, while sending an `autorelease` message adds the object to the local autorelease pool. The object will be released when the pool is destroyed, normally at the end of the current function.

If your object is a delegate of another object, you need to set the delegate property of that object to `nil` before you release your original object.

The dealloc Method

The `dealloc` method is called when an object is released. You should never call this method directly, but instead send a `release` message to the object, because the object may contain references to other objects that will not be deallocated.

As we did in the `HelloWorldViewController` class, you should always override the `dealloc` method in your own objects and in `release` objects you have created or retained:

```
- (void)dealloc {
    [label release];
    [button release]
    [super dealloc];
}
```

In this method, we released the `label` and `button` instance variables. We then called the `dealloc` method of the superclass. It is entirely permissible to send a `release` message to a `nil` object.

Responding to Memory Warnings

Your code must respond to memory warnings. Let's look at the `HelloWorldViewController` implementation from Chapter 3 again. It implements the `didReceiveMemoryWarning` method:

```
- (void)didReceiveMemoryWarning {
    [super didReceiveMemoryWarning];
}
```

This is where you should release any large blocks of memory—for instance, image or web caches—that you are using. If you ignore a memory warning, your application may crash. The iPhone does not have any sort of virtual memory or swap file; when the device runs out of memory there really is no more memory to allocate. It's possible, and advisable, to test your application by simulating a memory warning in iPhone Simulator, which you can do by selecting Hardware→Simulate Memory.

Fundamental iPhone Design Patterns

When you write code you're probably already using patterns, although possibly you're doing so without realizing it. A design pattern is just a reusable solution, a template, for how to approach commonly occurring problems. A pattern is not code, but instead describes how you should model the application in terms of the classes that are used, and how they should structure the interactions and relationships between these classes.

The Cocoa Touch framework underlying your iPhone applications is based on one of the oldest design patterns, the Model-View-Controller (MVC) pattern, which dates from the 1970s. The MVC pattern is used to separate the program logic from the UI, and is the generally accepted way to build iPhone applications. As it is used so extensively inside Apple's own frameworks, including the UIKit framework, it would be quite hard to write an iPhone application without using this pattern in your implementation. While you could write an iPhone application without referencing the MVC pattern, it is enormously difficult to fight the underlying frameworks; you should instead work with them. Attempting to write iPhone applications while ignoring the underlying MVC patterns is a pointless exercise in make-work.

The Model-View-Controller Pattern

The MVC pattern divides your application into three functional pieces:

Model
> The model manages the application state (and associated data) and is usually persistent. It is entirely decoupled from the UI or presentation of the application state to the user.

View
> The view is what the user sees, and it displays the model for the user. It allows the user to manipulate it and respond and generate events. In iPhone applications, the view is normally built inside Interface Builder rather than programmatically.

Controller
> The controller coordinates updates of the view and the model when user interaction with the view makes changes to the model, and vice versa. This is typically where most of the application logic lives.

We implemented our Hello World application from Chapter 3 using this pattern. We created the view using Interface Builder, and the `HelloWorldViewController` class managed the view. The application was too simple to require an explicit class to manage the application's state; effectively, the model was embedded in the `ViewController` class. If we were strictly adhering to the design pattern, we would have implemented a further class that our `sayHello:` method would have queried to ask what text should have been displayed.

The model class is usually a subclass of `NSObject` and has a set of instance variables and associated accessor methods, along with custom methods to associate the internal data model.

Views and View Controllers

I've talked about both views and view controllers quite a lot, and while so far we've built our views in Interface Builder and then handled them using our own view controller code, that isn't the only way to build a view. You can create views programmatically—in fact, in the early days of iPhone development you had to do things that way.

However, Interface Builder has made things a lot easier, and I recommend that in most cases you build your views using it if you can. When you used Interface Builder to construct your view you edited a NIB file, an XML serialization of the objects in the view. Using Interface Builder to create these objects, and to define the relationship between them and your own code, saves you from writing large amounts of boilerplate code that you would otherwise need to manage the view.

If you want to create your view manually, you should override the `loadView:` method of your view controller class, as this is the method the view controller calls when the `view` property is requested but is currently set to `nil`. Don't override this method if you've created your view using the `initWithNibName:` method, or set the `nibName` or `nibBundle` properties. If you're creating your view manually and you do override this method, however, you must assign the root view you create to the `view` property of your view controller class:

```
-(void) viewDidLoad {
    UIView* view = [[UIView alloc] initWithFrame:CGRectMake(0,0,320,480)];
        .
        .
        .
    self.view = view;
    [view release];
}
```

Your implementation of this method should not call [`super viewDidLoad`], as the default implementation of this method will create a plain `UIView` if no NIB information is present and will make this the main view.

The Delegates and DataSource Pattern

I talked briefly about delegates in Chapter 3. An object that implements a delegate protocol is one that acts on behalf of another object. To receive notification of an event to which it must respond, the delegate class needs to implement the notification method declared as the delegate protocol associated with that event. The protocol may, and usually does, specify a number of methods that the delegate class must implement.

Data sources are similar to delegates, but instead of delegating control, if an object implements a `DataSource` protocol it must implement one or more methods to supply data to requesting objects. The delegating object, typically something such as a `UITableView`, will ask the data source what data it should display; for instance, in the case of a table view, what should be displayed in the next `UITableViewCell` when it scrolls into the current view.

Declaring that a class is a data source or a delegate flags the object for Interface Builder so that you can connect the relevant UI elements to your code. (We'll be talking about UITableView in Chapter 5.) To declare that AnObject was *both* a table view data source and a delegate, we would note this in the @interface declaration:

```
@interface AnObject: UIViewController <UITableViewDataSource,
                                       UITableViewDelegate> {
    ...
}
```

This would mean that the AnObject object, a UIViewController, is responsible for both populating the table view with data and responding to events the table view generates. Another way to say this is that this object implements both the UITableViewData Source and the UITableViewDelegate protocols.

At this point, you would use Interface Builder, and we'll be doing that in the next chapter when we build a table-view-based application to connect the UITableView in our view to the data source and delegate object in our code.

Conclusion

This has been a dense chapter and fairly heavy going. However, our discussion of the MVC pattern should show you that this delegation of event handling and of populating data into the UI from the view to a controller class makes sense inside the confines of the pattern, and the availability of these features in Objective-C is one of the reasons why the MVC pattern has been widely adopted.

 In this chapter, I was able to give you only a brief overview of Objective-C and the Cocoa Touch framework. Added levels of subtlety are involved in many of the things I covered, but I didn't have the space to cover them here. My coverage of the basics should give you enough information so that you can pick up the rest as we go along. However, if you intend to develop for the iPhone on a serious level, you should read up on the language in more detail. Apple provides some excellent tutorial material on its Developer website (*http://developer.apple.com/ iphone/*), and that should certainly be your first port of call. However, I also suggest several other books for further reading in Chapter 14.

CHAPTER 5

Table-View-Based Applications

The `UITableView` and associated classes are perhaps the most commonly used classes when building UIs for your iPhone or iPod touch applications. Due to the nature of the applications, you can use these classes to solve a large cross section of problems, and as a result they appear almost everywhere. In this chapter, we're going to dive fairly deeply into the table view classes, and by the end of it you'll be able to produce `UITableView`-based applications on your own. We'll also discuss some features of Xcode and Interface Builder as we go along.

We're going to write a simple guidebook application. We'll start by displaying a list of cities in a table (using the `UITableView` class). Then we'll add the ability to click on the city name inside each table cell (each cell is a `UITableViewCell` object), which will take you to a page describing the city. Later in the chapter I'll show you how to add and delete cities to and from the guidebook. By the end of the chapter, we will have a working guidebook application. However, before we get to write some new code, we're going to do some helpful refactoring of the template code generated by Xcode.

Open Xcode and choose "Create a new Xcode project" in the startup window, and then choose the View-based Application template from the New Project pop-up window, the sample template we used for our Hello World application in Chapter 3. When prompted, name your new project *CityGuide*.

Simplifying the Template Classes

One of the annoying things about the Xcode templates is the long class names Xcode chooses for the default classes. While the default class names are OK for small programs, they can become somewhat unwieldy, and at times rather inappropriate, when the amount of code you have increases. So, we're going to modify the template Xcode provides before we add our own code, using a process known as *refactoring* the code.

Why are we doing this refactoring? Well, later in the chapter we're going to be using more than one view controller inside the project. The original name of the default view controller created by the Xcode template would be somewhat misleading. In addition to changing its name to something that reflects its purpose, we will shorten the `CityGuideAppDelegate` name.

Open the *CityGuideAppDelegate.h* file, right-click on the `CityGuideAppDelegate` class name in the interface declaration, and select Refactor, as shown in Figure 5-1. This will bring up the Refactoring window. Let's change the name of the main application delegate class from `CityGuideAppDelegate` to `CityGuideDelegate`.

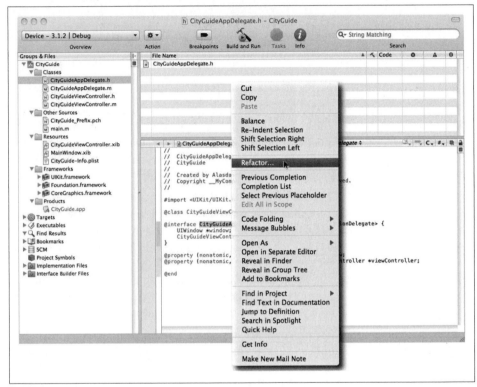

Figure 5-1. Select the class name, right-click, and select Refactor to access Xcode's intelligent refactoring tool

 Since Objective-C does not have namespaces, it's a common practice to prefix your class names with initials to avoid *namespace collision*, or the situation where two classes have the same name but do different things. For instance, the Apple classes have the prefix `NS` for historical reasons, as Cocoa was based on the NeXTSTEP frameworks.

Entering the new class name and clicking Preview, as I've done in Figure 5-2, shows us that three files will be affected by the change. Click Apply and Xcode will propagate the changes throughout the project. Remember to save the affected files before you refactor the next set of classes.

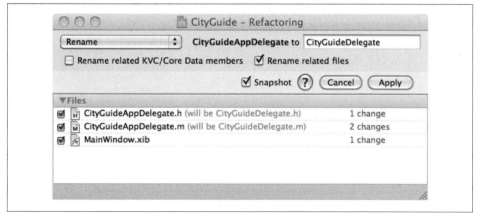

Figure 5-2. The Refactoring window

 If you find that the File→Save menu is grayed out in Xcode, click on the file you want to save and then click somewhere inside the file (it doesn't matter where). Then you'll be able to save the file.

You should also change the name of the `CityGuideViewController` class. Open the *CityGuideViewController.h* file and right-click on the `CityGuideViewController` class name in the interface declaration, and again choose to refactor. Let's change this class from `CityGuideViewController` to `RootController`. Entering the new class name and clicking Preview shows that this change is more extensive, with six files being affected by the change. Click Apply, and the changes will again propagate throughout the project.

Notice, however, that Xcode has not changed the *CityGuideViewController.xib* file to be more appropriately named *RootController.xib*. We'll have to make this change by hand. Click once on this file in the Groups & Files pane, wait a second, and click it again. You can then rename it to *RootController.xib*.

Unfortunately, since you had to make this change by hand, it hasn't been propagated throughout the project. You'll have to make some more manual changes. Double-click on the *MainWindow.xib* file to open it in Interface Builder. Click on the Root Controller icon in the main NIB window and open the Attribute pane of the Inspector window. As you can see in Figure 5-3, the NIB name associated with the root controller is still set as `CityGuideViewController`. Set this to `RootController`. You can either type the name of the controller into the window and Xcode will automatically perform name completion as you type, or use the control on the righthand side of the text entry box to get a drop-down panel where you'll find the `RootController` class listed. Remember to save the NIB file using ⌘-S, and then test your refactoring by clicking the Build and Run (or depending on your Xcode setup, the Build and Debug) button in Xcode's menu bar. You should see a bland gray screen pop up to prove that all is well.

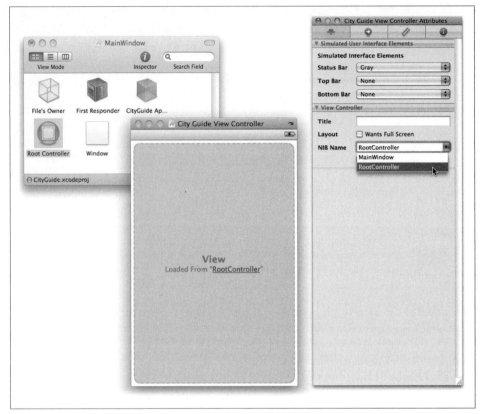

Figure 5-3. Changing the NIB name from CityGuideViewController to RootController

Creating a Table View

With refactoring out of the way, now it's time to put the UI together.

Double-click the *RootController.xib* file in Xcode to open it in Interface Builder. Then double-click on the View icon in the *RootController.xib* window to bring up the View window, and drag a table view from the Library window into the view. You'll find the table view under Cocoa Touch→Data Views in the Library window.

Center the UITableView in the view, as shown in Figure 5-4. You must confirm that you've dropped it as a subview of the main view by clicking the View Mode widget on the menu bar of the *RootController.xib* window and choosing List View. It should look as shown in Figure 5-4, with Table View appearing under View. Save the *.xib* file using ⌘-S.

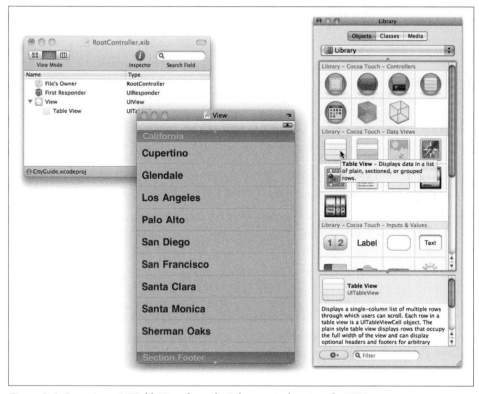

Figure 5-4. Dragging a UITableView from the Library window into the UIView

Switch back to Xcode to add the outlets and delegates Interface Builder needs so that you can connect the `UITableView` to your code. Open the *RootController.h* interface file and add a `UITableView` variable to the `@interface` declaration, then declare this as a property and an `IBOutlet`. You also need to declare that this class implements both the `UITableViewDataSource` and the `UITableViewDelegate` protocols. This means that it both provides the data to populate the table view and handles events generated by user interaction with the table view.

Once you've done this, the *RootController.h* file will look like this:

```
#import <UIKit/UIKit.h>

@interface RootController: UIViewController
  <UITableViewDataSource, UITableViewDelegate>
{
    UITableView *tableView;
}
```

```
@property (nonatomic, retain) IBOutlet UITableView *tableView;

@end
```

If you Option-double-click `UITableViewDataSource` in the declaration and then click the documentation icon in the upper-right corner of the window that appears (or ⌘-Option-double-click to go directly there), you'll see that the protocol has a number of optional methods, as well as two mandatory methods (you must implement the methods that aren't labeled as "optional"). Having declared that our view controller is a `UITableViewDataSource`, our `RootController` implementation must implement these two mandatory methods. These methods are `tableView:cellForRowAtIndexPath:` and `tableView:numberOfRowsInSection:`. The first of these methods returns a `UITableView Cell` object; the table view will ask the data source delegate for a cell each time a new cell is displayed in the view. The second method returns an `NSInteger` determining how many sections are in the table view. Table views can be divided into sections, and a title added to the top of each section. For now, we'll use just one section (the default).

Despite what the documentation for `UITableViewDelegate` seems to suggest, there aren't any mandatory methods. However, to obtain any sort of functionality from our table view we will at least have to implement the `tableView:didSelectRowAtIndexPath:` method.

Now we must add the implementation of those two mandatory data source methods to the `RootController` class (*RootController.m*). Once we have the code up and running we'll look at the `tableView:cellForRowAtIndexPath:` method in detail. This method returns a populated table view cell for each entry (index) in the table, and it's called each time the view controller wants to display a table view cell. For example, it's called as the table view is scrolled and a new cell appears in the view.

Here are the contents of *RootController.m*. I marked in bold the lines I added to the file that the Xcode template generated:

```
#import "RootController.h"

@implementation RootController

@synthesize tableView;

#pragma mark Instance Methods

(void)didReceiveMemoryWarning {
    // Releases the view if it doesn't have a superview.
    [super didReceiveMemoryWarning];

    // Release any cached data, images, etc that aren't in use.
}

- (void)viewDidUnload {
    // Release any retained subviews of the main view.
    // e.g. self.myOutlet = nil;
}
```

```
- (void)dealloc {
    [tableView release];
    [super dealloc];
}

#pragma mark UITableViewDataSource Methods

- (UITableViewCell *)tableView:(UITableView *)tv
    cellForRowAtIndexPath:(NSIndexPath *)indexPath
{
    UITableViewCell *cell =
      [tv dequeueReusableCellWithIdentifier:@"cell"];
    if( nil == cell ) {
        cell = [[[UITableViewCell alloc]
            initWithFrame:CGRectZero reuseIdentifier:@"cell"] autorelease];
    }
    return cell;
}

- (NSInteger)tableView:(UITableView *)tv
  numberOfRowsInSection:(NSInteger)section
{
    // Our table view will consist of only 3 cells
    return 3;
}

#pragma mark UITableViewDelegate Methods

@end
```

Organizing and Navigating Your Source Code

I introduced something new in the preceding code listing: the `#pragma mark` declaration. If you examine the lower-righthand pane of the Xcode interface you'll see that the title bar contains a filename, and immediately to the right of this is the name of the method inside which your cursor currently happens to be. If you click on this, you'll see a drop-down menu showing all the method names in the implementation (you can access this menu easily using the Ctrl-2 keyboard shortcut). You'll also see the text of the pragma marks I added to the code. For large classes, this is a convenient way to separate the methods involved in different jobs. In this case, I've added marks for the instance, data source, and delegate methods. You can also add a horizontal bar to the method list by adding the following:

```
#pragma mark -
```

Do not add a space after the -, as this will make Xcode think this is a text comment.

Connecting the Outlets

We now need to go back into Interface Builder and wire up the outlets to our code as we did in "Connecting the Outlets in Interface Builder" on page 36 in Chapter 3. Open the *RootController.xib* file, and when Interface Builder opens, set the *RootController.xib* main window's view mode to List, and then open the View list to reveal the table view.

Next, click the Table View icon and set the Inspector window to display the Connections Inspector (⌘-2). This reveals the `dataSource` and `delegate` outlets. Connect both of these to File's Owner in the main window, which in this case is the `RootController` class, as shown in Figure 5-5.

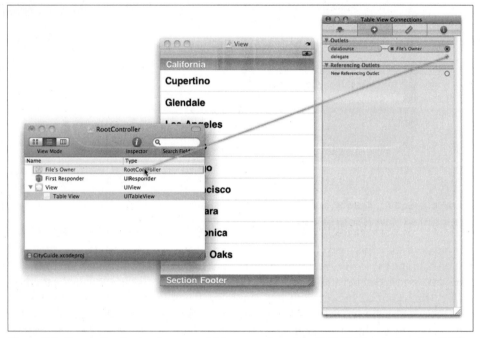

Figure 5-5. Connecting the dataSource and delegate outlets of the UITableView in Interface Builder to the RootController class (File's Owner)

Now click on the File's Owner icon. In the outlets section of the Connections Inspector (⌘-2) you'll see the `tableView` object that we flagged as an `IBOutlet` in the *RootController.h* file. Connect this with the `UITableView` as shown in Figure 5-6.

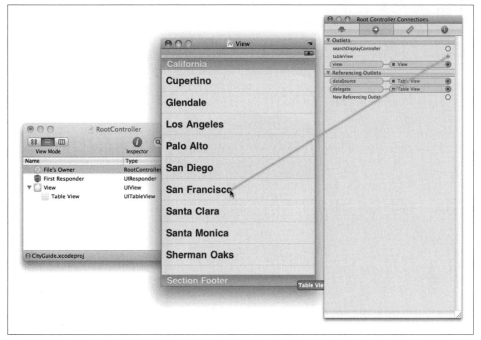

Figure 5-6. Connecting the tableView IBOutlet in the RootController to the UITableView subview

If you don't see the `tableView` object, quit Interface Builder (save your work so far), return to Xcode, and make sure you saved *RootController.h*. Then open *RootController.xib* in Interface Builder again; it should appear when you select the File's Owner icon and go to the Connections Inspector.

We've reached a natural point at which to take a break. Quit Interface Builder (be sure to save any changes) and return to Xcode. The code should now run without crashing, although it's not going to do very much. So, click Build and Run (or Build and Debug) to start the application in iPhone Simulator. Figure 5-7 shows what you should see.

OK, now we have the basic table view code working, so let's go back to the `RootController` implementation (*RootController.m*) and look at that `tableView:cellForRowAtIndexPath:` method where we were creating and then returning table view cells. For performance reasons, the `UITableView` can reuse cells to enhance scroll performance by minimizing the need to allocate memory during scrolling. However, to take advantage of this ability we need to specify a *reuse identifier string*. The `UITableView` uses this to look up existing cells with the same identifier using the `dequeueReusableCellWithIdentifier:` method. If it can't find an unused cell with the correct identifier, it will create one, but if an unused cell is available (perhaps it's scrolled out of the current view), it will reuse it:

```
UITableViewCell *cell =
  [tv dequeueReusableCellWithIdentifier:@"cell"];
if( nil == cell ) {
    cell = [[[UITableViewCell alloc]
      initWithFrame:CGRectZero reuseIdentifier:@"cell"] autorelease];
}
return cell;
```

Figure 5-7. The empty table view inside iPhone Simulator

So far our table view isn't that interesting, so let's push forward and add some content and some event handling. To do this, add an implementation for the **tableView:didSelectRowAtIndexPath:** delegate method to *RootController.m*. As the name suggests, this method is called when a user clicks on a table view cell. Because our cells are empty at the moment, we'll also add some text to a cell before returning it from this method. Added lines of code are shown in bold:

```
#pragma mark UITableViewDataSource Methods

- (UITableViewCell *)tableView:(UITableView *)tv
  cellForRowAtIndexPath:(NSIndexPath *)indexPath
{
    UITableViewCell *cell =
      [tv dequeueReusableCellWithIdentifier:@"cell"];
    if( nil == cell ) {
```

```
            cell = [[[UITableViewCell alloc]
                initWithFrame:CGRectZero reuseIdentifier:@"cell"] autorelease];
        }

        cell.textLabel.text = @"Testing";❶
        return cell;
    }

    - (NSInteger)tableView:(UITableView *)tv
      numberOfRowsInSection:(NSInteger)section
    {
        // Our table view will consist of only 3 cells
        return 3;
    }

    #pragma mark UITableViewDelegate Methods

    - (void)tableView:(UITableView *)tv❷
      didSelectRowAtIndexPath:(NSIndexPath *)indexPath
    {
        [tv deselectRowAtIndexPath:indexPath animated:YES];❸
    }
```

❶ This is where we added text to the cell we're returning from the `tableView:cellFor RowAtIndexPath:` method.

❷ Here's where we implemented the `tableView:didSelectRowAtIndexPath:` delegate method.

❸ Here we just told the table view to deselect the cell every time the user touches it and selects it. Because the `animated` argument is set to `YES`, the cell fades out as it deselects itself. Previously, if you touched the cell it would have stayed permanently selected.

You can see the results of these additions in Figure 5-8.

Building a Model

At this point, you should have a working `UITableView`. So far, you've implemented both the view and the controller parts of the MVC pattern. Now we're going to return to Xcode and implement the model. This needs to be separate from the view and the view controller, since we want to decouple the way the data is stored from the way it is displayed as much as possible. This will increase the reusability of both the classes that handle the UI and the classes that store the data behind the scenes, allowing us to change how parts of the application work while affecting as little code as possible.

Right-click on the Classes folder in the Groups & Files pane and select Add→New File. When you see the New File window shown in Figure 5-9, make sure Cocoa Touch Class is selected on the left side of the screen. Next, select "Objective-C class," make sure Subclass of NSObject is specified, and click on Next.

Figure 5-8. The new code running inside iPhone Simulator

You will then be asked for the filename of the new class. Type in *City.m* and click on Finish. Xcode will generate a pair of files, *City.h* and *City.m*, containing the template interface and the implementation of the new class, and will put them in the Classes folder. If you look at these files, you can see that since you specified that the class was a subclass of the base `NSObject` class, Xcode really hasn't created a lot of code. It didn't know what you wanted the object for, so you're going to have to write some code.

Open the *City.h* file and add variables to hold the name of our city, a short descriptive paragraph, and an image. Declare these variables as properties.

```
#import <Foundation/Foundation.h>

@interface City : NSObject {
    NSString *cityName;
    NSString *cityDescription;
    UIImage *cityPicture;
}

@property (nonatomic, retain) NSString *cityName;
@property (nonatomic, retain) NSString *cityDescription;
@property (nonatomic, retain) UIImage *cityPicture;

@end
```

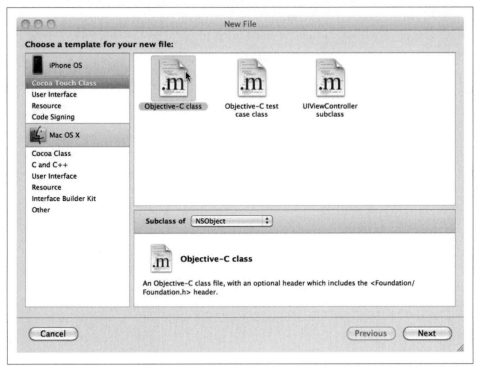

Figure 5-9. The New File window, which allows you to select the template Xcode will use to generate the new class interface and implementation file

I'm declaring the name and description as an `NSString`, and I'm declaring the variable used to hold the picture as a `UIImage`. `UIImage` is a fairly high-level class that can be directly displayed in a `UIImageView` that we can create inside Interface Builder.

I could have decided to use an `NSMutableString` rather than an `NSString`. An `NSMutableString` is a subclass of `NSString` that manages a *mutable string*, which is a string whose contents can be edited. Conversely, an `NSString` object manages an *immutable string*, which, once created, cannot be changed and can only be replaced. Using mutable strings here might give us a bit more flexibility later on, and if you decide you need it, you can always go back and change these definitions to mutable strings later. Changing from using an `NSString` to an `NSMutable String` is easy since mutable strings are a subclass and implement all of the methods provided by the `NSString` class. Going in the opposite direction is more difficult, unless you have not made use of the additional functionality offered by the mutable string class.

Open the *City.m* file and add code to `@synthesize` the `cityName`, `cityDescription`, and `cityPicture` accessor methods. After doing that, add a `dealloc:` method so that the variables will be released when the class is destroyed. Here's what your *City.m* file should contain:

```
#import "City.h"

@implementation City

@synthesize cityName;
@synthesize cityDescription;
@synthesize cityPicture;

-(void) dealloc {
    [cityName release];
    [cityDescription release];
    [cityPicture release];
    [super dealloc];
}

@end
```

Because we made use of properties, our accessor methods will be generated for us automatically. So, we're done now. Admittedly, this is just a fairly small class to hold some data, but it illustrates how useful properties will be for larger, more complex classes.

Let's go back to the `CityGuideDelegate` class and prepopulate it with a few cities. You can put in longer descriptions if you want. If you're just using it for personal testing, you could use text and images from Wikipedia. Later in the book I'll show you how to retrieve data like this directly from the network, but for now we'll *hardcode* (embed the data directly into the code; you normally will store your data outside the app) a few cities into the app delegate class and include the images inside the application itself rather than retrieving them from the network. Here's what the *CityGuideDelegate.h* file should look like now (added lines are shown in bold):

```
#import <UIKit/UIKit.h>

@class RootController; ❶

@interface CityGuideDelegate : NSObject <UIApplicationDelegate> {
    UIWindow *window;
    RootController *viewController;
    NSMutableArray *cities;
}

@property (nonatomic, retain) IBOutlet UIWindow *window;
@property (nonatomic, retain) IBOutlet RootController *viewController;
@property (nonatomic, retain) NSMutableArray *cities;

@end
```

❶ You should #import the header files for any classes you're using in the implementation. But if you need to reference a class in your header file, you should use the @class forward declaration instead of importing the class header file. Apple says in its documentation that the @class directive "minimizes the amount of code seen by the compiler and linker, and is therefore the simplest way to give a forward declaration of a class name. Being simple, it avoids potential problems that may come with importing files that import still other files."

In the application delegate interface file we declare our City class using the @class declaration, create an NSMutableArray to hold our list of cities, and declare this mutable array to be a property.

The changes to the application delegate implementation are slightly more extensive:

```
#import "CityGuideDelegate.h"
#import "RootController.h"
#import "City.h";❶

@implementation CityGuideDelegate

@synthesize window;
@synthesize viewController;
@synthesize cities;❷

- (void)applicationDidFinishLaunching:(UIApplication *)application {

    City *london = [[City alloc] init];❸
    london.cityName = @"London";
    london.cityDescription =
      @"The capital of the United Kingdom and England.";
    london.cityPicture = [UIImage imageNamed:@"London.jpg"];

    City *sanFrancisco = [[City alloc] init];
    sanFrancisco.cityName = @"San Francisco";
    sanFrancisco.cityDescription = @"The heart of the San Francisco Bay Area.";
    sanFrancisco.cityPicture = [UIImage imageNamed:@"SanFrancisco.jpg"];

    City *sydney = [[City alloc] init];
    sydney.cityName = @"Sydney";
    sydney.cityDescription = @"The largest city in Australia.";
    sydney.cityPicture = [UIImage imageNamed:@"Sydney.jpg"];

    City *madrid = [[City alloc] init];
    madrid.cityName = @"Madrid";
    madrid.cityDescription = @"The capital and largest city of Spain. ";
    madrid.cityPicture = [UIImage imageNamed:@"Madrid.jpg"];

    self.cities = [[NSMutableArray alloc]
      initWithObjects:london, sanFrancisco, sydney, madrid, nil]; ❹
    [london release]; ❺
    [sanFrancisco release];
    [sydney release];
    [madrid release];
```

```
    // Override point for customization after app launch
    [window addSubview:viewController.view];
    [window makeKeyAndVisible];
}

- (void)dealloc {
    [viewController release];
    [window release];
    [cities release]; ❻
    [super dealloc];
}

@end
```

❶ First, we imported the *City.h* interface file.

❷ Next, we synthesized the `cities` property to automatically create the accessor methods.

❸ Following this, we declared and populated four instances of the `City` class. For each one, we allocated and initialized the instance object and then used the accessor methods to populate the instance. We could also have written an `initWithName:with Description:andImage:` method for the class and achieved the same result by using this method to initialize the class. However, I do not discuss that sort of approach to class initialization until later in the book; the first time you'll meet this is when I talk about web views near the start of Chapter 7.

❹ Here, we initialized an `NSMutableArray` and populated it with the four cities. The trailing `nil` in the object list passed to the `initWithObjects:` method is essential. You must ensure that the last object in a comma-separated list of objects is the `nil` object; otherwise, when iterating through the array your code will end up pointing to un-allocated memory, which will lead to an exception.

❺ Here, we released the initial reference to each of the four instances of the `City` class. You'll notice that previous to this we assigned references to these instances to the `self.cities` array. Remembering our discussion of the alloc-retain-release cycle in Chapter 4, we are therefore safe to reduce the count by releasing the initial reference, which reduces the reference count from two back to one, as adding an object to an array will increase its retain count. The memory allocated to these objects will therefore now be released when the `self.cities` array is released.

❻ Here, we released the reference to the object instances that we are responsible for before releasing the reference to the class itself. If we did not do this, memory allocated for these objects would not be released until the application itself terminated. When this happens, especially with many objects, the condition is referred to as a *memory leak*.

If you create a `UIImage` using the `imageNamed:` method as shown in this example, it is added to the default autorelease pool rather than the event loop autorelease pool. This means the memory associated with such images will be released only when the application terminates. If you use this method with many large images, you'll find that your application may quickly run out of memory. Since these images are part of an autorelease pool, you'll be unable to free the memory they use when the device's operating system calls the `didReceiveMemoryWarning:` method in the application delegate when it runs short on memory. You should use the `imageNamed:` method sparingly, and generally only for small images.

Adding Images to Your Projects

As you can see, we retrieve the `UIImage` by name using the `imageNamed:` class method, but from where are we retrieving these images? The answer is, from somewhere inside the application itself. For testing purposes, I sorted through my image collection, found a representative image for each city (and then scaled and cropped the images to be the same size [1,000×750 pixels] and aspect ratio using my favorite image editing software), and copied them into the Xcode project. To do this yourself, drag and drop each image into the Resources folder in the Groups & Files pane. This brings up the copy file dropdown pane, as shown in Figure 5-10. If you want to copy the file into the project's directory rather than create a link to wherever the file is stored, click on the relevant checkbox. If you do not copy the files to the project's directory, they will still be collected in the application bundle file when Xcode compiles the application; however, if you later move or delete the file, Xcode will lose the reference to it and will no longer be able to access it. This is especially important when copying source code files. In general, I advocate always checking the box and copying the file into your project, unless you have a very good reason not to do so.

 There are other ways to add a file to a project. You can also right-click on the Resources folder and select Add→Existing Files to add a file to the project.

After you copy the downloaded images into the project, they become accessible from your code (see Figure 5-11). It's generally advisable not to copy large images into the project. For example, if your binary gets too large you'll have distribution problems. Among other problems, applications above a certain size cannot be downloaded directly from the App Store on the iPhone unless it is connected to the Internet via WiFi. Depending on the demographic you're targeting, this may limit the market for your application. However, despite this, bundling images into your application is a good way to get easy access to small icons and logos that you may want to use in your project.

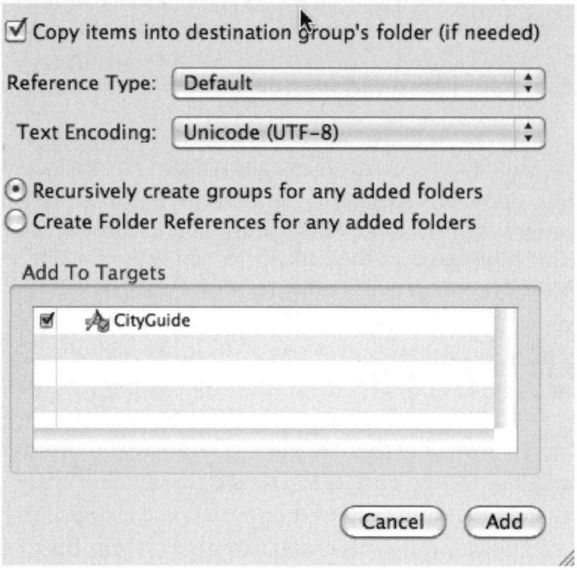

☑ Copy items into destination group's folder (if needed)

Reference Type: Default ⬍

Text Encoding: Unicode (UTF–8) ⬍

◉ Recursively create groups for any added folders
○ Create Folder References for any added folders

Add To Targets

☑ 🅰 CityGuide

Cancel   Add

Figure 5-10. The drop down brought up when you drag and drop a file into the project

Figure 5-11. The downloaded images inside my Xcode project

Connecting the Controller to the Model

Now that we've built the model, we have to go back to the `RootController` class and build the bridge between the view controller and the model. To do this we need to make only one change in the `RootController` interface declaration (*RootController.h*). Add a pointer to an `NSMutableArray` that you'll then populate inside the `viewDidLoad:` method:

```
@interface RootController : UIViewController
  <UITableViewDataSource, UITableViewDelegate> {
    UITableView *tableView;
    NSMutableArray *cities;
}
```

Changes to the implementation (*RootController.m*) are only slightly more extensive. You need to `#import` both the *City.h* and *CityGuideDelegate.h* interface files, as you'll be using both of these classes inside the updated implementation:

```
#import "RootController.h"
#import "CityGuideDelegate.h"
#import "City.h"
```

As I mentioned earlier, you must implement the `viewDidLoad:` method. This `UIViewController` method is called after the controller's view is loaded into memory, and is the method we'll normally use to set up things that the view needs. You'll find that the Xcode template included a stub for `viewDidLoad` (not far from the `#pragma mark`-labeled instance methods), but it's *commented out* (wrapped inside a comment, so it doesn't compile). Replace it with the following (be sure to remove the /* and */ so that it's no longer commented out):

```
- (void)viewDidLoad {
    CityGuideDelegate *delegate =
     (CityGuideDelegate *)[[UIApplication sharedApplication] delegate];
    cities = delegate.cities;
}
```

Here, we acquired a reference to the application delegate by using the `[[UIApplication sharedApplication] delegate]` method call. Since this method returns a generic `id` object, we had to cast it to be a `CityGuideDelegate` object before assigning it. We then grabbed a pointer to the array of cities managed by the app delegate.

Since our code now declares a new variable, we also have to remember to release it in the `dealloc:` method:

```
- (void)dealloc {
    [tableView release];
    [cities release];
    [super dealloc];
}
```

Finally, we must use the model to populate the table view. The number of rows in the table view should now be determined by the number of cities in the `NSMutableArray` instead of simply returning "3" all the time. We must now go ahead and change the `tableView: numberOfRowsInSection:` method to reflect that by replacing the line `return 3;` (and the comment above it). Here's how the method should look now:

```
- (NSInteger)tableView:(UITableView *)tv
  numberOfRowsInSection:(NSInteger)section
{
    return [cities count];
}
```

Finally, we need to change the `tableView:cellForRowAtIndexPath:` method to label the cell with the correct city name. To do this, add the following code shown in bold, which figures out which row of the table we're trying to populate and looks up the appropriate element of the `cities` array:

```
- (UITableViewCell *)tableView:(UITableView *)tv
  cellForRowAtIndexPath:(NSIndexPath *)indexPath
{
    UITableViewCell *cell =
      [tv dequeueReusableCellWithIdentifier:@"cell"];
    if( nil == cell ) {
        cell = [[[UITableViewCell alloc]
                initWithFrame:CGRectZero reuseIdentifier:@"cell"] autorelease];
    }

    City *thisCity = [cities objectAtIndex:indexPath.row];
    cell.textLabel.text = thisCity.cityName;
    return cell;
}
```

We've now reached a point where we have a functional, buildable application. However, while our table view now reflects our model, we still can't access any of the information we entered about our cities. When we click on a city we want the application to tell us about the city, and for that we need to modify the `tableView:didSelectRowAtIndexPath:` method. But for now, click the Build and Run button on the Xcode toolbar, and your iPhone Simulator should pop up, looking like Figure 5-12.

Mocking Up Functionality with Alert Windows

Before I go on to show how to properly display the city descriptions and images using the `UINavigationController` class, let's do a quick hack and get the application to pop up an alert window when we click on a table view cell. Go back to *RootController.m* and add the highlighted lines in the following code to the `didSelectRowAtIndexPath:` method:

```
- (void)tableView:(UITableView *)tv
  didSelectRowAtIndexPath:(NSIndexPath *)indexPath {
    City *thisCity = [cities objectAtIndex:indexPath.row];
    UIAlertView *alert = [[UIAlertView alloc]
      initWithTitle:thisCity.cityName message:thisCity.cityDescription
      delegate:self cancelButtonTitle:nil otherButtonTitles:@"OK", nil];
    [alert show];
    [alert autorelease];
```

```
    [tv deselectRowAtIndexPath:indexPath animated:YES];
}
```

Figure 5-12. Populating the UITableView of our application using the new model

In this method, we create a `UIAlertView` window with an OK button, and set the title to be the city name and the contents to be the city description. You can see how this looks in Figure 5-13.

Adding Navigation Controls to the Application

Next, back out the changes you just made to the `tableView:didSelectRowAtIndex` `Path:` method by deleting the lines you added in the preceding section (be careful to not remove the call to `deselectRowAtIndexPath`).

Now, let's wrap this app up properly. This means we have to add a `UINavigationCon` `troller` to the application. If you've used many iPhone apps, you'll be familiar with this interface; it's one of the most commonly used iPhone design interface patterns. Clicking on a cell in the table view makes the current view slide to the left and a new view is displayed. You return to the original table view by clicking on the Back button.

Figure 5-13. After you modify the tableView:didSelectRowAtIndexPath: method, a UIAlertView pop up appears when you click on a city name

The first thing you need to do is add an `IBOutlet` to a `UINavigationController` to the app delegate interface (*CityGuideDelegate.h*):

```
#import <UIKit/UIKit.h>

@class RootController;

@interface CityGuideDelegate : NSObject <UIApplicationDelegate> {
    UIWindow *window;
    RootController *viewController;
    NSMutableArray *cities;
    UINavigationController *navController;
}

@property (nonatomic, retain) IBOutlet UIWindow *window;
@property (nonatomic, retain) IBOutlet RootController *viewController;
@property (nonatomic, retain) IBOutlet UINavigationController *navController;
@property (nonatomic, retain) NSMutableArray *cities;

@end
```

You also need to make some modifications to the app delegate implementation (*City-GuideDelegate.m*). Add a new line of code near the top to @**synthesize** the new property:

```
@synthesize window;
@synthesize viewController;
@synthesize cities;
@synthesize navController;
```

Now you need to replace the section of the code that adds the `RootController` main view as a subview of the main window. Delete the following line from the bottom of the `applicationDidFinishLaunching:` method:

```
[window addSubview:viewController.view];
```

Next, replace it with the code shown in bold in the following code snippet. This new code adds the `RootController` to the `NavController`'s stack of view controllers, making its view the current view of the `NavController`. Then it sets the current `NavController` view as the subview of the main window. The end of the `applicationDidFinishLaunch ing:` method should look like this now:

```
    // Override point for customization after app launch
    navController.viewControllers = [NSArray arrayWithObject:viewController];
    [window addSubview:navController.view];
    [window makeKeyAndVisible];
}
```

As the current view of the `NavController` changes, it will automatically update the sub-view of the main window, and thus what the user sees on his screen. Let's get this working first, and afterward I'll discuss exactly how the `NavController` manipulates its stack of views.

Open the *MainWindow.xib* file in Interface Builder and drag and drop a navigation controller (`UINavigationController`) into the main NIB window (titled "MainWindow" or "MainWindow.xib"). The navigation controller is found on the Library (⌘-Shift-L) under Cocoa Touch→Controllers.

After doing so, you should see something similar to Figure 5-14. Note the navigation bar that appears at the top (with the title "City Guide").

After adding the `UINavigationController` to the NIB, click on the CityGuide App Delegate icon in the main NIB window and switch to the Connections pane (⌘-2) of the Inspector window. Connect the `navController` outlet to the `UINavigationController`, as shown in Figure 5-15.

After performing this step, save the NIB file and return to Xcode. Open the *RootController.m* file and add the following snippet at the top of the `viewDidLoad:` method:

```
self.title = @"City Guide";
```

We've reached another good time to take a break, so click Build and Run. If you've followed all the steps, you should see what I see, something that looks a lot like Figure 5-16.

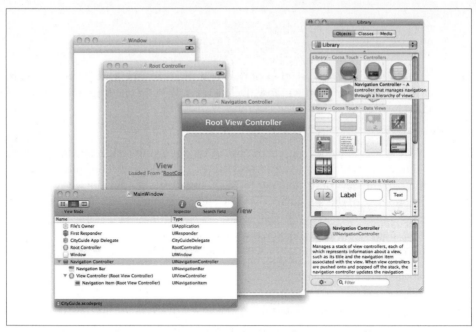

Figure 5-14. Adding a UINavigationController to the MainWindow.xib NIB file

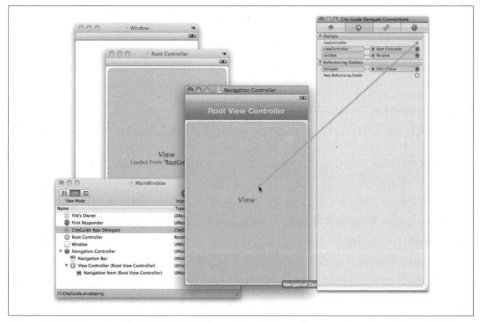

Figure 5-15. Connecting the UINavigationController to the outlet created in the application delegate code earlier

Figure 5-16. The CityGuide application is starting to look more like an iPhone application after adding a navigation bar

Adding a City View

You might have a nice navigation bar, but it doesn't do any navigation yet, and after backing out of the changes you made to the `tableView:didSelectRowAtIndexPath:` method to present a pop up, the code doesn't tell you about the selected city anymore. Let's fix that now and implement a view controller and associated view to present the city information to the application user.

Right-click on the Classes folder in the Groups & Files pane and select Add→New File. Choose a `UIViewController` subclass and tick the checkbox to ask Xcode to generate an associated NIB file, as shown in Figure 5-17. When prompted, name the new class `CityController.m`, as this will be the view controller we're going to use to present the information about our cities.

This will generate three new files: *CityController.h*, *CityController.m*, and *CityController.xib*. For neatness you might want to drag the *CityController.xib* file into the Resources folder of the project along with the other project NIB files.

Figure 5-17. Select a UIViewController subclass and tick the checkbox for Xcode to create an associated XIB for the user interface

Right now, the new NIB file is just a blank view. We'll fix that later, but first we need to add code to the `tableView:didSelectRowAtIndexPath:` method in the *RootController.m* class to open the new view when a city is selected in the table view:

```
- (void)tableView:(UITableView *)tv
  didSelectRowAtIndexPath:(NSIndexPath *)indexPath
{

    CityGuideDelegate *delegate =
     (CityGuideDelegate *)[[UIApplication sharedApplication] delegate];
    CityController *city = [[CityController alloc] init];

    [delegate.navController pushViewController:city animated:YES];
    [city release];

    [tv deselectRowAtIndexPath:indexPath animated:YES];
}
```

Here we grabbed a reference to the application delegate and initialized a new `CityCon troller` instance. We then pushed this view controller onto the top of the `UINaviga tionController` stack, making its view the current view.

Additionally, at the top of the *RootController.m* class, since we're now making use of the `CityController` class, we'll also need to import its interface file into this class:

```
#import "CityController.h"
```

This is another good point to stop and try things out, so click the Build and Run button in the Xcode menu bar. If all has gone well, when you click on a city your table view should slide neatly to the left and reveal a blank white view created by the `CityControl ler` view controller, with a navigation bar at the top and a Back button provided by your `UINavigationController` that will take you back to the city table view, as shown in Figure 5-18.

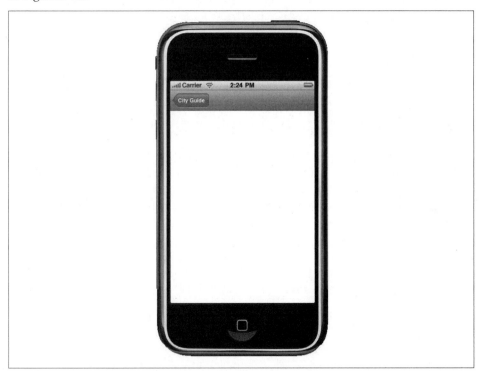

Figure 5-18. The blank view generated by the CityController view controller

From here we need to modify the `CityController` class so that we can populate its view from the model held by the app delegate; then we need to build that view in Interface Builder by modifying the *CityController.xib* file. The first question we need to ask, however, is "How does the controller class know which city to display?" An easy way to make this happen is to override the `init` method. In the interface file (*CityControl ler.h*), we'll declare the following method:

```
- (id)initWithIndexPath:(NSIndexPath *)indexPath;
```

I plan to initialize the class by passing in the index (`NSIndexPath`) of the selected `UITableViewCell` in the main table view. From this you can figure out which `City` to use to populate the view. As you can imagine, this is one of a number of different ways to approach this problem.

In our view, we'll be using the navigation bar to display the city name as the view title, a `UITextView` element to display the city description, and finally a `UIImageView` to display the picture of the city that we added to the project earlier. The interface file therefore has to declare these as variables and make them available to Interface Builder by also declaring them as an `IBOutlet`. Here's what *CityController.h* should look like with these changes (including the line of code just listed):

```
#import <UIKit/UIKit.h>

@interface CityController : UIViewController {
    NSIndexPath *index;

    IBOutlet UIImageView *pictureView;
    IBOutlet UITextView *descriptionView;
}

- (id)initWithIndexPath:(NSIndexPath *)indexPath;

@end
```

You'll notice that we declared our variables as an `IBOutlet` inside the `@interface` declaration instead of doing so while declaring them as a property. There really isn't any need to make these variables a property, as we don't need accessor methods for them, and making the `IBOutlet` declaration as part of the variable declaration is perfectly fine.

 Even when working with properties, you can put the `IBOutlet` declaration in the property's variable declaration instead of the `@property` statement if you wish (it's a matter of style).

I implemented the `init` method in *CityController.m* as follows:

```
- (id)initWithIndexPath: (NSIndexPath *)indexPath {

    if ( self == [super init] ) {
        index = indexPath;
    }
    return self;
}
```

This invokes the superclass `init` method and assigns the result to the `self` variable. If the call to the superclass is unsuccessful, `self` will be set to `nil` and this will be returned by the `initWithIndexPath:` method. This is very unlikely to occur, and if it does your application will crash. However, normally our line of custom initializer code will be executed: it sets the `index` variable to point to the `NSIndexPath` we passed into the object. We then initialize the view inside the `viewDidLoad:` method.

```
- (void)viewDidLoad {
    CityGuideDelegate *delegate = (CityGuideDelegate *)
      [[UIApplication sharedApplication] delegate];
    City *thisCity = [delegate.cities objectAtIndex:index.row];

    self.title = thisCity.cityName;
    descriptionView.text = thisCity.cityDescription;
    descriptionView.editable = NO;
    pictureView.image = thisCity.cityPicture;

}
```

Inside the `viewDidLoad:` method we grabbed a reference to the application's app delegate, and then used this and the `index` variable to retrieve the correct city. Then we set the `text` and `image` properties of the two subviews to hold the city data, and the `title` of the main view to be the city name. The title of the view will be displayed in the navigation bar. We also set the `editable` property of the `descriptionView` to `NO`, as we don't want the user to be able to edit the text describing the city.

Since we've made use of both the `CityGuideDelegate` and the `City` classes in this method, we must also remember to import them in our implementation. Add these lines to the top of *CityController.m*:

```
#import "CityGuideDelegate.h"
#import "City.h"
```

Apart from the changes shown so far, the only other change to the default `CityControl ler` implementation is to make sure we release our declared variables in the `dealloc:` method. Find the `dealloc:` method at the bottom of *CityController.m* and add the lines shown in bold:

```
- (void)dealloc {
    [index release];
    [descriptionView release];
    [pictureView release];
    [super dealloc];
}
```

Now we have to go back to the `RootController` implementation and make one quick change: substitute the new `initWithIndexPath:` method for the default `init` method call we originally used. In the `tableView:didSelectRowAtIndexPath:` method of *RootController.m*, replace the following line:

```
CityController *city = [[CityController alloc] init];
```

with this line, making use of the new initialization method:

```
CityController *city =
            [[CityController alloc] initWithIndexPath:indexPath];
```

At this point, all we need to do is go into Interface Builder and build the view, and then connect the view to the outlets we declared and implemented inside the `CityControl ler` class.

Opening the *CityController.xib* file in Interface Builder will present you with a blank view. Drag an image view (`UIImageView`) and text view (`UITextView`) element from the Library window (⌘-Shift-L) onto the view. These controls are available under Cocoa Touch→Data Views.

Since I resized my images to be the same aspect ratio, we're going to change the size of our `UIImageView` to reflect that. In the Size tab of the Inspector window (⌘-3), resize the `UIImageView` to have a width of 250 pixels and a height of 188 pixels. Next, position it at X = 25 and Y = 37. Turning to the Attributes tab of the Inspector window (⌘-1), change the mode of the view to Aspect Fill. This means the image will be scaled to the size of the view, and if the aspect ratio of the image is not the same as the aspect ratio of the view, some portion of the image will be clipped so that the view is filled.

Turning to the `UITextView` element, use the Size tab of the Inspector window (⌘-3) to position it at X = 0 and Y = 223 with a width of W = 320 and a height of H = 256. This fills the main view below the image, as shown in Figure 5-19.

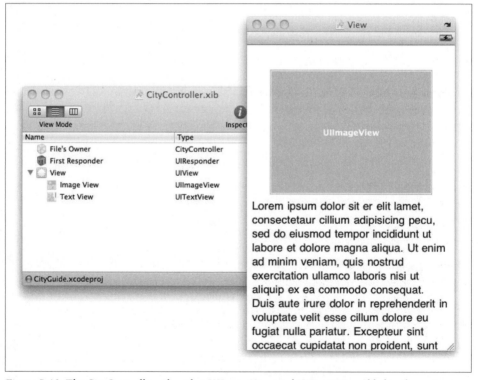

Figure 5-19. The CityController.xib with a UIImageView and UITextView added to the main view

The only thing left to do is connect the UIImageView and UITextView elements to the two IBOutlet variables we created in code. In the main XIB window (titled CityControl-ler.xib), click on File's Owner and go to the Connections tab in the Inspector window (⌘-2). Connect the descriptionView outlet to the text view and the pictureView outlet to the image view, as shown in Figure 5-20.

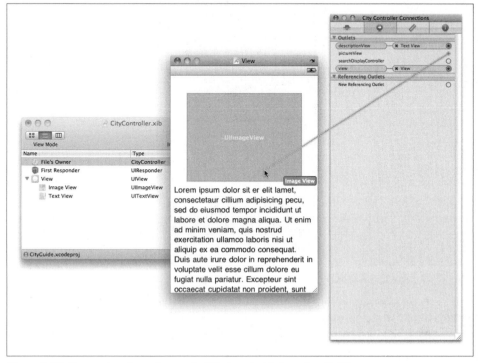

Figure 5-20. Connecting the outlets to the UI views inside Interface Builder

At this point we're done, so make sure the NIB file is saved and go back into Xcode and click the Build and Run button on the toolbar. After the application starts tap one of the city names and you should see something like Figure 5-21.

Edit Mode

So far, so good. But it would be nice if we could add more cities to our guide and, if we're not interested in a particular city, delete it as well. Let's implement a first cut at that using the UITableViewController edit mode. You'll have seen this many times when using iPhone applications such as the Mail application. There is an Edit button on the top right on the navigation bar. When tapped, it will drop the table view into edit mode, allowing you to delete mail messages. In some applications, the Edit button lets you add entries to the table view.

Figure 5-21. The city guide to London

This is such a commonly implemented pattern that there are hooks inside the `UIView` `Controller` to simplify things. In the `viewDidLoad:` method of *RootController.m*, you need to add the following line of code:

```
self.navigationItem.rightBarButtonItem = self.editButtonItem;
```

This will add an Edit button to the navigation bar. Clicking on this button calls a method called `setEditing:animated:` on the view controller, which sets the table view into edit mode and changes the Edit button to a Done button. Clicking on the Done button will take the table view out of edit mode, and calls the `setEditing:animated:` method again, although this time to different effect (ending the edits and changing the button back to an Edit button).

Since we want to be able to add new cities, when the table view is put into editing mode we're going to add another cell to our table view prompting us to "Add New City...". When this is clicked, we'll open a new view allowing us to enter the details of the city.

To do that we need to change the `tableView:numberOfRowsInSection:` method in *RootController.m* to return `cities.count+1` when our table view has been put into editing mode. We'll need to delete the one line (`return cities.count;`) in that method and replace it with the code shown in bold:

```
- (NSInteger)tableView:(UITableView *)tv
  numberOfRowsInSection:(NSInteger)section {
    NSInteger count = cities.count;
    if(self.editing) {
        count = count + 1;
    }
    return count;
}
```

We also need to edit the `tableView:cellForRowAtIndexPath:` method to return that extra cell when in edit mode:

```
- (UITableViewCell *)tableView:(UITableView *)tv
  cellForRowAtIndexPath:(NSIndexPath *)indexPath {

    UITableViewCell *cell =
      [tv dequeueReusableCellWithIdentifier:@"cell"];
    if( nil == cell ) {
        cell = [[[UITableViewCell alloc]
          initWithFrame:CGRectZero reuseIdentifier:@"cell"] autorelease];
    }
    if (indexPath.row < cities.count ) {
        City *thisCity = [cities objectAtIndex:indexPath.row];
        cell.textLabel.text = thisCity.cityName;
    } else {
        cell.textLabel.text = @"Add New City...";
        cell.textLabel.textColor = [UIColor lightGrayColor];
        cell.editingAccessoryType =
          UITableViewCellAccessoryDisclosureIndicator;
    }
    return cell;
}
```

Next, we need to override the `setEditing:animated:` method to put the table view into edit mode and display the extra cell needed to prompt us to add a new city. Add this method to *RootController.m* somewhere above the `#pragma mark`–labeled `UITableView DataSource` methods:

```
-(void)setEditing:(BOOL)editing animated:(BOOL) animated {
    [super setEditing:editing animated:animated];
    [tableView setEditing:editing animated:animated];
    [tableView reloadData];
}
```

This code calls the **super** method and notifies the subview (the `UITableView` we are attempting to put into edit mode) that we have been put into edit mode. It then reloads the data in the table view to update the view the user sees.

By default, when you put the table view into edit mode, the edit control that appears next to the table view cell is of style `UITableViewCellEditingStyleDelete`, a red circle enclosing a minus sign, to signify that editing this row will delete the item in question. This is fine for our existing cities, but for the newly added "Add New City..." cell we need to set this to a different style. To do so, we need to implement the `tableView:editingStyleForRowAtIndexPath:` method that is part of the `UITableViewDelegate` protocol.

This should go somewhere below the #pragma mark–labeled UITableViewDelegate methods:

```
- (UITableViewCellEditingStyle)tableView:(UITableView *)tv
  editingStyleForRowAtIndexPath:(NSIndexPath *)indexPath {
    if (indexPath.row < cities.count ) {
        return UITableViewCellEditingStyleDelete;
    } else {
        return UITableViewCellEditingStyleInsert;
    }

}
```

In this method, we tell the table view that for cells occupied by existing cities we want the delete style; otherwise, we want the insert style, a green circle enclosing a plus sign.

Bearing in mind that we haven't actually implemented the backend logic for editing yet, we've reached a good point to see if everything's working. Click the Build and Run button in the Xcode toolbar, and when the City Guide application starts tap on the Edit button on the navigation bar. Your app should look just like Figure 5-22.

Figure 5-22. The City Guide table view in editing mode

You've probably noticed that putting the table view into editing mode wasn't really very pretty, as no animation was carried out while the table view reloaded the view. It's actually fairly simple to change this by making use of two methods: `insertRowsAtIn dexPaths:withRowAnimation:` and `deleteRowsAtIndexPaths:withRowAnimation:`.

Going back to our overridden `setEditing:animated:` method, we need to modify it to use these two methods as shown here:

```
-(void)setEditing:(BOOL)editing animated:(BOOL) animated {
    if( editing != self.editing ) {
        [super setEditing:editing animated:animated];
        [tableView setEditing:editing animated:animated];

        NSArray *indexes =
          [NSArray arrayWithObject:
            [NSIndexPath indexPathForRow:cities.count inSection:0]];
        if (editing == YES ) {
            [tableView insertRowsAtIndexPaths:indexes
               withRowAnimation:UITableViewRowAnimationLeft];
        } else {
            [tableView deleteRowsAtIndexPaths:indexes
               withRowAnimation:UITableViewRowAnimationLeft];
        }
    }
}
```

This code now checks to see whether we are changing editing modes; if we are, we call the **super** method and then notify our subview as before. However, instead of just calling `[tableView reloadData]` we now need to build an array containing the `NSIndexPath` of each cell we wish to insert (or delete) with animation. In our case, the array will hold only a single object since we intend to animate only a single cell; we then insert or delete with animation depending on whether we are entering or leaving editing mode, respectively.

After clicking Build and Run again, you should still see something that looks a lot like Figure 5-22; however, this time the "Add New City…" cell, as well as the + and – buttons, will be nicely animated and fly in and out. Note that you still won't be able to do anything with these buttons, but at least they make a nice entrance and exit.

Deleting a City Entry

To actually delete a table view cell, we need to add the table view data source method `tableView:commitEditingStyle:forRowAtIndexPath:` to the code. Add this method to *RootController.m* between the `#pragma mark`-labeled `UITableViewDataSource` methods and the `#pragma mark`-labeled `UITableViewDelegate` methods:

```
- (void) tableView:(UITableView *)tv
  commitEditingStyle:(UITableViewCellEditingStyle) editing
  forRowAtIndexPath:(NSIndexPath *)indexPath {
    if( editing == UITableViewCellEditingStyleDelete ) {
        [cities removeObjectAtIndex:indexPath.row];
        [tv deleteRowsAtIndexPaths:[NSArray arrayWithObject:indexPath]
          withRowAnimation:UITableViewRowAnimationLeft];
```

```
    }
  }
```

In this method, we check that the editing style is set to delete, and if that's the case, we remove the item from the `cities` array. We figure out which item to remove by checking the `indexPath.row`, and delete the relevant table view cell with animation.

You can now delete cities from the City Guide application. Click Build and Run and try it out. Tap the Edit button on the navigation bar, and then tap the edit control to the left of a city name. Tap the Delete button that appears, as shown in Figure 5-23. The city will be deleted. Tap the Done button.

Figure 5-23. Deleting a city

The nice part about implementing things in this way is that you don't have to drop the table into edit mode to delete a city; swiping from left to right will also bring up the Delete button.

Adding a City Entry

Before you can add a new city, you must implement an interface to allow the user to enter city metadata: the city name, a description, and an image. I'm going to put off adding the ability to add a picture to the city entry until the next chapter, where we look at various view controllers including the `UIImagePickerController`; for now, let's implement the basic framework to allow us to add a new city by allowing the user to enter a city name and description.

Right-click on the Classes folder in the Groups & Files pane and select Add→New File. Choose a `UIViewController` class and tick the checkbox to ask Xcode to generate an associated XIB file, as shown in Figure 5-17. When prompted, name the new class `AddCityController.m`. You may want to drag the *.xib* file from the Classes group into the Resources group, just to keep things organized consistently.

As we did when we created the `CityController` class earlier, let's add the hooks in the code which will allow us to open the new view when we click on the "Add New City..." cell after putting the table view into edit mode.

First we need to make some changes to the `RootController` class. Since we're going to be using the new `AddCityController` class, we need to import the declaration into the implementation. Add this line to the top of *RootController.m*:

```
#import "AddCityController.h"
```

We also have to make some changes to the `tableView:didSelectRowAtIndexPath:` method in that same file:

```
- (void)tableView:(UITableView *)tv
  didSelectRowAtIndexPath:(NSIndexPath *)indexPath
{
    CityGuideDelegate *delegate =
      (CityGuideDelegate *)[[UIApplication sharedApplication] delegate];

    if (indexPath.row < cities.count && !self.editing ) {❶

        CityController *city =
                [[CityController alloc] initWithIndexPath:indexPath];
        [delegate.navController pushViewController:city animated:YES];
        [city release];
    }

    if( indexPath.row == cities.count && self.editing ) {❷

        AddCityController *addCity = [[AddCityController alloc] init];
        [delegate.navController pushViewController:addCity animated:YES];
        [addCity release];
    }

    [tv deselectRowAtIndexPath:indexPath animated:YES];
}
```

❶ We execute the commands within this `if` statement for cells whose row is less than the number of entries in the `cities` array, but only if the table view *is not* in editing mode.

❷ We execute the commands within this `if` statement for cells whose row is equal to the number of entries in the `cities` array, but only if the table view *is* in editing mode.

Because Objective-C is derived from C, its array indexes start at zero. So, the only cell in our table view whose row number is *greater* than the number of entries in the city array is the "Add New City…" cell. Therefore, the code in the first `if` block uses the `cities` array to display each cell; the code in the second block uses a new city that the user is adding.

The first code branch, for city cells, is unchanged from the original implementation. While the second branch is very similar to the first, in this case we create an `AddCity Controller` instance rather than a `CityController` instance.

Click the Build and Run button on the Xcode toolbar. Running the application at this point shows us that we've forgotten something. Right now clicking on any of the table view cells when the table is in edit mode, including the "Add New City…" cell, doesn't do anything, despite having implemented code inside the `tableView:didSelectRowAtIn dexPath:` method.

You need to go back to the *RootController.xib* file inside Interface Builder, select the `UITableView` element, and in the Attributes tab of the Inspector window (⌘-1) tick the Allow Selection While Editing box.

If you rerun the application after setting this flag inside Interface Builder and click on a city cell when the table view is in edit mode, you should see that it is briefly selected and then deselected. Clicking on the "Add New City…" cell, however, should slide in a blank view: the one associated with the *AddCityController.xib* file.

However, the brief selection effect you get when you click on one of the normal city cells inside edit mode is annoying. These cells shouldn't be selectable in edit mode, but unfortunately there isn't a way to tell our table view that only the last cell is selectable. There are several ways to fool the user into thinking that this is the case, though. One of these is to extend our `setEditing:animated` method in the `RootController` class to set the selection style of these cells to `UITableViewCellSelectionStyleNone` when the table view is in edit mode, and then set the style back to `UITableViewCellSelectionSty leBlue` when we leave edit mode. The changes you need to make to the `setEditing:ani mated:` method in the *RootController.m* file are significant, so you can simply replace the method with the following:

```
-(void)setEditing:(BOOL)editing animated:(BOOL) animated {
    if( editing != self.editing ) {
        [super setEditing:editing animated:animated];
        [tableView setEditing:editing animated:animated];

        NSMutableArray *indices = [[NSMutableArray alloc] init];
        [indices autorelease];
        for(int i=0; i < cities.count; i++ ) {❶
            [indices addObject:[NSIndexPath indexPathForRow:i inSection:0]];
        }
        NSArray *lastIndex = [NSArray
          arrayWithObject:[NSIndexPath
                            indexPathForRow:cities.count inSection:0]];❷
```

```
        if (editing == YES ) {
            for(int i=0; i < cities.count; i++ ) {❸
                UITableViewCell *cell =
                  [tableView
                    cellForRowAtIndexPath:[indices objectAtIndex:i]];
                  [cell setSelectionStyle:UITableViewCellSelectionStyleNone];
            }
            [tableView insertRowsAtIndexPaths:lastIndex
                withRowAnimation:UITableViewRowAnimationLeft];
        } else {
            for(int i=0; i < cities.count; i++ ) {❹
                UITableViewCell *cell =
                  [tableView
                    cellForRowAtIndexPath:[indices objectAtIndex:i]];
                  [cell setSelectionStyle:UITableViewCellSelectionStyleBlue];
            }
            [tableView deleteRowsAtIndexPaths:lastIndex
                withRowAnimation:UITableViewRowAnimationLeft];
        }
    }
}
```

❶ Inside this loop, we build an NSMutableArray containing the NSIndexPath of all the cells where we want to modify the selection style, that is, normal cells that contain cities.

❷ Here we build an NSArray containing the NSIndexPath of the final "Add New City..." cell.

❸ We have just entered edit mode, so inside this loop we retrieve the UITableView Cell for each NSIndexPath in our array and set the selection style to "None".

❹ Leaving edit mode we do the opposite, and set the selection style back to the default for each cell in the array.

Build and run the application and you'll see that this gets you where you want to go: inside edit mode the only (apparently) selectable cell is the "Add New City..." cell. None of the other cells show any indication that they have been selected when they are clicked on. However, outside edit mode these cells are selectable, and will take you (as expected) to the view describing the city.

The "Add New City..." Interface

There are a number of ways we could build an interface to allow the user to enter metadata about a new city. I'm going to take the opportunity to show you how to customize a UITableViewCell inside Interface Builder and load those custom cells into a table view.

Open the *AddCityController.xib* file in Interface Builder. Open the Library (⌘-Shift-L) and choose Cocoa Touch→Data Views. Drag and drop a table view (UITableView) into the view. Next, grab a UITableViewCell from the Library window and drag and drop that into the main `AddCityController` NIB window (not the View window). Repeat this step and your AddCityController.xib window will look like Figure 5-24. Here you can see the main view with its table view and the two table view cells, which are not part of the main view. Double-clicking on a table view cell in this window will open the cell in a new view window. Each table view cell is a separate subview.

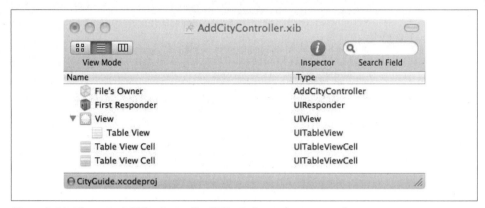

Figure 5-24. The main AddCityController NIB window in list view mode

We now need to customize these two cells to give users the ability to enter text. To do this, we're going to build a table view similar to the one Apple uses when we write a new mail message. Yes, in case you didn't release it, that's just a highly customized table view. It's actually pretty amazing how far you can get writing iPhone applications just using the `UITableView` and associated classes.

Since you're going to be using these cells to enter text, you don't want them to be selectable, so you should open the Attributes tab for both of the cells (click on the cell's name and press ⌘-1) and change the selection type from "Blue" to "None" in both cases.

At the top of the table view, we'll have a normal-size table view cell with an embedded `UITextField` to allow users to enter the city name. Below that we'll have a super-size table view cell with an embedded `UITextView` to allow users to enter the much longer description.

Double-click on the first of your two table view cells, grab a label (`UILabel`) from the Library window (Cocoa Touch→Inputs and Values), and drop it onto the Table View Cell window. Make sure the label is selected, and in the Attributes tab (⌘-1) of the Inspector window change the text to "City:". Then switch to the Size tab (⌘-3) and position the label at X = 10 and Y = 11 with width W = 42 and height H = 21.

Now grab a Text field (`UITextField`) from the Library window and drag and drop it onto the same Table View Cell window. Click on the Text field, and in the Attributes tab of the Inspector window select the dotted-line border for the field. This represents the "no border" style. In the Text Input Traits section of the Attributes tab set Capitalize to "None" and Correction to "No". With the Text field still selected, go to the Size tab of the Inspector window and resize the element to have origin X = 60 and Y = 0 with width W = 260 and height H = 44. In the Attributes tab you may want to add some placeholder text to the Text field to prompt the user to enter a city name. I went with "e.g. Paris, Rome".

Next, double-click on the second of the two table view cells. You need to resize this to fill the remaining part of the main view. The navigation bar at the top of the view is 54 pixels high, and a standard table view cell is 44 pixels high. Since the iPhone's screen is 460 pixels high, to fill the view we want the table view cell to be 362 pixels high. So, go to the Size tab in the Inspector window and set H = 362. The view window containing the table view cell will automatically grow to reflect its new size.

 Apple explicitly warns developers in the documentation that we should not rely on the number of pixels in the iPhone screen staying constant. The next revision of the iPhone after the 3GS may have a larger screen, and our careful sizing of the table view cells based on the size of the screen in the current models will break our application's interface. Instead of hardwiring the sizes of the table view cells as we have done here, in production code you should make use of the UIScreen class to determine the size of the main window. For more information, see Apple's SDK documentation for UIScreen.

Grab another UILabel from the Library window and drop it onto the Table View Cell window. In the Attributes tab of the Inspector window change the text to "Description" and then switch to the Size tab. Position the label at X = 11 and Y = 1 with width W = 86 and height H = 21.

Now grab a UITextView from the Library window (Cocoa Touch→Data Views), drag and drop it into this new expanded table view cell, resize it to the remaining extent of the cell using the Size tab in the Inspector window (X = 11, Y = 29, W = 297, H = 332), and delete the default text from the Attributes tab. After doing so, you should have a collection of views that resembles that seen in Figure 5-25.

Finally, click on the UITextView, and in the View section of the Attributes tab (⌘-1) of the Inspector window set the Tag attribute to 777. Go to your other table view cell and do the same for its UITextField. The Tag attribute is a UIView property that Interface Builder is exposing to us; this is used to uniquely identify views (or in this case a subview) to our application. We'll be able to grab the UITextView and UITextField easily using this tag directly from our code after setting it here in Interface Builder.

We're done with Interface Builder for now, so save your changes to the NIB file, return to Xcode, and open the *AddCityController.h* file. Add the code shown in bold:

```
#import <UIKit/UIKit.h>

@interface AddCityController : UIViewController
  <UITableViewDataSource, UITableViewDelegate> {
    IBOutlet UITableView *tableView;
```

```
    IBOutlet UITableViewCell *nameCell;
    IBOutlet UITableViewCell *descriptionCell;
}

@end
```

Figure 5-25. Interface Builder with the two modified UITableViewCells

Here we declare the view controller class to be both a data source and a delegate for the table view. We also declare three variables: a `UITableView` variable and two `UITableViewCell` variables. We declare each of these variables to be an `IBOutlet`; we'll connect these variables to our views inside Interface Builder in a little while.

However, before we return to Interface Builder to do that, we need to implement a number of table view data source and delegate methods inside the *AddCityController.m* class implementation. Here is the full listing for that file:

```objc
#import "AddCityController.h"

@implementation AddCityController

#pragma mark ViewController Methods

- (void)didReceiveMemoryWarning {
    // Releases the view if it doesn't have a superview.
    [super didReceiveMemoryWarning];

    // Release any cached data, images, etc that aren't in use.
}

- (void)viewDidLoad {
    self.title = @"New City";❶
}

- (void)viewDidUnload {
    // Release any retained subviews of the main view.
    // e.g. self.myOutlet = nil;
}


- (void)dealloc {❷
    [tableView release];
    [nameCell release];
    [descriptionCell release];
    [super dealloc];
}

#pragma mark UITableViewDataSource Methods

- (UITableViewCell *)tableView:(UITableView *)tv
  cellForRowAtIndexPath:(NSIndexPath *)indexPath
{
    UITableViewCell *cell = nil;
    if( indexPath.row == 0 ) {❸
        cell = nameCell;
    } else {
        cell = descriptionCell;
    }
    return cell;

}

- (NSInteger)tableView:(UITableView *)tv
  numberOfRowsInSection:(NSInteger)section
{
    return 2; ❹
}

#pragma mark UITableViewDelegate Methods

- (CGFloat)tableView:(UITableView *)tv
  heightForRowAtIndexPath:(NSIndexPath *)indexPath {
```

```
        CGFloat height;
        if( indexPath.row == 0 ) {❺
            height = 44;
        } else {
            height = 362;
        }
        return height;

    }

    @end
```

❶ As we did for the `CityController` view controller, we need to add a title to the view inside the `viewDidLoad:` method. This title will be displayed in the navigation bar at the top of the view.

❷ Since we have declared variables, we need to remember to release them inside the `dealloc:` method.

❸ Instead of using the `dequeueReusableCellWithIdentifier:` method to obtain a cell, we check which row we are being asked to display, and return either our custom cell to enter the city name or the custom cell to enter the city description.

❹ Since we have only two cells in our table view, we just return 2 from this method.

❺ Since the table view cells are different heights, we have to return the correct height in pixels depending on which cell we are being asked about.

The only method you haven't seen before is the `tableView:heightForRowAtIndexPath:` method. As you would expect, this delegate returns the height of the individual table view cell in a specified location.

Double-click the *AddCityController.xib* file to open it in Interface Builder. Click on File's Owner and open the Connections tab (⌘-2) of the Inspector window. Connect the `descriptionCell` outlet to the super-size table view cell and the `nameCell` outlet to the smaller table view cell. If you aren't sure which table view cell is which by looking at the AddCityController.xib window, you can open each one and drag the outlet to their open windows.

Finally, connect the `tableView` outlet to the table view in the main View window. Now click on the table view in the main View window and connect both the `dataSource` and the `delegate` outlets of the table view to File's Owner. After doing this, click on File's Owner, and the Connections tab of the Inspector window should look the same as in Figure 5-26.

We've reached a point where we should have a working application. Save the XIB, then click on the Build and Run button in the Xcode toolbar to compile and start the application in the simulator. Once it has started successfully, click on the Edit button to put your table view into edit mode and then click on the "Add New City..." cell. If everything has gone according to plan, you should see something like Figure 5-27.

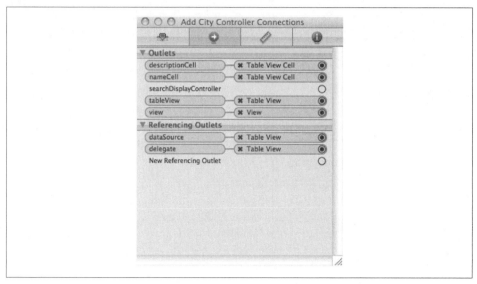

Figure 5-26. The Connections tab of the Inspector window after making all the necessary connections inside Interface Builder between the various components

Figure 5-27. The new "New City" UI in iPhone Simulator

If we tap inside one of the custom table view cells, the keyboard will appear and we can start typing. However, right now we don't have any way to save the information we enter in these fields. Let's implement that right now.

Capturing the City Data

Both the UITextField and the UITextView we're using to capture the name and description of the city have delegate protocols. However, we don't need to look into those quite yet, although I will be talking about them later in the book. The first step is to add a Save button to the interface.

That's actually pretty easy to do from the viewDidLoad: method of the view controller. We can use the same technique we used to add the Edit and Done buttons to the main view controller to add our Save button to the AddCityController. However, instead of declaring the navigation item to be self.editButtonItem, we make use of the UIBarButtonItem method's initWithBarButtonSystemItem:target:action: to create the navigation item:

```
self.navigationItem.rightBarButtonItem = [[UIBarButtonItem alloc]
 initWithBarButtonSystemItem:UIBarButtonSystemItemSave
 target:self action:@selector(saveCity:)];
```

We must add the preceding code to the viewDidLoad: method of *AddCityController.m*. In this method call, we declare that the button delegate is self (the AddCityController class) and that, when clicked, the event will be handled by the saveCity: method in this class, which is shown next. We must add the following to *AddCityController.m*. This should go directly below the #pragma mark–labeled instance methods:

```
- (void)saveCity:(id)sender {

    CityGuideDelegate *delegate =
      (CityGuideDelegate *)[[UIApplication sharedApplication] delegate];
    NSMutableArray *cities = delegate.cities; ❶

    UITextField *nameEntry = (UITextField *)[nameCell viewWithTag:777]; ❷
    UITextView *descriptionEntry =
      (UITextView *)[descriptionCell viewWithTag:777];

    if ( nameEntry.text.length > 0 ) { ❸
        City *newCity = [[City alloc] init];
        newCity.cityName = nameEntry.text;
        newCity.cityDescription = descriptionEntry.text;
        newCity.cityPicture = nil;
        [cities addObject:newCity];

        RootController *viewController = delegate.viewController;
        [viewController.tableView reloadData]; ❹
    }
    [delegate.navController popViewControllerAnimated:YES]; ❺

}
```

❶ This gets a pointer to the `cities` array (the data model) held by the application delegate class.

❷ Here the xxxTag property is used to obtain references to the `UITextField` and `UIText View` in the two custom table view cells.

❸ If the city name text field holds some text, we must assume there is a new city to add to the guide. We need to create a new `City` object, populate it, and push it onto the `cities` array.

❹ Because we have changed the size of the `cities` array, we need to reload the data held by the main view controller. The current view held by the object is not correct anymore.

❺ We are done with this view, so we ask the navigation controller to remove it from its stack of views. This will mean that the current (displayed) view becomes the next view down in the navigation controller's stack of views. In this specific case, this will be our previous view.

Since we're making use of the `CityGuideDelegate`, `RootController`, and `City` classes in this method we must also remember to import their definitions into our implementation. Add these lines to the top of *AddCityController.m*:

```
#import "CityGuideDelegate.h"
#import "RootController.h"
#import "City.h";
```

We could actually compile and run the application at this point and it would work, mostly. But there are a few UI loose ends we need to clear up before everything works correctly.

When we click the Save button and return to the main table view, we will be reusing the table view cell which previously held the "Add New City…" cell to hold a city name in the newly expanded list of cities. This will cause some problems: while we explicitly set the color and accessory properties for this cell in `cellForRowAtIndexPath:` we don't do the same for the other cells. We therefore have to make a small change to the `tableView:cellForRowAtIndexPath:` method and set the `textLabel.textColor` and `editingAccessoryType` for the other cells as well as the "Add New City…" cell. Make the changes shown here to the `tableView:cellForRowAtIndexPath:` method in *Root-Controller.m*:

```
- (UITableViewCell *)tableView:(UITableView *)tv
  cellForRowAtIndexPath:(NSIndexPath *)indexPath
{

    UITableViewCell *cell =
     [tv dequeueReusableCellWithIdentifier:@"cell"];
    if( nil == cell ) {
        cell = [[[UITableViewCell alloc]
            initWithFrame:CGRectZero reuseIdentifier:@"cell"] autorelease];
    }
```

```
        NSLog( @"indexPath.row = %d, cities.count = %d",
          indexPath.row, cities.count );
    if (indexPath.row < cities.count ) {
        City *thisCity = [cities objectAtIndex:indexPath.row];
        cell.textLabel.text = thisCity.cityName;
        cell.textLabel.textColor = [UIColor blackColor];
        cell.editingAccessoryType = UITableViewCellAccessoryNone;
        if (self.editing) {
            [cell setSelectionStyle:UITableViewCellSelectionStyleNone];❶
        }

    } else {
        cell.textLabel.text = @"Add New City...";
        cell.textLabel.textColor = [UIColor lightGrayColor];
        cell.editingAccessoryType =
                UITableViewCellAccessoryDisclosureIndicator;
    }
    return cell;
}
```

❶ Since we are creating an extra cell while in edit mode, and as the table view has been flagged as allowing selection in edit mode, the selection style for this cell will be the default. The selection style will not be set implicitly since the `setEditing:anima ted:` method has already been called on this table view. We therefore have to set the selection style explicitly, to "None", as the table view is already in edit mode when we return to it from the Add City view and the cell is created.

We're done! Click the Build and Run button on the Xcode toolbar to compile and start the application in the simulator. Once it has started, click on the Edit button to put the table view into edit mode and then click on the "Add New City..." cell. Enter a name for the new city, as shown in Figure 5-28, and click Save. You should see something that looks a lot like Figure 5-29. Click Done, and take the table view out of edit mode. Clicking on the new city will take you to the city page; apart from the blank space where the picture will be placed it should look the same as the other city pages in the guide.

If you don't enter a city name in the Add City view, or if you click on the Back button on the left rather than the Save button, no changes will be made to either the `cities` array or the data model held by the application delegate.

The blank space where the image should be on our newly added city is a bit annoying; the easiest way to get around this is to add a default image. The image you choose to use for this placeholder image isn't really relevant. I used the classic image of a question mark on top of a folder, the image Mac OS X would display if it could not find my boot disk, but you can use anything. Remember to keep your aspect ratio the same as you scale your image, and copy it into your project, as we did with the other city images.

Figure 5-28. The Add New City view

Figure 5-29. The City Guide view in edit mode with our new city added to the list

You can add the image to the `viewDidLoad:` method of the `CityController` class. You'll be replacing the last line of code in the method (`pictureView.image = thisCity.city Picture;`) with the code shown in bold:

```
- (void)viewDidLoad {
    CityGuideDelegate *delegate = (CityGuideDelegate *)
      [[UIApplication sharedApplication] delegate];
    City *thisCity = [delegate.cities objectAtIndex:index.row];

    self.title = thisCity.cityName;
    descriptionView.text = thisCity.cityDescription;
    descriptionView.editable = NO;

    UIImage *image = thisCity.cityPicture;
    if ( image == nil ) {
        image =[UIImage imageNamed:@"QuestionMark.jpg"];
    }
    pictureView.image = image;

}
```

Here we added a check to see whether the `cityPicture` returned by the `City` object is equal to `nil`. If so, we simply substitute the default image; this should produce something similar to Figure 5-30.

Figure 5-30. The default image displayed in the CityController view

We're done, at least for this chapter. We'll come back to the City Guide application to fix the remaining problems later. For instance, we'll return to it briefly in the next chapter where I'll show you how to use the UIImagePickerController to attach images to your new City Guide entries. We'll also come back to it again in Chapter 8 where I'll address how to store your data. At the moment, while users can add new cities and delete cities, if they quit the application and restart it they'll be back to the original default set of cities.

CHAPTER 6

Other View Controllers

Now that we've discussed the `UITableView` and `UINavigationController` (as well as their associated classes and views) and built an iPhone application using them, you've actually come a long way toward being able to write applications on your own. With these classes under your belt, you have the tools to attack a large slice of the problem space that iPhone applications normally address.

In this chapter, we'll look at some of the other view controllers and classes that will be useful when building your applications: simple two-screen views (utility applications), single-screen tabbed views (tab bar applications), a view controller that takes over the whole screen until dismissed (modal view controller), and a view controller for selecting video and images (image picker view controller).

Utility Applications

Utility applications perform simple tasks: they have a one-page main view and another window that is brought into view with a flip animation. The Stocks and Weather applications that ship with the iPhone and iPod touch are examples of applications that use this pattern. Both are optimized for simple tasks that require the absolute minimum of user interaction. Such applications are usually designed to display a simple list in the main view, with preferences and option settings on the flip view. You access the flip view by clicking a small *i* icon from the main view.

The Xcode Utility Application template implements the main view and gives the user access to a flipside view. It is one of the most extensive templates in Xcode and it implements a fully working utility application, which is fortunate as the documentation Apple provides regarding this type of application is otherwise somewhat lacking in details.

Open Xcode and start a new project. Click Application under the iPhone OS group, and then select Utility Application from the New Project window as the template (see Figure 6-1). Click Choose, and name the project "BatteryMonitor" when requested.

Figure 6-1. Selecting Utility Application in the New Project window

Figure 6-2 shows the Project window in Xcode and lists the files the template generates. The names of the classes the template generates are meant to hint strongly at what each of them does, but if not, Xcode has conveniently put the relevant classes into groups. Since the template implements all the logic necessary to control the application's interface, we only need to implement our own UI and some basic logic to control it.

Click Build and Run to compile and run the application. You'll find that it's a fully working utility application, although with blank main and flipside views.

Making the Battery Monitoring Application

The somewhat descriptive name of the application has probably revealed its purpose already. We're going to implement a simple battery monitoring application, and to do so I'm going to introduce you to the UIDevice class. This is a *singleton class* that provides information relating to your hardware device. From it you can obtain information about your device such as its unique ID, assigned name, device model, and operating system name and version. More importantly, you can also use the class to detect changes in the device's characteristics such as physical orientation, and register for notifications about when these characteristics change.

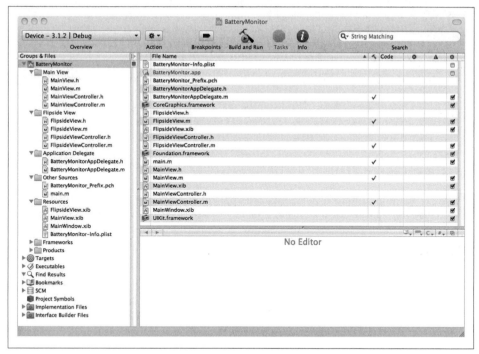

Figure 6-2. The new Utility Application project open in Xcode

A *singleton class* is restricted in some manner such that only one instance of the class can be created. This design pattern can be used to coordinate actions or information across your application. Although some argue that because use of singleton classes introduces global state into your application, and is therefore almost by definition a bad thing, I think that when it is used correctly the pattern can simplify your architecture considerably.

Information—and notifications—about the device battery state weren't introduced until the 3.0 update of the SDK. Even now the implementation is somewhat coarse-grained (notifications regarding charge level changes occur in only 5% increments).

The `UIDevice` class has several limitations, and some developers have resorted to the underlying IOKit framework to obtain more information about the device (e.g., better precision to your battery measurements). However, while Apple marked the IOKit as a public framework, no documentation or header files are associated with it.

If you use this framework and try to publish your application on the App Store, it is possible that Apple will reject it for using a private framework despite its apparent public status. In the official documentation, IOKit is described as "Contain[ing] interfaces used by the device. Do not include this framework directly."

Building our interface

First we're going to build our interface. Double-click on the *MainView.xib* file (located in the Resources group in the Groups & Files pane) to open it in Interface Builder. You'll see that the default view that Xcode generated already has the Info button to switch between the main and flipside views. Not only is it there, but it's connected to the template code, so it's already working.

The UI will consist of just three `UILabel` elements, so drag and drop three labels from the Library (⌘-Shift-L, then choose Cocoa Touch→Inputs & Values) onto the Main View window, and position them roughly as shown in Figure 6-3.

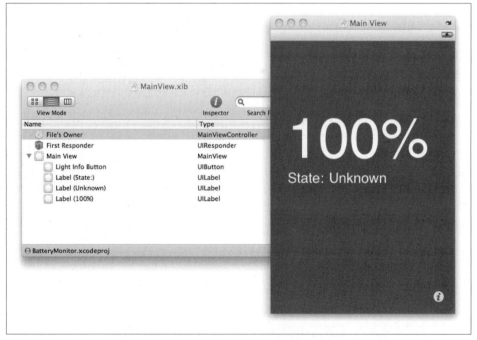

Figure 6-3. The Main View NIB file being edited in Interface Builder

You can use the Attributes Inspector (⌘-1) to change the font size and color as I have done with my view. We'll be setting the text of the labels from inside our code, but for now I've added placeholder text ("100%", "State:", and "Unknown") using the Attributes tab so that I can position the labels more neatly and get a better idea of how my UI will look.

That's all we're going to do to the main view. Save the file and return to Xcode. Open the *FlipsideView.xib* file. You'll see that this time the default view that Xcode generates already has a navigation bar and a Done button present and connected to the template code. You need to add a label (`UILabel`) and switch (`UISwitch`) to this interface, as shown in Figure 6-4.

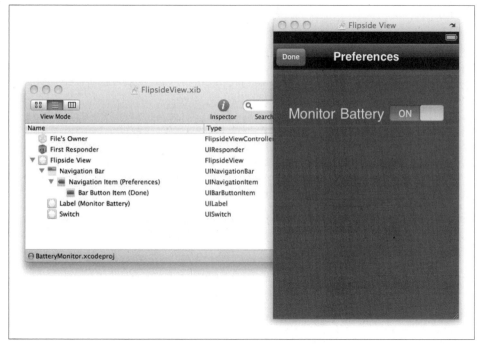

Figure 6-4. The flipside view being edited in Interface Builder

Drag and drop the two elements from the Library window (⌘-Shift-L, then choose Cocoa Touch→Inputs & Values) into the Flipside View window and position them as shown in Figure 6-4. Set the text of the label to "Monitor Battery", and using the Attributes pane of the Inspector window set the label text color to white. The default black text won't show up well against the dark gray background of the view. That's all that's needed. Save the file in Interface Builder, and open the *BatteryMonitorAppDelegate.h* file in Xcode (it's in the Application Delegate folder in the Groups & Files pane).

Writing the code

In the interface, we need to add a Boolean variable that stores the flag that indicates whether the app is currently monitoring the battery state. Add the following inside the `@interface` declaration:

```
BOOL monitorBattery;
```

We also need to make this a property. Add the following next to the existing `@property` declarations (but before the `@end`):

```
@property (nonatomic) BOOL monitorBattery;
```

This means that in the *BatteryMonitorAppDelegate.m* implementation file, we also need to synthesize the property to create the accessor methods. Open that file and add the following next to the existing `@synthesize` statements:

```
@synthesize monitorBattery;
```

By default, we're going to make it so that the application starts with battery monitoring turned off, so in the `applicationDidFinishLaunching:` method we must set the flag to `NO`. Add the following to the top of the method:

```
self.monitorBattery = NO;❶
```

❶ Note that we access the variable by using the accessor method generated by the `@synthesize` statement. It's important to realize that accessing the instance variable directly using `monitorBattery` and accessing the property via a call to `self.monitor Battery:` are completely different in Objective-C since you are sending a message when you invoke the property, rather than directly accessing the variable.

Next, open the *FlipSideViewController.h* interface file (you can find it in the Flipside View folder in the Groups & Files pane) and add the lines shown in bold:

```
@class BatteryMonitorAppDelegate;❶

@interface FlipsideViewController : UIViewController {
    id <FlipsideViewControllerDelegate> delegate;
    BatteryMonitorAppDelegate *appDelegate;❷
    IBOutlet UISwitch *toggleSwitch;❸
}
```

❶ This is a forward declaration of the `BatteryMonitorAppDelegate` class, which allows you to refer to it elsewhere in this file.

❷ We're going to be using the switch (`UISwitch`) we added to the NIB file to toggle battery monitoring on and off. Because we're storing the state of that switch in the application delegate, we need this variable so that we can refer to the application delegate.

❸ Finally, we need to add a `UISwitch` variable and mark it as an `IBOutlet` for Interface Builder.

In the *FlipSideViewController.m* implementation file, you first need to import the application delegate header file (using the `@class` forward declaration in the interface file does not remove the need to `#import` this header file). See Chapter 4 for details on the `#import` statement. Add the following line to the top of *FlipSideViewController.m*:

```
#import "BatteryMonitorAppDelegate.h"
```

Next, make the changes shown in bold to the `viewDidLoad:` method:

```
- (void)viewDidLoad {
    [super viewDidLoad];
    self.view.backgroundColor = [UIColor viewFlipsideBackgroundColor];
    self.title = @"Preferences";❶

    appDelegate = (BatteryMonitorAppDelegate *)
      [[UIApplication sharedApplication] delegate]; ❷
    toggleSwitch.on = appDelegate.monitorBattery; ❸
}
```

❶ This sets the title of the view.

❷ We grab a reference to the application delegate here.

❸ Here, we set the status of the toggle switch to reflect whether we're currently monitoring the battery.

Now modify the `done:` method to save the status of the toggle switch back to the application delegate when you close the flipside view:

```
- (IBAction)done {
    appDelegate.monitorBattery = toggleSwitch.on;
    [self.delegate flipsideViewControllerDidFinish:self];
}
```

Finally, add the following code to the `dealloc:` method (this releases the `toggleSwitch` variable):

```
- (void)dealloc {
    [toggleSwitch release];
    [super dealloc];
}
```

The modifications we need to make to the main view controller are a bit more extensive than those we've made thus far. Open the *MainViewController.h* interface file in Xcode and make the changes shown in bold. You can find this file in the Main View folder of the Groups & Files pane.

```
#import "FlipsideViewController.h"

@class BatteryMonitorAppDelegate; ❶

@interface MainViewController : UIViewController
  <FlipsideViewControllerDelegate>
{
    BatteryMonitorAppDelegate *appDelegate;❷
    IBOutlet UILabel *levelLabel; ❸
```

```
    IBOutlet UILabel *stateLabel;
}

- (IBAction)showInfo;

- (void)batteryChanged:(NSNotification *)note;❹
- (NSString *)batteryLevel;❺
- (NSString *)batteryState:(UIDeviceBatteryState )batteryState;❻

@end
```

❶ This is a forward declaration of the `BatteryMonitorAppDelegate` class, which allows you to refer to it elsewhere in this file.

❷ This is a reference to the application delegate.

❸ Here, we've added an `IBOutlet` for each of the two labels in the main view that we're going to be updating: one for the battery charge level and the other for the current charging state.

❹ This method will be called when we receive a notification that there has been a change in the state of the battery.

❺ This is a convenience method to wrap the call to `UIDevice` to query the current battery level and return an `NSString` that we can use for the text of one of the `UILabel`s.

❻ This is another convenience method to convert a `UIDeviceBatteryState` into an `NSString` that we can use for the text of one of the other `UILabel`s.

Save the interface file, and then open the *MainViewController.m* implementation file in Xcode. We declared a reference to the application delegate in the interface file, so now we need to import the relevant header file. Add this line at the top:

```
#import "BatteryMonitorAppDelegate.h"
```

We also need to grab a reference to the application delegate in the `viewDidLoad:` method. Uncomment the method (remove the lines that consist solely of /* and */ immediately before and after the method) and add the lines shown in bold:

```
- (void)viewDidLoad {
    [super viewDidLoad];
    appDelegate = (BatteryMonitorAppDelegate *)
        [[UIApplication sharedApplication] delegate];

}
```

Next, we need to implement the `viewWillAppear:` method. At this point, you may be wondering what the difference is between this method and the previous `viewDidLoad:` method. The answer is that they're called at different times: `viewWillAppear:` will be called each time the view becomes visible, while `viewDidLoad:` is called only when the view is first loaded. Because the changes we make to the preferences (on the flip side) affect the main view, we need to use `viewWillAppear:`, which is triggered each time we flip back from the preferences view to the main view. Add the following to *MainView-Controller.m*:

```
- (void)viewWillAppear:(BOOL)animated {
    UIDevice *device = [UIDevice currentDevice];
    device.batteryMonitoringEnabled = appDelegate.monitorBattery; ❶

    if (device.batteryMonitoringEnabled) {❷
        [[NSNotificationCenter defaultCenter] addObserver:self
            selector:@selector(batteryChanged:)
            name:@"UIDeviceBatteryLevelDidChangeNotification" object:nil];

        [[NSNotificationCenter defaultCenter] addObserver:self
            selector:@selector(batteryChanged:)
            name:@"UIDeviceBatteryStateDidChangeNotification" object:nil];
    } else {❸

        [[NSNotificationCenter defaultCenter] removeObserver:self
            name:@"UIDeviceBatteryLevelDidChangeNotification" object:nil];
        [[NSNotificationCenter defaultCenter] removeObserver:self
            name:@"UIDeviceBatteryStateDidChangeNotification" object:nil];
    }
    levelLabel.text = [self batteryLevel];❹
    stateLabel.text = [self batteryState:device.batteryState];

    [super viewWillAppear:animated];

}
```

❶ This sets the current battery monitoring state in the singleton `UIDevice` object to correspond to our current battery monitoring state, as determined by the switch on the flipside view.

❷ If battery monitoring is enabled, we're going to add our object as an observer to receive notifications when either the battery level or the battery state changes. If either of these events occurs, the `batteryChanged:` method will be called.

❸ If battery monitoring is disabled, we're going to remove the object as an observer for these notifications.

❹ In either case, we'll populate the text of our two `UILabel`s using the convenience methods (`batteryState:` and `batteryLevel:`, which we'll define shortly).

Since the object may be registered as an observer when we deallocate this view, we also need to make sure we remove ourselves as an observer of any notifications in the `dealloc:` method. Add the lines shown in bold to the `dealloc:` method:

```
- (void)dealloc {
    [[NSNotificationCenter defaultCenter] removeObserver:self];
    [levelLabel release];
    [stateLabel release];
    [super dealloc];
}
```

We also need to implement the `batteryChanged:` method; this method is called when our application is notified of a change in battery state. Here, all we're doing is updating the text of our two labels when we receive a notification of a change. Add the following to *MainViewController.m*:

```
- (void)batteryChanged:(NSNotification *)note {
    UIDevice *device = [UIDevice currentDevice];
    levelLabel.text = [self batteryLevel];
    stateLabel.text = [self batteryState:device.batteryState];
}
```

Finally, we need to implement those convenience methods. Add the following to *MainViewController.m*:

```
- (NSString *)batteryLevel {
    UIDevice *device = [UIDevice currentDevice];

    NSString *levelString = nil;
    float level = device.batteryLevel;
    if ( level == -1 ) {
        levelString = @"---%";
    } else {
        int percent = (int) (level * 100);
        levelString = [NSString stringWithFormat:@"%i%%", percent];
    }
    return levelString;
}

- (NSString *)batteryState:(UIDeviceBatteryState )batteryState {

    NSString *state = nil;
    switch (batteryState) {
        case UIDeviceBatteryStateUnknown:
            state = @"Unknown";
            break;
        case UIDeviceBatteryStateUnplugged:
            state = @"Unplugged";
            break;
        case UIDeviceBatteryStateCharging:
            state = @"Charging";
            break;
        case UIDeviceBatteryStateFull:
            state = @"Full";
            break;
        default:
            state = @"Undefined";
            break;
    }
    return state;
}
```

We're done in Xcode; let's go back into Interface Builder to make all the necessary connections. Locate *FlipsideView.xib* under Resources in the Groups & Files pane and double-click it to open it in Xcode.

Wiring the application in Interface Builder

In the *FlipsideView.xib* file we need to make only one connection: between the `tog` `gleSwitch` outlet and the `UISwitch`. To make the connection, click File's Owner in the *FlipsideView.xib* window, and then drag the `toggleSwitch` outlet from the Connections Inspector (⌘-2) to the switch, as shown in Figure 6-5.

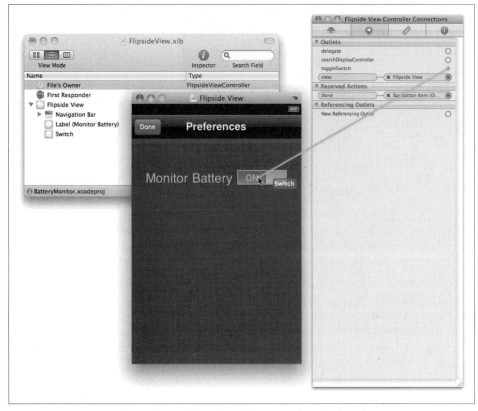

Figure 6-5. Connecting the toggleSwitch outlet to the UISwitch in the flipside view

Save the *FlipsideView.xib* file and open the *MainView.xib* file. This time we need to make two connections. Just as you did in *FlipsideView.xib*, select File's Owner and use the Connections Inspector to make connections between the `levelLabel` and `stateLa` `bel` outlets and their corresponding `UILabel` in the main view, as shown in Figure 6-6.

At this point, we're done. We've implemented everything we need to in code, and we've linked all of our outlets to our interface. Unfortunately, since this application makes use of the `UIDevice` battery monitoring API, and iPhone Simulator doesn't have a battery, we're going to have to test it directly on the device. We covered deploying applications onto your iPhone or iPod touch at the end of Chapter 3.

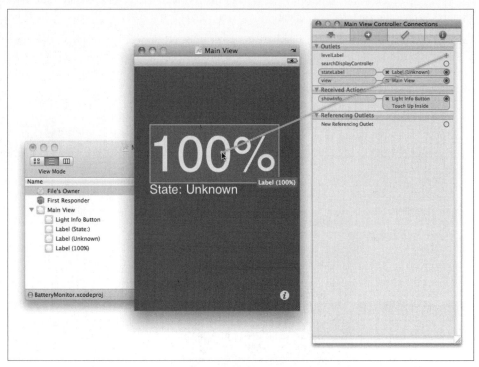

Figure 6-6. Connecting the two outlets in our code to the UILabels in the main view

To deploy the application onto your device, you need to edit the Bundle Identifier inside the *BatteryMonitor-Info.plist* file to something appropriate, and you need to set the Code Signing Identity associated with the project in the Project Info window (although in most cases Xcode will select an appropriate signing identity automatically, if you have more than one developer profile installed this isn't guaranteed). For more information, see "Putting the Application on Your iPhone" on page 37 in Chapter 3. Once this is done, change the Active SDK in the overview window to "iPhone Device" and click Build and Run. Xcode should compile and deploy the application onto your iPhone.

Click the Info button in the bottom-lefthand corner to switch to the flip side and enable battery monitoring in the preferences pane. Click the Done button and return to the main view. Both the battery level and the state should have changed. While the battery level only changes every 5%, you can get some immediate feedback by plugging and unplugging your device from your Mac. The state should change from "Full" or "Charging" (see Figure 6-7) to "Unplugged".

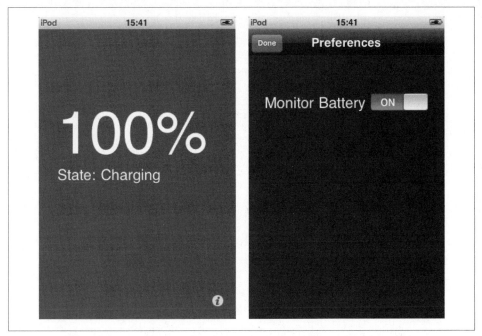

Figure 6-7. The main view and the flipside view of the Battery Monitor application

Tab Bar Applications

If you need to provide a number of different views on the same data set, or separately present a number of different tasks relating to your application, Apple recommends using a tab bar application. Both the iTunes and the App Store applications that ship with the iPhone and iPod touch are examples of applications that use this pattern.

To create a tab bar application, open Xcode and start a new project. Select Tab Bar Application from the New Project window as the template and name it "TabExample" when requested.

Unlike some of the other application templates provided by Apple, there are actually several different approaches you can take to building a tab bar application: loading a tab's view from a secondary NIB, managing the tab's view entirely from a view controller, or using a hybrid of these two approaches.

The default template provides a tab bar application with two tab items, but the way the view is managed for each of these items is very different. Double-click *Main-Window.xib* (it's in the Resources group) to open it in Interface Builder. Next, make sure MainWindow.xib is the foremost window and switch to List Mode (⌘-Option-2), then fully expand Tab Bar Controller by Option-clicking the disclosure triangle to its left.

In Figure 6-8 you can see that under the Tab Bar Controller entry is the tab bar itself, and then two view controllers, each with a tab bar item.

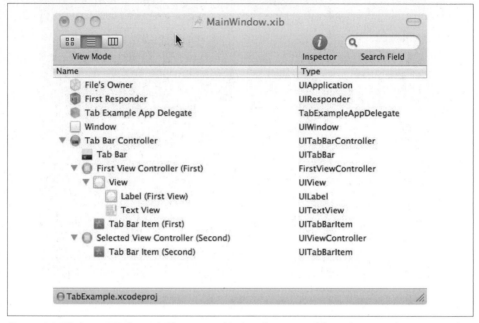

Figure 6-8. The MainWindow.xib file generated by Xcode as part of the Tab Bar Application template

Notice that the "Selected View Controller (Second)" view controller has type `UIView Controller`. Select it and open the Attributes Inspector window (⌘-1) and you'll also see that it loads its view from the *SecondView.xib* file that Xcode generated when you created the new project.

However, the "First View Controller (First)" entry is of type `FirstViewController` rather than `UIViewController`. The view here is managed slightly differently. It has no linked NIB file, and the custom view controller manages its own view.

The template generated by Apple therefore illustrates two very different ways to manage views inside a tab bar application. However, I recommend that you use neither of these two. Instead, I usually approach view management in a slightly different manner: by using a custom view controller class to manage the view, but storing the view outside the *MainWindow.xib* in a separate NIB file.

Refactoring the Template

Let's refactor the current template to reflect my prejudices. Don't worry if you think one of the other approaches sounds better; you should learn enough while refactoring the template to manage your views in either of the other two ways.

Creating the first tab

In Xcode, create a new View NIB called *FirstView.xib*. Then back in Interface Builder (*MainWindow.xib*, not the newly created NIB) click on the `UIView` managed by "First View Controller (First)" and press the Backspace key to delete it. This will also delete its children (a label and text view).

Next, click on "First View Controller (First)" and navigate to the Attributes Inspector (⌘-1). Using the NIB Name drop down, select your newly created FirstView NIB from the list of NIB files in the project.

 To add a new View XIB to the project, right-click or Ctrl-click on the Resources group in the lefthand pane in Xcode and select Add→New File. When the New File window opens select User Interface from under iPhone OS, then choose View XIB and click Next. Enter the name for the new NIB and then click Finish.

Now open the *FirstView.xib* file and click File's Owner in the main window. Then, using the Identity Inspector (⌘-4), change the Class identity of File's Owner from `NSObject` to `UIViewController`. Next, use the Connections Inspector (⌘-2) to connect the view outlet to the view in *FirstView.xib*.

Save both of the NIB files and return to Xcode.

Creating the second tab

We also need to create a custom view controller for the second tab view. Go back into Xcode and right-click or Ctrl-click on the Classes group and select Add→New File. When the File window opens select a `UIViewController` subclass from the Cocoa Touch Class panel, but unlike earlier examples in this book, uncheck the "With XIB for user interface" box (we already have a *SecondView.xib* file in the project). Click Next. When asked, name the new view controller "SecondViewController.m".

Go back to *MainWindow.xib* in Interface Builder and click on the "Second View Controller (Second)" entry. In the Identity Inspector (⌘-4) change the Class identity from `UIViewController` to `SecondViewController`. You don't need to connect the view outlet as you did for the *FirstView.xib* file because Xcode created the second tab bar item with its outlets connected correctly by default.

Wrapping up the refactoring

After doing this refactoring, you should end up with a *MainWindow.xib* file that looks a lot like that shown in Figure 6-9. Make sure you save the NIB file after finishing the refactoring.

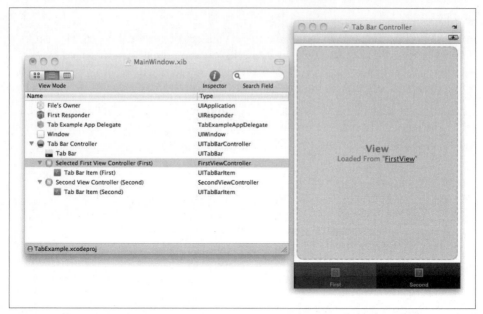

Figure 6-9. The MainWindow.xib file after refactoring

Adding Another Tab Bar Item

Let's add another tab bar item so that you can see how to create one from scratch. With *MainWindow.xib* open in Interface Builder, drag and drop a new tab bar item (not a tab bar) from the Library window (under Cocoa Touch→Windows, Views, & Bars) onto the tab bar controller in the MainWindow.xib window. Click the disclosure triangle next to the new tab bar item, and you'll notice that it generates another view controller with an associated tab bar item. The new view controller is similar to "Second View Controller (Second)" before refactoring, with a type of `UIViewController`. If you check the Attributes tab of the Inspector window, however, you'll notice that the new controller currently has no view associated with it in Interface Builder, as shown in Figure 6-10.

We now need to add a view controller to manage this tab. Go back into Xcode and right-click or Ctrl-click on the Classes group and select Add→New File again. When the File window opens, select a `UIViewController` subclass from the Cocoa Touch Class panel; this time check the "With XIB for user interface" box, as you need Xcode to generate a NIB. When asked, name the new view controller "ThirdViewController.m".

> For neatness, you may want to drag the *ThirdViewController.xib* file from the Classes group to the Resources group. You may also want to rename the *ThirdViewController.xib* file to *ThirdView.xib* to keep your naming conventions consistent throughout the application.

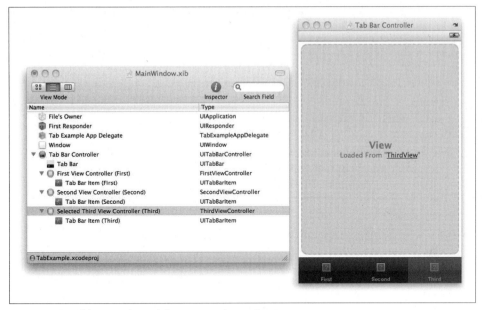

Figure 6-10. Adding another tab bar item to the application

After doing this, edit *MainWindow.xib* in Interface Builder by changing the type of the newly created "View Controller (Item)" from `UIViewController` to `ThirdViewControl ler` in the Identity tab of the Inspector window, and then set the NIB name to `Third View` in the Attributes Inspector (⌘-1).

You should explore some of the standard tab bar items that Apple provides; for example, expand the newly added third view controller's disclosure triangle in the MainWindow.xib window. Next, select the tab bar item underneath it and open the Attributes Inspector (⌘-1). Try selecting something other than Custom for its identifier and see what happens.

This example assumes you use the Custom identifier, so make sure you set it back to Custom when you're done exploring.

After selecting Custom, you should change the name of the item from "Item" to "Third". Although currently our tab bar item doesn't have an image, we could associate one with (each of) our tabs using the Image drop down in the Attributes tab. Just drag and drop the image you want to use into the project in the same way you added the images for the City Guide application in Chapter 5. To look like Apple's icons, your images cannot be larger than 32×32 pixels in size and they must have a transparent background. I've found that PNG images between 20 and 30 pixels work well as tab bar icons.

Creating Tab Bar Icons

Creating tab-bar-based applications means you must create icons for the bar. You may be able to use the system-supplied icons, either by setting the Identifier by clicking on the `UITabBarItem` on the *MainWindow* NIB file and changing the Identity value in the Attributes tab of the Inspector window inside Interface Builder, or directly via code inside your view controller's `init:` method, as shown here:

```
self.tabBarItem = [[UITabBarItem alloc]
        initWithTabBarSystemItem:UITabBarSystemItemSearch tag:0];
```

However, the selection of available icons is fairly limited and you will inevitably have to resort to creating your own. Apple has this to say on tab bar icons: "The unselected and selected images displayed by the tab bar are derived from the images that you set. The alpha values in the source image are used to create the other images—opaque values are ignored."

Effectively the alpha channel of your image will determine the shading of your icon. Tab bar icons should therefore be in PNG format, be no larger than 30×30 pixels in size, and have a transparent background. Multicolor icons are ignored as the icons themselves are an opaque mask which the iPhone will use to generate the actual tab bar icon.

Finishing Up

Finally, edit the three NIB files—*FirstView.xib*, *SecondView.xib*, and *ThirdView.xib*—and add a large (in 144 pt font) label saying "1", "2", and "3" to each respective view. This way you can confirm that the correct one is being activated. *SecondView.xib* will have some labels on it that were placed there when Xcode generated the project from its template; you can delete these labels.

Make sure you save all the NIB files. Then, click Build and Run to compile, deploy, and run the application in iPhone Simulator, as shown in Figure 6-11.

Despite the fact that we haven't written a single line of code in this section, you should now have a working, if rather basic, tab bar application.

Although I haven't walked you through the process of building a full-blown application, you should have begun to see the commonalities and familiar patterns emerging in this application. Our application has an application delegate along with three custom view controllers managing each view. This is a very similar arrangement to both the table view application we wrote in Chapter 5 and the utility application we wrote earlier in this chapter.

At this point, you may want to try building your own application on top of the infra-structure we have created so far. Start with something simple where changing something in one view affects the contents of another view. Don't worry; take your time, and I'll be here when you get back.

124 | Chapter 6: Other View Controllers

Figure 6-11. The tab bar application running in the simulator with SecondView selected as the active tab

Modal View Controllers

So far in this chapter we've looked at two of Apple's application templates. However, in this section we're going to focus once again on an individual view controller—or rather, a way to *present* a view controller to the user. After table views and the `UINavigationController` it's probably one of the most heavily used ways to present data: it's the modal view controller.

You'll have seen a modal controller in action many times when using your iPhone. A view slides in from the bottom of the screen and is usually dismissed with a Done button at the top of the screen. When dismissed, it slides back down the screen, disappearing at the bottom.

In the main controller we would generally have a button or other UI element; tapping this would trigger an event linked to the following method in the view controller, which would bring up the modal view:

```
-(void)openNewController:(id)sender {
    OtherController *other = [[OtherController alloc] init];❶
    [self presentModalViewController:other animated:YES];❷
    [other release];❸
}
```

❶ We instantiate the view controller that manages the view we wish to display.

❷ We present the view managed by the view controller. Note that presenting a view controller modally will explicitly retain it, hence the need for the release in the next line.

❸ We release the view controller. Once it is dismissed, the *retain count* (see "The alloc, retain, copy, and release Cycle" on page 48 in Chapter 4) will drop to zero.

In the modal view itself, we would implement a button or some other way to close the view, which would call this method in the view controller:

```
-(void)doneWithController:(id)sender {
    [self dismissModalViewControllerAnimated:YES];
}
```

This dismisses the current modal view.

Modifying the City Guide Application

The best way to explain the modal view is to show it in action. For that we're going to go back to the City Guide application we built in Chapter 5. We're going to make some fairly extensive changes to it, so you should make a copy of the project first and work with the copy while you make your modifications. In this section, I'll show you how to take your code apart and put it back together again in an organized fashion. This occurs a lot when writing applications, especially for clients who have a tendency to change their mind about what they want out of the application in the first place.

Open the Finder and navigate to the location where you saved the *CityGuide* project; see Figure 6-12.

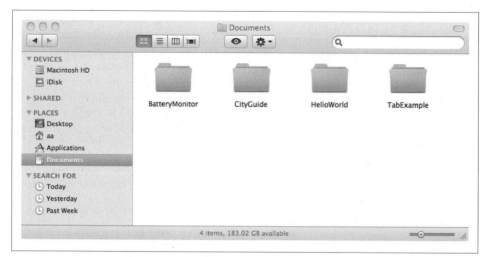

Figure 6-12. The CityGuide project folder in the Finder

Right-click or Ctrl-click on the folder containing the project files and select Duplicate. A folder called *CityGuide copy* will be created containing a duplicate of our project. You should probably rename it to something more sensible. I suggest *CityGuide2*. Now open the new version of the project in Xcode and select Project→Rename from the Xcode menu bar. Enter **CityGuide2** when prompted and click on the Rename button to rename the project.

In Chapter 5, we built an application that lets users both add and delete city entries in our table view. Adding the functionality to delete table view cells was fairly simple; the complicated part was adding the ability to add cities. So, let's take a step back and look at another way to implement that functionality.

First we're going to go into the `RootController` implementation and back out of the changes that allowed users to edit the table view. We're going to replace the Edit button and the associated implementation with an Add button, reusing the `AddCityControl ler` code and associated view, but presenting the Add City view modally instead of using the navigation controller.

You may wonder about deleting lots of perfectly good code, but refactoring functionality like this is a fairly common task when you change your mind about how you want to present information to the user, or if the requirements driving the project change. This is good practice for you.

 If you want to do a global find (and replace) over the entire project for a word or phrase you can do so from the Edit menu. Selecting Edit→Find→Find in Project will bring up the Project Find window.

To remove functionality like this, first you need to figure out what needs to be removed. If you don't know the author of the original application this can sometimes be difficult. Do a project-wide search for "editing", as shown in Figure 6-13. If you do that you'll see that the only mention of "editing" is in the *RootController.m* file. The changes we'll need to make are actually fairly tightly constrained inside a single class. We'll have to make some minor changes elsewhere in the project. Limiting the scope of necessary changes when refactoring code in this way is one of the main benefits of writing code in an object-oriented manner.

Open the *RootController.m* file in Xcode. Begin the refactoring by deleting the following methods in their entirety:

- `setEditing:animated:`
- `tableView:commitEditingStyle:forRowAtIndexPath:`
- `tableView:editingStyleForRowAtIndexPath:`

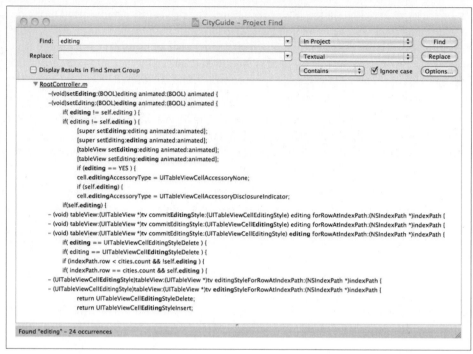

Figure 6-13. The results of a global find across the CityGuide2 project for "editing"

 Remember that the methods as they appear in the file have longer, more complicated names. For example, setEditing:animated: is (void)setEditing:(BOOL)editing animated:(BOOL) animated.

Next, do the following:

1. In the viewDidLoad: method, remove the line that adds the self.editButtonItem to the navigation bar.

2. In the tableView:cellForRowAtIndexPath: method, remove the section enclosed in the if(self.editing) { ... } conditional statement, and the else { ... } statement that adds the "Add New City..." cell. Additionally, you should remove the line that sets the editingAccessoryType inside the conditional statement.

3. Similarly, remove the if(self.editing) { ... } conditional statement in the tableView:numberOfRowsInSection: method.

4. Finally, in the tableView:didSelectRowAtIndexPath: method remove the && !self.editing expression from the first if block. Remove the second if block (which deals with what happens if we are editing) in its entirety.

We're done. If you do a global find in the project for "editing" you should now come up blank, and the class should appear as shown here:

```objc
#import "RootController.h"
#import "CityGuideDelegate.h"
#import "City.h"
#import "CityController.h"
#import "AddCityController.h"

@implementation RootController

@synthesize tableView;

#pragma mark UIViewController Methods

- (void)didReceiveMemoryWarning {
    [super didReceiveMemoryWarning];
}

- (void)viewDidLoad {
    self.title = @"City Guide";
    CityGuideDelegate *delegate =
     (CityGuideDelegate *)[[UIApplication sharedApplication] delegate];
    cities = delegate.cities;
}

- (void)dealloc {
    [tableView release];
    [cities release];
    [super dealloc];
}

#pragma mark UITableViewDataSource Methods

- (UITableViewCell *)tableView:(UITableView *)tv
   cellForRowAtIndexPath:(NSIndexPath *)indexPath
{
    UITableViewCell *cell =
     [tv dequeueReusableCellWithIdentifier:@"cell"];
    if( nil == cell ) {
        cell = [[[UITableViewCell alloc]
         initWithFrame:CGRectZero reuseIdentifier:@"cell"] autorelease];
    }

    if (indexPath.row < cities.count ) {
        City *thisCity = [cities objectAtIndex:indexPath.row];
        cell.textLabel.text = thisCity.cityName;
        cell.textLabel.textColor = [UIColor blackColor];
    }
    return cell;
}

- (NSInteger)tableView:(UITableView *)tv
  numberOfRowsInSection:(NSInteger)section
{
    NSInteger count = cities.count;
    return count;
}
```

```
#pragma mark UITableViewDelegate Methods

- (void)tableView:(UITableView *)tv
  didSelectRowAtIndexPath:(NSIndexPath *)indexPath
{
    CityGuideDelegate *delegate =
     (CityGuideDelegate *)[[UIApplication sharedApplication] delegate];

    if (indexPath.row < cities.count ) {
        CityController *city =
         [[CityController alloc] initWithIndexPath:indexPath];
        [delegate.navController pushViewController:city animated:YES];
        [city release];
    }
    [tv deselectRowAtIndexPath:indexPath animated:YES];
}

@end
```

Since you've now made fairly extensive changes to the view controller, you should test it to see if things are still working. Click the Build and Run button on the Xcode toolbar, and if all is well you should see something very similar to Figure 6-14. Tapping on one of the city names should take you to its city page as before.

We've deleted a lot of code, so let's write some more. In the `viewDidLoad:` method we need to replace the Edit button that we deleted with an Add button.

Let's add a button of style `UIBarButtonSystemItemAdd` and set things up so that when it is clicked it will call the `addCity:` method in this class. Add the following code to the `viewDidLoad:` method:

```
self.navigationItem.rightBarButtonItem = [[UIBarButtonItem alloc]
    initWithBarButtonSystemItem:UIBarButtonSystemItemAdd target:self
    action:@selector(addCity:)];
```

Since there isn't an `addCity:` method right now, we need to declare it in the *RootController.h* interface file. Open that file, and add this line after the `@interface { ...}` declaration but before the `@end` directive:

```
- (void)addCity:(id)sender;
```

Now add the implementation to the *RootController.m* file:

```
- (void)addCity:(id)sender {
    AddCityController *addCity = [[AddCityController alloc] init];
    [self presentModalViewController:addCity animated:YES];
    [addCity release];
}
```

This looks almost identical to the snippet of code I showed you at the beginning of this section, but the modal view we're going to display is the one managed by our `AddCity Controller` class.

Figure 6-14. The stripped-down City Guide application, looking a lot like it did in Figure 5-16 in Chapter 5

Now we need to make a couple of small changes to our `AddCityController` class. Open the *AddCityController.h* interface file in Xcode and declare the `saveCity:` method as an `IBAction`. Add this line after the `@interface { ... }` statement but before the `@end` directive:

```
- (IBAction)saveCity:(id)sender;
```

Open the implementation file (*AddCityController.m*), and remove the last line (where we pop the view controller off the navigation controller) and replace it with a line dismissing the modal view controller. You'll also change the return value of the `saveCity:` method from `void` to `IBAction` here just as you did in the interface file:

```
- (IBAction)saveCity:(id)sender {
    CityGuideDelegate *delegate =
      (CityGuideDelegate *)[[UIApplication sharedApplication] delegate];
    NSMutableArray *cities = delegate.cities;

    UITextField *nameEntry = (UITextField *)[nameCell viewWithTag:777];
    UITextView *descriptionEntry =
                     (UITextView *)[descriptionCell viewWithTag:777];

    if ( nameEntry.text.length > 0 ) {
        City *newCity = [[City alloc] init];
```

```
        newCity.cityName = nameEntry.text;
        newCity.cityDescription = descriptionEntry.text;
        [cities addObject:newCity];

        RootController *viewController = delegate.viewController;
        [viewController.tableView reloadData];
    }
    [self dismissModalViewControllerAnimated:YES];

}
```

We're pretty much there at this point; however, before we finish with our changes here we also need to go up to the `viewDidLoad:` method and delete the lines where we add the Save button to the view (it's a single statement beginning with `self.naviga tionItem.rightBarButtonItem` that spans multiple lines).

Make sure you save the changes you made to the `AddCityController` class, and open the *AddCityController.xib* file inside Interface Builder.

First, drag and drop into the view a navigation bar (`UINavigationBar`) from the Library window (select Cocoa Touch→Windows, Views & Bars). Position it at the top of the view, and resize the table view so that it fits in the remaining space. While you're there, change the title of the navigation bar from "title" to "Add New City".

Next, drag and drop a bar button item (`UIBarButtonItem`) onto the navigation bar and position it to the left of the title. In the Attributes Inspector (⌘-1) change the Identifier from Custom to Done. You'll see that this changes both the text and the style of the button.

Finally, click on File's Owner in the AddCityController.xib window and switch to the Connections Inspector (⌘-2). Connect the `saveCity:` received action to the Done button, as I've done in Figure 6-15. Save your changes to the NIB file, as we've now finished refactoring our City Guide application.

Click Build and Run on the Xcode toolbar to compile and start the application in iPhone Simulator. When the application starts you should see something like Figure 6-16. Clicking the Add button in the navigation bar should bring up our "Add City" view; when it does, enter some information and click Done. You should see your test city appear in the main table view.

Well done. We've just taken the City Guide application apart, put it back together again, and made it work slightly differently. But what if you disliked the way we implemented the ability to add cities in the first version of the application, preferring this approach, but you still want to retain the ability to delete cities? You could still implement things so that a left-to-right swipe brought up the Delete button for the row; for instance, Apple's Mail application that ships with the iPhone and iPod touch takes this approach. Just adding the following method back into *RootController.m* will reimplement this functionality:

```
- (void) tableView:(UITableView *)tv
  commitEditingStyle:(UITableViewCellEditingStyle) editing
```

```
forRowAtIndexPath:(NSIndexPath *)indexPath {
    if( editing == UITableViewCellEditingStyleDelete ) {
        [cities removeObjectAtIndex:indexPath.row];
        [tv deleteRowsAtIndexPaths:[NSArray arrayWithObject:indexPath]
            withRowAnimation:UITableViewRowAnimationLeft];
    }
}
```

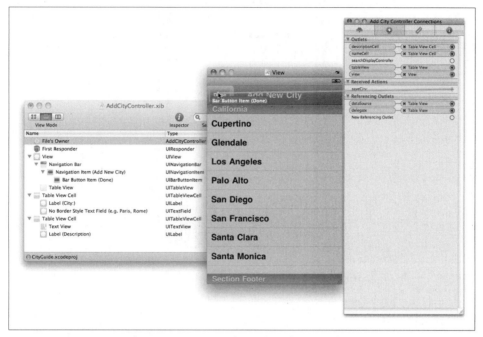

Figure 6-15. Connecting the SaveCity: received action to the Done button in our newly modified AddCityController.xib file

The Image Picker View Controller

As I promised in Chapter 5, I'm going to talk about the image picker view controller. This view controller manages Apple-supplied interfaces for choosing images and movies, and on supported devices it takes new images or movies with the camera. As this class handles all of the required interaction with the user, it is very simple to use. All you need to do is tell it to start, and then dismiss it after the user selects an image or movie.

Adding the Image Picker to the City Guide Application

In this section, we'll continue to build on our City Guide application. Either of the two versions of the application we now have will do, as all of the changes we're going to

Figure 6-16. The newly rewritten City Guide application, with our Add button on the right of the navigation bar

make will be confined to the `AddCityController` class. In the preceding section, we made only relatively minor changes in this class that won't affect our additions here.

However, if you want to follow along, I'm going to return to our original version and work on that. As we did in the preceding section, you should work on a copy of the project, so right-click or Ctrl-click on the folder containing the project files and select Duplicate. A folder called *CityGuide copy* will be created containing a duplicate of our project. You should probably rename the folder to something more sensible. I suggest *CityGuide3*, and renaming the project by selecting Project→Rename from the Xcode menu bar.

The first thing we need to do is build an interface to allow the user to trigger the image picker. If you remember from Chapter 5, our "Add City" view was built out of two custom table view cells. The easiest way to add this ability is to add another table view cell.

Open the *AddCityController.xib* file in Interface Builder. Drag and drop a table view cell (`UITableViewCell`) from the Library window into the *AddCityController.xib* window. We need to resize this cell so that it can hold a small thumbnail of our selected image, so go to the Size Inspector (⌘-3) and change its height from the default 44 pixels to H = 83 pixels. At this point, we also need to resize the super-size table view cell for entering the description to account for this new cell. So, click on the description cell and go to the Size tab of the Inspector window and change the height from H = 362 to H = 279 pixels.

Go back to the new cell and grab a label (UILabel) from the Library window and drop it onto the Table View Cell window (if the window is not open already, double-click on the new cell in the *AddCityController.xib* window to open it). In the Attributes Inspector (⌘-1) change the label's text to "Add a picture:" and then switch to the Size tab and position the label at X = 10 and Y = 28 with W = 126 and H = 21 pixels.

Next, grab an image view (UIImageView) from the Library window and drop it onto the cell, then position it at X = 186 and Y = 7 and resize it to be W = 83 and H = 63 using the Size tab of the Inspector window. In the Attributes tab, set the Tag attribute to 777 (this lets us easily refer to this subview from our code) and set the view mode to Aspect Fill.

Finally, drop a round rect button (UIButton) onto the cell, and in the Attributes tab change its type from Rounded Rect to Add Contact. The button should now appear as a blue circle enclosing a plus sign. Position it to the right of the UIImageView, at X = 274 and Y = 25.

After doing this, you should have something that looks a lot like Figure 6-17. Set the cell selection type to None in the Attributes tab, make sure you've saved your changes to the NIB, and then open the *AddCityController.h* and *AddCityController.m* files in Xcode.

In the *AddCityController.h* interface file, the first thing we need to do is add an IBOutlet to allow us to connect our code to the new table view cell inside Interface Builder. We must also add an instance variable of type UIImage called cityPicture, which we'll use to hold the image passed back to us from the image picker, along with an addPicture: method that we'll connect to the UIButton in the cell, allowing us to start the image picker. Add the lines shown in bold to the file:

```
#import <UIKit/UIKit.h>

@interface AddCityController : UIViewController
  <UITableViewDataSource, UITableViewDelegate> {
    IBOutlet UITableView *tableView;
    IBOutlet UITableViewCell *nameCell;
    IBOutlet UITableViewCell *pictureCell;
    IBOutlet UITableViewCell *descriptionCell;

    UIImage *cityPicture;
}

- (void)saveCity:(id)sender;
- (IBAction)addPicture:(id)sender;

@end
```

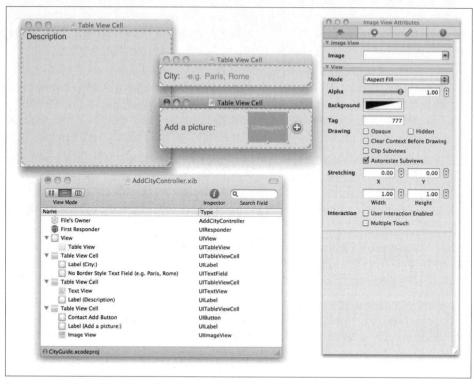

Figure 6-17. The Add Picture table view cell in Interface Builder with the UIImageView tagged as view 777 so that we can access its subview from code more easily

Before implementing the code to go with this interface, we need to quickly go back into Interface Builder and make those two connections. Open the *AddCityController.xib* file and click on File's Owner, then use the Connections Inspector (⌘-2) to connect the `pictureCell` outlet to your new `UITableViewCell`. Next, click on the `addPicture:` received action and connect it to the `UIButton` in your table view cell; see Figure 6-18. When you release the mouse button you'll be presented with a pop-up menu of possible events the button can generate (just like the Hello World example back in Chapter 3). We want just a simple button click, so select the Touch Up Inside event.

We now need to save this file, and then go back into Xcode to finish our implementation. In the *AddCityController.m* implementation file, first we have to provide a default image for the `UIImage` in the cell (otherwise, it will appear blank). We can do this inside the `viewDidLoad:` method by adding this line (you'll need an image called *QuestionMark.jpg* for this to work; see "Capturing the City Data" on page 100 in Chapter 5 for information on using this image in your project):

```
cityPicture = [UIImage imageNamed:@"QuestionMark.jpg"];
```

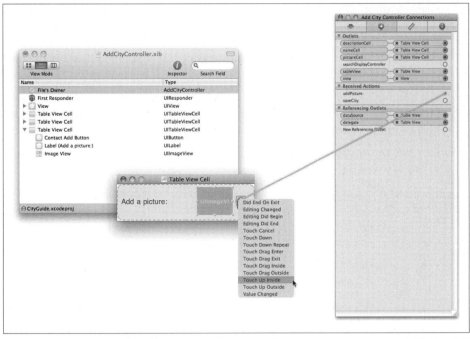

Figure 6-18. Connecting the addCity: received action to the UIButton in our new UITableViewCell to allow it to trigger the image picker

We also have to make some changes to the table view delegate and data source methods (in the *AddCityController.m* implementation file) to take account of the new cell. First we need to change the number of rows returned by the `tableView:numberOfRowsInSec tion:` method from two to three. Make the change shown in bold:

```
- (NSInteger)tableView:(UITableView *)tv
     numberOfRowsInSection:(NSInteger)section
{
    return 3;
}
```

Now we need to modify the `tableView:cellForRowAtIndexPath:` method to return the extra cell in the correct position in our table view. Make the changes shown in bold:

```
- (UITableViewCell *)tableView:(UITableView *)tv
     cellForRowAtIndexPath:(NSIndexPath *)indexPath {
    UITableViewCell *cell = nil;
    if( indexPath.row == 0 ) {❶
        cell = nameCell;
    } else if ( indexPath.row == 1 ) {❷
        UIImageView *pictureView = (UIImageView *)[pictureCell viewWithTag:777];
        pictureView.image = cityPicture;
        cell = pictureCell;
    } else {❸
        cell = descriptionCell;
```

```
    }
    return cell;

}
```

❶ In the first row of the table view, we return a `nameCell`, configured to allow the user to enter the city name.

❷ In the second row of the table view, we return the cell we just added. We first populate the `UIImageView` with the image held by the `cityPicture` variable that we initialized in the `viewDidLoad:` method earlier.

❸ Finally, we return the table view cell that we set up to allow the user to enter a description for the city.

We also need to change the `tableView:heightForRowAtIndexPath:` method to take account of the new cell. Make the changes shown in bold:

```
- (CGFloat)tableView:(UITableView *)tv
    heightForRowAtIndexPath:(NSIndexPath *)indexPath
{
    CGFloat height;
    if( indexPath.row == 0 ) {
        height = 44;
    } else     if( indexPath.row == 1 ) {
        height = 83;
    } else {
        height = 279;
    }
    return height;

}
```

We also need to remember to release the `pictureCell` variables in the `dealloc:` method. We don't have to release the `cityPicture` variable because it will be part of the autorelease pool. Add the following to the `dealloc:` method:

```
[pictureCell release];
```

Finally, we need to add a placeholder implementation (after the instance methods pragma mark) for our `addPicture:` method, which we'll fill in later:

```
- (IBAction)addPicture:(id)sender {
    NSLog(@"addPicture: called.");
}
```

We're done, at least for now. Click Build and Run in the Xcode toolbar to compile and run the application in iPhone Simulator. Once the application has started, tap the Edit button in the navigation bar and click Add New City (if you chose to modify the second version of the guide, click the Add button). Figure 6-19 shows the new view.

Now we have an interface to trigger the image picker for us, so let's implement the code to do that. First we need to add a `UIImagePickerController` variable to the *AddCity-Controller.h* interface file, along with a `UIImage` variable to hold the image returned by

Figure 6-19. The New City view with our new UITableViewCell

the image picker. We also need to declare the class to be a delegate. Make the changes shown in bold:

```
@interface AddCityController : UIViewController
  <UITableViewDataSource, UITableViewDelegate,
  UIImagePickerControllerDelegate, UINavigationControllerDelegate> {❶
    IBOutlet UITableView *tableView;
    IBOutlet UITableViewCell *nameCell;
    IBOutlet UITableViewCell *pictureCell;
    IBOutlet UITableViewCell *descriptionCell;

    UIImage *cityPicture;
    UIImagePickerController *pickerController;
}

- (void)saveCity:(id)sender;
- (IBAction)addPicture:(id)sender;

@end
```

❶ We need to declare the class as both a `UIImagePickerControllerDelegate` and a `UINavigationControllerDelegate`. Both declarations are necessary for the class to interact with the `UIImagePickerController`.

In the *AddCityController.m* implementation file, we need to modify the `viewDidLoad:` method to initialize our `UIImagePickerController`. Make the changes shown in bold:

```
- (void)viewDidLoad {
    self.title = @"New City";
    self.navigationItem.rightBarButtonItem = [[UIBarButtonItem alloc]
      initWithBarButtonSystemItem:UIBarButtonSystemItemSave
      target:self action:@selector(saveCity:)];
    cityPicture = [UIImage imageNamed:@"QuestionMark.jpg"];

    pickerController = [[UIImagePickerController alloc] init];❶
    pickerController.allowsImageEditing = NO;❷
    pickerController.delegate = self;❸
    pickerController.sourceType =
      UIImagePickerControllerSourceTypeSavedPhotosAlbum;❹
}
```

❶ We allocate and initialize the `UIImagePickerController` (this means we're responsible for it and we must release it inside our `dealloc:` method).

❷ When using the image picker, the user may be allowed to edit the selected image before it is passed to our code. This disables that option here.

❸ We set the delegate class to be this class.

❹ Finally, we select the image source. There are three: `UIImagePickerControllerSourceTypeCamera`, `UIImagePickerControllerSourceTypePhotoLibrary`, and `UIImagePickerControllerSourceTypeSavedPhotosAlbum`. Each presents different views to the user, allowing him to take an image with the camera, pick it from the image library, or choose something from his photo album.

We also need to implement the `addPicture:` method, the method called when we tap the button in our interface. This method simply starts the image picker interface, presenting it as a modal view controller. Replace the placeholder `addPicture:` method you added to the *AddCityController.m* file as part of the instance methods pragma section with the following:

```
- (IBAction)addPicture:(id)sender {
    [self presentModalViewController:pickerController animated:YES];
}
```

Next, we need to implement the delegate method that will tell our code the user has finished with the picker interface, the `imagePickerController:didFinishPickingMedia WithInfo:` method. Add the following to *AddCityController.m* inside the `UIImagePickerController` method's pragma section:

```
- (void)imagePickerController:(UIImagePickerController *)picker
    didFinishPickingMediaWithInfo:(NSDictionary *)info
{
    [self dismissModalViewControllerAnimated:YES];❶
    cityPicture = [info objectForKey:@"UIImagePickerControllerOriginalImage"];❷

    UIImageView *pictureView = (UIImageView *)[pictureCell viewWithTag:777];❸
```

```
pictureView.image = cityPicture;
[tableView reloadData];
```

    }

❶ We dismiss the image picker interface.

❷ We grab the `UIImage` selected by the user from the `NSDictionary` returned by the image picker and set the `cityPicture` variable.

❸ We grab a reference to the thumbnail `UIImageView`, populate it with the chosen image, and reload the table view so that the displayed image is updated.

Finally, in the `saveCity:` method, we need to add a line just before we add the `newCity` to the `cities` array. Add the line shown in bold:

```
newCity.cityPicture = nil;
newCity.cityPicture = cityPicture;
[cities addObject:newCity];
```

This will take our new picture and serialize it into the data model for our application.

It's time to test our application. Make sure you've saved your changes and click Build and Run.

> If you test the application in iPhone Simulator, you'll notice that there are no images in the Saved Photos folder. There is a way around this problem. In the simulator, tap the Safari icon and drag and drop a picture from your computer (you can drag it from the Finder or iPhoto) into the browser. You'll notice that the URL bar displays the file path to the image. Click and hold down the cursor over the image and a dialog will appear allowing you to save the image to the Saved Photos folder.

Once the application has started, tap the Edit button in the navigation bar and go to the New City view. Tapping the blue button will open the image picker, as shown in Figure 6-20, and allow you to select an image. Once you've done this, the image picker will be dismissed and you'll return to the New City interface.

Is everything working? Not exactly; depending on how you tested the interface you may have noticed the problem. Currently, if you enter text in the City field and then click on the "Add a picture" button before clicking on the Description field, the text in the City field will be lost when you return from the image picker. However, if you enter text in the City field and *then* enter text in (or just click on) the Description field, the text will still be there when you return from the image picker. Any text entered in the Description field will remain in any case.

This is actually quite a subtle bug and is a result of the different ways in which a `UITextField` and `UITextView` interact as first responders. We're going to talk about the *responder chain* in Chapter 8 when we deal with data handling in more detail. However,

Figure 6-20. The UIImagePickerController and the New City view with a new image

to explain this without getting into too much detail, the first responder is the object in the application that is the current recipient of any UI events (such as a touch). The UIWindow class sends events to the registered first responder, giving it the first chance to handle the event. If it fails to do so, the event will be passed to the next object.

By default, the UITextField doesn't commit any changes to its text until it is no longer the first responder, which is where the problem comes from. While we could change this behavior through the UITextFieldDelegate protocol, there is a simpler fix. Add the lines shown in bold to the addPicture: method:

```
- (IBAction)addPicture:(id)sender {
    UITextField *nameEntry = (UITextField *)[nameCell viewWithTag:777];
    [nameEntry resignFirstResponder];

    [self presentModalViewController:pickerController animated:YES];
}
```

With this change, we force the UITextField to resign as first responder before we open the image picker. This means that when the image picker is dismissed, the text we entered before opening it will remain when we are done.

Save your changes, and click on the Build and Run button in the Xcode toolbar. When the application starts up, return to the New City view and confirm that this simple change fixes the bug.

We're done with the City Guide application for a while. However, we'll be back in Chapter 8, where I'll fix the last remaining problem with the application and talk about data storage. (Until then, cities you add will not be saved when you exit the application, so don't enter all your favorite cities just yet.)

CHAPTER 7

Connecting to the Network

The iPhone and iPod touch platforms are designed for always-on connectivity in mind. Developers have taken advantage of this to create some innovative third-party applications. Most iPhone applications will make a network connection at some point, and many are so fundamentally tied to web services that they need a network connection to function.

Detecting Network Status

Before your application attempts to make a network connection, you need to know whether you have a network available, and depending on what you want to do you might also want to know whether the device is connected to a WiFi or cellular network.

One of the more common reasons for Apple to reject an application submitted for review is that the application doesn't correctly notify the user when the application fails to access the network. Apple requires that you detect the state of the network connection and report it to the user when the connection is unavailable, or otherwise handle it in a graceful manner.

Apple's Reachability Class

Helpfully, Apple has provided some sample code to deal with detecting current network status. The Reachability code is available at *http://developer.apple.com/iphone/library/samplecode/Reachability/*.

Two different versions of the Apple Reachability code are in general circulation. The earlier version, which appears in many web tutorials and has been widely distributed, dates from the pre-2.0 SDK. The newer version, released in August 2009, is much improved and supports asynchronous connection monitoring. However, the interface offered by the two versions is very different, so to avoid confusion you need to be aware which version of the Reachability code you're using.

Download the *Reachability.zip* file from Apple, and unzip it. Open the *Reachability/Classes* directory and grab the *Reachability.h* and *Reachability.m* files from the Xcode project and copy them onto your Desktop (or any convenient location). This is the `Reachability` class that we want to reuse in our projects.

To use the `Reachability` class in a project, you must do the following after you create the project in Xcode:

1. Drag and drop both the header and implementation files into the Classes group in your project, and be sure to tick the "Copy items into destination group's folder (if needed)" checkbox in the pop-up dialog that appears when you drop the files into Xcode.

2. Right-click or Ctrl-click on the Frameworks group, select Add→Existing Frameworks, and then select *SystemConfiguration.framework* in the Frameworks selector pop up, as shown in Figure 7-1. The Reachability code needs this framework and it has to be added to your projects where you use it.

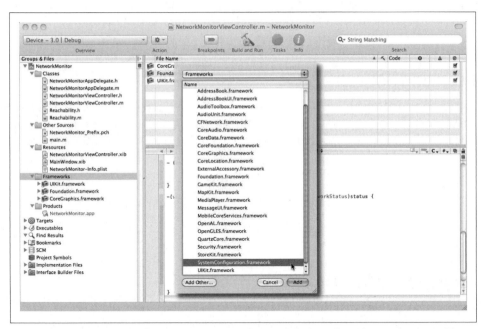

Figure 7-1. Selecting SystemConfiguration.framework from the list offered by Xcode when adding a new framework to a project

There are two ways to make use of Apple's Reachability code: synchronously or asynchronously.

Synchronous reachability

The synchronous case is the simpler of the two approaches; here we import the *Reachability.h* header file into our code and then carry out a "spot-check" as to whether the network is reachable, and whether we have a wireless or WWAN connection:

```
#import "Reachability.h"

... some code omitted ...

Reachability *reach = [[Reachability reachabilityForInternetConnection] retain];
NetworkStatus status = [reach currentReachabilityStatus];
```

or alternatively, whether a specific host is reachable:

```
Reachability *reach =
            [[Reachability reachabilityWithHostName: @"www.apple.com"] retain];
NetworkStatus status = [reach currentReachabilityStatus];
```

We can then use a simple `switch` statement to decode the network status. The following code turns the `status` flag into an `NSString`, perhaps to update a `UILabel` in the application interface, but of course you can trigger any action you need to (disabling parts of your user interface, perhaps?) depending on the current network status:

```
- (NSString *)stringFromStatus:(NetworkStatus ) status {

    NSString *string;
    switch(status) {
        case NotReachable:
            string = @"Not Reachable";
            break;
        case ReachableViaWiFi:
            string = @"Reachable via WiFi";
            break;
        case ReachableViaWWAN:
            string = @"Reachable via WWAN";
            break;
        default:
            string = @"Unknown";
            break;
    }
    return string;
}
```

We can easily put together a quick application to illustrate use of the Reachability code. Open Xcode and start a new project. Choose a view-based iPhone OS application, and when prompted, name it "NetworkMonitor". Import the Reachability code, add the *SystemConfiguration.framework* into your new project (as discussed in the preceding section), open the *NetworkMonitorAppDelegate.h* interface file in the Xcode editor, and declare the `stringFromStatus:` method as shown in the following code:

```
#import <UIKit/UIKit.h>
#import "Reachability.h"

@class NetworkMonitorViewController;
```

```
@interface NetworkMonitorAppDelegate : NSObject <UIApplicationDelegate> {
    UIWindow *window;
    NetworkMonitorViewController *viewController;
}

@property (nonatomic, retain) IBOutlet UIWindow *window;
@property (nonatomic, retain) IBOutlet
    NetworkMonitorViewController *viewController;

- (NSString *)stringFromStatus:(NetworkStatus )status;

@end
```

Save your changes, and open the *NetworkMonitorAppDelegate.m* implementation file in the Xcode editor and modify the `applicationDidFinishLaunching:` method:

```
- (void)applicationDidFinishLaunching:(UIApplication *)application {

    // Override point for customization after app launch
    [window addSubview:viewController.view];
    [window makeKeyAndVisible];

    Reachability *reach =
                [[Reachability reachabilityForInternetConnection] retain];
    NetworkStatus status = [reach currentReachabilityStatus];

    UIAlertView *alert = [[UIAlertView alloc]
                          initWithTitle:@"Reachability"
                          message:[self stringFromStatus: status]
                          delegate:self
                          cancelButtonTitle:@"OK"
                          otherButtonTitles:nil];
    [alert show];
    [alert release];
}
```

The final step is to add the `stringWithStatus:` method I showed earlier to *Network-MonitorAppDelegate.m*. Save your changes and click the Build and Run button on the Xcode toolbar to compile your code and deploy it into iPhone Simulator. You should see something similar to Figure 7-2.

Asynchronous reachability

The asynchronous approach is (only slightly) more complicated, but using the `Reacha bility` class in this way means your application can be notified of changes in the current network status. You must first import the *Reachability.h* header file into your code. After that, you need to register the class that must monitor the network as an observer for the `kReachabilityChangedNotification` event:

```
[[NSNotificationCenter defaultCenter] addObserver: self
    selector: @selector(reachabilityChanged:)
    name: kReachabilityChangedNotification
    object: nil];
```

Figure 7-2. The NetworkMonitor application in iPhone Simulator

Then you need to create a `Reachability` instance and start event notification:

```
Reachability *reach =
  [[Reachability reachabilityWithHostName: @"www.apple.com"] retain];
[reach startNotifer];
```

When the network reachability status changes, the `Reachability` instance will notify your code by calling the `reachabilityChanged:` method. What you do in that method of course very much depends on *why* you're monitoring the network status in the first place; however, the stub of such a method would look like this:

```
- (void) reachabilityChanged: (NSNotification *)notification {
    Reachability *reach = [notification object];
    if( [reach isKindOfClass: [Reachability class]]) {❶
        NetworkStatus status = [reach currentReachabilityStatus];
        // Insert your code here
    }
}
```

❶ The `isKindOfClass:` method returns a Boolean that indicates whether the receiver is an instance of a given class. Here we check whether the `Reachability` object passed as part of the notification is indeed of type `Reachability`.

Using Reachability directly

The Apple `Reachability` class is just a friendly wrapper around the `SCNetworkReacha bility` programming interface, which is part of *SystemConfiguration.framework*. While I recommend using Apple's sample code if possible, you can use the interfaces directly if you need to do something out of the ordinary.

 If you are interested in alternative approaches to checking for network reachability, I recommend looking at the `UIDevice-Reachability` extensions provided by Erica Sadun in *The iPhone Developer's Cookbook* (Addison-Wesley). The Reachability code is available for download from the GitHub source repository that accompanies the book (*http:// github.com/erica/iphone-3.0-cookbook-*). It is located in the *013- Networking/02-General Reachability/* folder of the repository.

Embedding a Web Browser in Your App

The `UIWebView` class allows you to embed web content inside your application. This class is the simplest but least flexible way of getting network content into your application. A `UIWebView` is best used to display content. If you want to manipulate the content programmatically, you should skip ahead a couple of sections and look at the discussion of the `NSURLConnection` class. However, there are a few tricks you can play to retrieve the displayed content from the `UIWebView` once it has been downloaded, and I'll talk about them later in the section.

A Simple Web View Controller

There are a number of cases where you might want to load a URL and display a web page, but keep users inside your application rather than closing it and opening Safari. If this is what you need to do, you should be using a `UIWebView`.

So, let's build some code that you'll be able to reuse in your own applications later. The specification for this code is a view controller that we can display modally, which will display a `UIWebView` with a specified web page, and can then be dismissed, returning us to our application.

I'm going to prototype the code here, hanging it off a simple view with a button that will pull up the modal view. However, the view controller class is reusable without modification; just drag and drop the code out of this project and into another. This is also a good exercise in writing reusable code.

Open Xcode and start a new project, choose a view-based iPhone OS application, and when prompted, name it "Prototype". The first thing we want to do is set up our main view; this is going to consist of a single button that we'll click to bring up the web view. Click on the *PrototypeViewController.h* interface file to open it in the editor, and add a UIButton flagged as an IBOutlet and an associated method (flagged as an IBAction) to the interface file. The added code is shown in bold:

```
#import <UIKit/UIKit.h>

@interface PrototypeViewController : UIViewController {
    IBOutlet UIButton *goButton;
}

-(IBAction) pushedGo:(id) sender;

@end
```

Now, open the *PrototypeViewController.m* implementation file and add a stub for the pushedGo: method. As always, you have to remember to release the goButton in the dealloc: method:

```
-(IBAction) pushedGo:(id) sender {
    // Code goes here later
}

- (void)dealloc {
    [goButton release];
    [super dealloc];
}
```

Next, we need to add a new view controller class to the project. This is the class we're going to use to manage our UIWebView. Right-click on the Classes group in the Groups & Files pane in Xcode and select Add→New File, select the UIViewController subclass template from the Cocoa Touch Class category, and check the "With XIB for user interface" box. When prompted, name the new class "WebViewController".

Three files will be created: the interface file *WebViewController.h*, the implementation file *WebViewController.m*, and the view NIB file *WebViewController.xib*.

 At this point, I normally rename the NIB file, removing the "Controller" part of the filename and leaving it as *WebView.xib*, as I feel this is a neater naming scheme. I also usually move it from the Classes group to the Resources group to keep it with the other NIBs.

After creating this new view controller, we need to leave Xcode for a moment. Double-click on the *PrototypeViewController.xib* file to open the NIB file in Interface Builder. Drag and drop a round rect button (UIButton) into the view and change its text to something appropriate; I picked "Go!". (You can find the button in the Inputs & Values category of the Library.)

Next, click on File's Owner in the *WebView.xib* window. In the Connections Inspector (⌘-2), connect both the goButton outlet and the pushedGo: received action to the button that you just dropped into the view, choosing Touch Up Inside as the action; see

Figure 7-3. Make sure you save your changes to the *PrototypeViewController.xib* file and close it. We're done with the `PrototypeViewController` class for now.

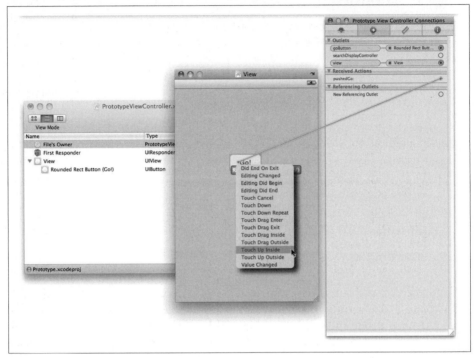

Figure 7-3. Connecting the UIButton to File's Owner, the PrototypeViewController

Now we need to build our web view. Double-click on *WebView.xib* to open the NIB file in Interface Builder. Drag and drop a navigation bar (`UINavigationBar`) from Library→Windows, Views & Bars, and position it at the top of the view. Then drag a web view (`UIWebView`) from Library→Data Views into the view and resize it to fill the remaining portion of the View window. Check the box marked Scales Page to Fit in the Attributes Inspector (⌘-1). Finally, drag a bar button item (`UIBarButton`) onto the navigation bar, and in the Attributes tab of the Inspector window change its identifier to Done. Once you're done, your view will look similar to Figure 7-4.

After saving the changes to the *WebView.xib* file, close it and return to Xcode. We now need to implement the `WebViewController` class before we can connect the new UI to our code.

Open the *WebViewController.h* interface file. We want to make this class self-contained so that we can reuse it without any modifications. Therefore, we're going to override the `init:` function to pass in the URL when instantiating the object. Make the following changes to the file (notice that I've added `<UIWebViewDelegate>` to the interface declaration):

```
#import <UIKit/UIKit.h>

@interface WebViewController : UIViewController <UIWebViewDelegate> {
    NSURL *theURL;
    NSString *theTitle;
    IBOutlet UIWebView *webView;
    IBOutlet UINavigationItem *webTitle;

}

- (id)initWithURL:(NSURL *)url;
- (id)initWithURL:(NSURL *)url andTitle:(NSString *)string;
- (IBAction) done:(id)sender;

@end
```

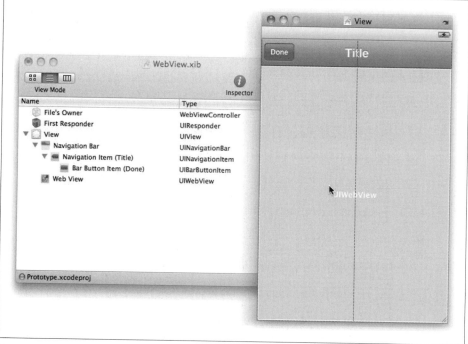

Figure 7-4. Creating our web view in Interface Builder

In fact, to give a bit more flexibility to the class, I provided two different init: functions: initWithURL: and initWithURL:andTitle:. There's also a done: method flagged as an IBAction that we can connect to our Done UIBarButtonItem when we go back into Interface Builder.

We've declared an NSURL and an NSString to store the URL and view title passed to our init methods, along with a UIWebView and a UINavigationItem flagged as IBOutlet to connect to the UI elements we created previously in Interface Builder.

Now, open the *WebViewController.m* implementation file. We'll start by implementing the two initWith methods. Add the following code to the file:

```
- (id)initWithURL:(NSURL *)url andTitle:(NSString *)string {
    if( self = [super init] ) {
        theURL = url;
        theTitle = string;
    }
    return self;
}

-(id)initWithURL:(NSURL *)url {
    return [self initWithURL:url andTitle:nil]; ❶
}
```

❶ We implemented the initWithURL: method by calling the initWithURL:andTitle: method with an empty (nil) title. Doing it this way means that if we need to change the implementation of the initialization method later, we have to do so in only one place.

Next, we have to load the URL into the view, and we'll do that in the viewDidLoad: method. Uncomment the viewDidLoad: method and add the lines shown in bold:

```
- (void)viewDidLoad {
    [super viewDidLoad];
    webTitle.title = theTitle; ❶
    NSURLRequest *requestObject = [NSURLRequest requestWithURL:theURL]; ❷
    [webView loadRequest:requestObject]; ❸
}
```

❶ We set the title property of the NSNavigationBarItem to the title string we passed earlier in the initWithURL:andTitle: method.

❷ We *marshal* (gather together along with the other necessary data) the URL we passed in the `initWithURL:andTitle:` method to form an `NSURLRequest` object.

❸ Here, we load the requested URL into the `UIWebView`.

Now we have to deal with what happens when the user dismisses the view by tapping the Done button. Add the following to the file:

```
- (IBAction) done:(id)sender {
    [self dismissModalViewControllerAnimated:YES];❶
}

- (void)viewWillDisappear:(BOOL)animated {
    [super viewWillDisappear:animated];
    webView.delegate = nil;❷
    [webView stopLoading];❸
}
```

❶ In the `done:` method, we dismiss the modal view, which will trigger the `viewWillDisappear:animated:` method.

❷ In the `viewWillDisappear:animated:` method, we have to set the delegate class for our `UIWebView` to `nil`. We're about to deallocate our object, and if we don't set the `delegate` property to `nil` before this happens, messages sent to the nonexistent object by the `UIWebViewDelegate` protocol will cause our application to crash.

❸ We also have to stop loading from our URL because the events generated as the web page continues to load will cause the application to crash.

Finally, we have to make sure we release our declared variables in the `dealloc:` method. Add the lines shown in bold to this method:

```
- (void)dealloc {
    [webView release];
    [webTitle release];
    [super dealloc];
}
```

We're not quite done yet. Back in the *PrototypeViewController.m* file we still need to implement the `pushedGo:` method. Replace `// Code goes here later` with the code shown in bold:

```
-(IBAction) pushedGo:(id)sender {
    NSURL *url = [NSURL URLWithString:@"http://www.apple.com/"];
    WebViewController *webViewController =
        [[WebViewController alloc] initWithURL:url andTitle:@"Apple"];❶
    [self presentModalViewController:webViewController animated:YES];❷
    [webViewController release];
}
```

❶ We create an instance of our `WebViewController` using `initWithURL:andTitle:`.

❷ We present the new controller modally.

Remember that since we've used the class in the `pushedGo:` method, we also now need to import the *WebViewController.h* header file into the `PrototypeViewController`. So, go to the top of *PrototypeViewController.m* and add this line:

```
#import "WebViewController.h"
```

We're done in Xcode. Now we have to go back into Interface Builder and connect the web view to our controller code. Open the *WebView.xib* file in Interface Builder. Make sure you are in List view mode (Option-⌘-2) and expand the view completely, then click on File's Owner. In the Connection Inspector:

1. Connect the `webTitle` outlet to the `UINavigationItem` "Navigation Item (Title)".
2. Connect the `webView` outlet to the `UIWebView` "Web View".
3. Connect the `done:` received action to the `UIBarButtonItem` "Bar Button Item (Done)".

Finally, click on the web view and connect the `delegate` outlet back to File's Owner.

At this point, if you click on File's Owner in the main NIB window and check the Connections tab, you should see something similar to Figure 7-5.

Save the NIB and return to Xcode. Click on the Build and Run button in the Xcode toolbar to compile and start the application in iPhone Simulator, as shown in Figure 7-6. Tap the Go! button and the Apple website should load in your view. Remember that you're making a network connection here, so you might have to be a bit patient depending on the speed of your network connection.

Of course, users don't like to be patient, and we currently don't have a way to indicate to them that our application is doing something they need to be patient about. This is where the `UIWebViewDelegate` protocol comes in; we declared `WebViewController` as a web view delegate, but so far we haven't taken advantage of that.

The delegate protocol offers two methods: `webViewDidStartLoad:` and `webViewDidFinish Load:`. We can use these to start and stop the network activity indicator in the iPhone's toolbar to indicate that we're transferring data and the user should be patient. Add these two methods to *WebViewController.m*:

```
- (void)webViewDidStartLoad:(UIWebView *)wv {
    [UIApplication sharedApplication].networkActivityIndicatorVisible = YES;
}

- (void)webViewDidFinishLoad:(UIWebView *)wv {
    [UIApplication sharedApplication].networkActivityIndicatorVisible = NO;
}
```

But what happens if our URL fails to load? Even if we checked reachability before creating the view controller, what if we lose the network connection while the page itself is loading? The delegate protocol also provides the `webView:didFailLoad WithError:` method to inform us that something has gone wrong. Add the following to *WebViewController.m*:

```
- (void)webView:(UIWebView *)wv didFailLoadWithError:(NSError *)error {
    [UIApplication sharedApplication].networkActivityIndicatorVisible = NO;

    NSString *errorString = [error localizedDescription];
    NSString *errorTitle =
                [NSString stringWithFormat:@"Error (%d)", error.code];

    UIAlertView *errorView = [[UIAlertView alloc]
        initWithTitle:errorTitle
        message:errorString
        delegate:self
        cancelButtonTitle:nil
        otherButtonTitles:@"OK", nil];❶
    [errorView show];
    [errorView autorelease];
}
```

❶ Here we grab the error description and open an alert view to display the error. We declare our view controller class to be the alert's delegate.

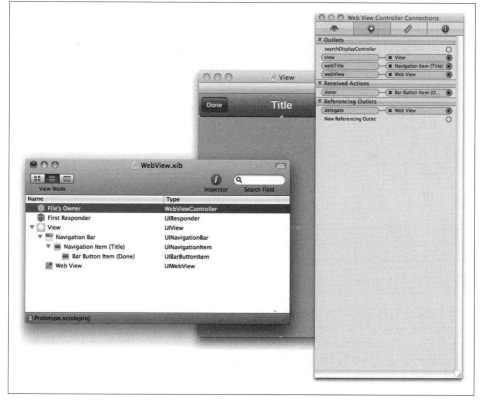

Figure 7-5. The web view NIB file connected to the WebViewController

Figure 7-6. The initial main view (left) and the web view (right)

Since we said our view controller class is the `UIAlertView` delegate, we also have to declare the class as a `UIAlertViewDelegate` in the *WebViewController.h* interface file:

```
@interface WebViewController :
  UIViewController <UIWebViewDelegate, UIAlertViewDelegate> {
    ... no changes to the code inside the declaration ...
}
```

With this change made, we can make use of the `UIAlertViewDelegate` protocol back in our implementation to dismiss the web view pane when an error is received loading our URL. Add the following to *WebViewController.m*:

```
- (void)didPresentAlertView:(UIAlertView *)alertView {
    [self dismissModalViewControllerAnimated:YES];
}
```

We're done. With these changes, the application can tell the user that it is doing something, and can handle any errors that occur when loading the URL. Click on the Build and Run button in the Xcode toolbar to compile and start the application in iPhone Simulator. Tap the Go! button and you should see the activity indicator spinning in the toolbar next to the WiFi signal strength icon as the application loads Apple's web page. When it finishes, the spinner should stop.

Click Done, and then either turn Airport off or unplug your Ethernet cable. Now try again, and you should get something that looks like Figure 7-7, informing you that you no longer have an Internet connection.

Figure 7-7. The webView:didFailLoadWithError: method creates a UIAlertView and dismisses the web view when we fail to load the URL we passed to it

At this point, you have a reusable `WebViewController` class and associated NIB file that you can copy and drop directly into your own projects. You might also want to think about improvements if you do that, of course. For instance, the only error checking we do occurs after we attempt to load the view. Perhaps you could make use of the `Reach ability` class we looked at earlier in the chapter inside the `viewWillAppear:` method, before the web view is even displayed, to check the network connection. Then you can pop up an alert view if you are unable to reach `theURL` (which we passed to the view controller as part of the `initWithURL:` or `initWithURL:andTitle:` method) before the view is displayed to the user rather than afterward.

Displaying Static HTML Files

We can use the `UIWebView` class to display HTML files bundled into our project. In fact, we can add HTML documents to our project in the same way we dragged and dropped the images into the City Guide application; see "Adding Images to Your Projects" on page 71 in Chapter 5.

Suppose we're going to use a web view to display a help document for our application. We could do so as follows:

```
NSString *filePath =
   [[NSBundle mainBundle]
      pathForResource:@"HelpDocument" ofType:@"html"];

NSData *htmlData = [NSData dataWithContentsOfFile:filePath];

if (htmlData) {
   [webView loadData:htmlData
             MIMEType:@"text/html"
             textEncodingName:@"UTF-8"
             baseURL:[NSURL URLWithString:@"http://www.babilim.co.uk"]];
}
```

We grab the file path to our bundled resource, create an `NSData` object, and pass this to our web view.

Embedding Images in the Application Bundle

Since we can specify the base URL of our web view, we can use a trick to embed small images directly into our application bundle by setting this base URL for our HTML document correctly. For instance, if we have an HTML document in the `NSString` variable `htmlDocument`, we could add this snippet:

```
NSString *filePath = [[NSBundle mainBundle] bundlePath];
NSURL *baseURL = [NSURL fileURLWithPath:filePath];
[webView loadHTMLString:htmlDocument baseURL:baseURL];
```

This will load the HTML document into our `UIWebView`. However, it will also set the base URL to the root of the application bundle and allow us to add images (or other content) into our application and refer to them directly in our document (or an associated CSS file):

```
<img src="image.png">
```

You should note that even if you store your images inside a folder in your Xcode project, they will be at the root of the application bundle file when you build and deploy your application.

Getting Data Out of a UIWebView

A `UIWebView` is primarily intended to display a URL, but if need be you can retrieve the content that has been loaded into the view using the `stringByEvaluatingJavaScript FromString:` method:

```
NSString *content =
   [webView stringByEvaluatingJavaScriptFromString:@"document.body.outerHTML"];❶
```

❶ Here we retrieve the contents of the HTML <body> ... </body> tag.

Sending Email

The `MFMailComposeViewController` class provides access to the same interface used by the Mail client to edit and send an email. The most common way to present this interface is to do so modally using the `presentModalViewController:animated:` method, just as we did in the preceding section to create a reusable web view class.

We can therefore reuse our Prototype application code from the preceding section to demonstrate how the mail composer works; we'll just drop in a class that displays the mail interface instead of the web interface. Open the Finder and navigate to the location where you saved the *Prototype* project. Right-click on the folder containing the project files and select Duplicate; a folder called *Prototype copy* will be created containing a duplicate of our project. Rename the folder *Prototype2*, and then open the new (duplicate) project inside Xcode and use the Project→Rename tool to rename the project itself.

Next, prune back the code:

1. Open the copy of the project in Xcode and delete the *WebViewController.h*, *Web-ViewController.m*, and *WebView.xib* files by right-clicking on each file in the Groups & Files pane and selecting Delete from the pop-up menu. When prompted, click Also Move to Trash. If you moved *WebView.xib* into your Resources folder with the rest of the NIBs, look for it there.

2. Now click on the *PrototypeViewController.m* file to open it in the editor. Delete the line where you import the *WebViewController.h* file and delete all the code in the `pushedGo:` method, but not the method itself.

At this point, we have just the stub of the application, with that Go! button and associated `pushedGo:` method we can use to trigger the display of our mail composer view. So, let's write the code to do that now.

The first thing we need to do is add the *MessageUI.framework* framework to the project. As you did earlier for the *SystemConfiguration.framework*, right-click on the Frameworks group and select Add→Existing Frameworks. Then select the *MessageUI.framework* from the list presented in the framework selection pop-up window.

 If you have upgraded your Xcode (and iPhone SDK) distribution in the middle of developing a project, *MessageUI.framework* may not show up in the list of frameworks presented to you by Xcode in the framework selection pop up. If this turns out to be the case, you may be able to resolve the problem by opening the Targets group in the Groups & Files pane in Xcode, right-clicking on the application's target, and selecting Get Info. Navigate to the Build pane of the Target Info window and set the Base SDK of your project to the SDK you currently have installed (rather than the SDK with which you initially developed the project).

We're going to present our mail composer view when the Go! button is clicked using our pushedGo: method. However, before we do, we need to see if the device is even configured to send email, using the canSendMail: class method. If it isn't, we need to inform the user that the device isn't able to send mail. When writing a real application that relies on email being available, you might want to do this check when the application starts inside your application delegate, and then either inform the user that there is a problem or disable the parts of your application that depend on it being able to send mail. Add the following code to the pushedGo: method in *PrototypeViewController.m*:

```
-(IBAction) pushedGo:(id)sender {
  if (![MFMailComposeViewController canSendMail]) {❶
      NSString *errorTitle = @"Error";
      NSString *errorString =
      @"This device is not configured to send email.";
      UIAlertView *errorView = [[UIAlertView alloc] initWithTitle:errorTitle
         message:errorString
         delegate:self
         cancelButtonTitle:nil
        otherButtonTitles:@"OK", nil];
      [errorView show];
      [errorView release];
  } else {
      MFMailComposeViewController *mailView =
      [[[MFMailComposeViewController alloc] init] autorelease];❷
      mailView.mailComposeDelegate = self;❸
      [mailView setSubject:@"Test"];
      [mailView setMessageBody:@"This is a test message" isHTML:NO];
      [self presentModalViewController:mailView animated:YES];❹
  }
}
```

❶ Here we check to see if the device is capable of sending mail. If it isn't, we present a UIAlertView to inform the user.

❷ We allocate and initialize an instance of the mail composer view controller.

❸ We set the delegate for the controller to be this class, which implies that we have to implement the delegate protocol for the mail composer view controller.

❹ After setting the subject and the message body, we present the view controller modally.

Unlike the web view we implemented earlier in the chapter, the mail composer view won't dismiss itself when the user clicks the Send or Cancel button. We need to know when it is dismissed by the user; for that to happen we must implement the MFMailCom poseViewControllerDelegate protocol. We therefore need to import the framework headers into the *PrototypeViewController.h* interface file, which we do by importing the *MessageUI.h* header file:

```
#import <MessageUI/MessageUI.h>
```

We also have to declare our `PrototypeViewController` as a delegate class for the mail view by changing the declaration in *PrototypeViewController.h*, as shown here:

```
@interface PrototypeViewController : UIViewController
  <MFMailComposeViewControllerDelegate> {
  ... no changes to the code in here ...
}
```

The delegate protocol implements only one method, which dismisses the view controller and handles any errors: the `mailComposeController:didFinish WithResult:error:` method. Let's implement that now as part of our `PrototypeViewCon troller` class. Add the following method to *PrototypeViewController.m*:

```
-(void)mailComposeController:(MFMailComposeViewController *)controller
  didFinishWithResult:(MFMailComposeResult)result error:(NSError *)error {
    if (error) {❶
        NSString *errorTitle = @"Mail Error";
        NSString *errorDescription = [error localizedDescription];
        UIAlertView *errorView = [[UIAlertView alloc]
          initWithTitle:errorTitle
          message:errorDescription
          delegate:self
          cancelButtonTitle:nil
          otherButtonTitles:@"OK", nil];
        [errorView show];
        [errorView release];

    } else {❷
        // Add code here to handle the MFMailComposeResult
    }

    [controller dismissModalViewControllerAnimated:YES];❸
}
```

❶ If the controller returns an error, we use a `UIAlertView` to inform the user.

❷ If no error is returned, we should handle the `MFMailComposeResult` instead.

❸ In either case, we need to dismiss the controller's view and release the controller.

Before we discuss how to handle the `MFMailComposeResult`, let's test our code. Click the Build and Go button on the Xcode toolbar to compile and start the application in iPhone Simulator. Once the application opens, click the Go! button. If all goes well, you should see something very similar to Figure 7-8.

Now that the application is working, let's handle that `MFMailComposeResult`. The simplest way to illustrate how to handle the result is to add a label to the `PrototypeView Controller` NIB file, and display the result returned by the mail composer view there.

The first thing you need to do is to add a `UILabel` to the *PrototypeViewController.h* interface file and declare it as an `IBOutlet`. Add the line shown in bold:

```
#import <UIKit/UIKit.h>
#import <MessageUI/MessageUI.h>
```

```
@interface PrototypeViewController : UIViewController
<MFMailComposeViewControllerDelegate> {
    IBOutlet UIButton *goButton;
    IBOutlet UILabel *resultLabel;
}

-(IBAction) pushedGo:(id)sender;

@end
```

Figure 7-8. The MFMailMailComposeViewController

Remember that now we've declared the label variable, so we also need to release it
inside the `dealloc:` method. Add the following to the `dealloc:` method in *Prototype-
ViewController.m*:

```
[resultLabel release];
```

We also need to open the *PrototypeViewController.xib* file in Interface Builder and add
the label. Open the NIB file and then drag and drop a label (`UILabel`) from the Library
window onto the view. Now right-click on File's Owner and connect the `resultLabel`
outlet to the new `UILabel`. Make sure you save your changes to the NIB file, and then
return to Xcode.

Now we can use the label to display the results. Inside the mail composer delegate method, replace the line that reads `// Add code here to handle the MFMailCompo` `seResult` with the following code:

```
NSString *string;
switch (result) {
    case MFMailComposeResultSent:
        string = @"Mail sent.";
        break;
    case MFMailComposeResultSaved:
        string = @"Mail saved.";
        break;
    case MFMailComposeResultCancelled:
        string = @"Mail cancelled.";
        break;
    case MFMailComposeResultFailed:
        string = @"Mail failed.";
        break;
    default:
        string = @"Unknown";
        break;
}
resultLabel.text = string;
```

The `switch` statement we just added enumerates the possible results, and then sets the label string to a human-readable result. We're done. If you build the application again and send an email from the composer view, you should see something very much like Figure 7-9.

Attaching an Image to a Mail Message

You can attach an image to your mail message by using the `addAttachmentData:mime` `Type:Filename:` method. This should be called before displaying the mail composer interface, directly after the call to the `setMessageBody:isHTML:` method. You should not call this method after displaying the composer interface to the user.

If necessary, you can change the image type using the `UIImageJPEGRepresentation()` or `UIImagePNGRepresentation()` UIKit function, as shown here:

```
UIImage *image = [UIImage imageNamed:@"Attachment.png"];
NSData *data = UIImageJPEGRepresentation(image, 1.0);
[mailView addAttachmentData:data mimeType:@"image/jpeg"
    fileName:@"Picture.jpeg"];
```

This example will look for *Attachment.png* at the root of the application bundle (to put a file there, drag it into the top level of the Groups & Files pane), convert it to a JPEG, and attach it under the filename *Picture.jpeg*.

Figure 7-9. We successfully sent the mail message

Getting Data from the Internet

If you want to retrieve data from the Internet and process it programmatically, rather than just display it in a view, you should use the NSURLConnection class. While it's more complicated than the UIWebView we looked at earlier in the chapter, it's inherently more flexible.

The NSURLConnection class can make both synchronous and asynchronous requests to download the contents of a URL, and the associated delegate methods provide feedback and control for asynchronous requests.

Synchronous Requests

The easiest, but not the best, way to use the NSURLConnection class is to make a synchronous request for data:

```
NSString *url = @"http://www.apple.com";
NSURLRequest *request =
    [NSURLRequest requestWithURL:[NSURL URLWithString:url]];

NSURLResponse *response = nil;
NSError *error = nil;
```

```
NSData *content = [NSURLConnection sendSynchronousRequest:request
  returningResponse:&response error:&error];

NSString *string = [[NSString alloc] initWithData:content
  encoding:NSUTF8StringEncoding];
NSLog(@"response: %@", string);
```

sendSynchronousRequest: is a convenience method built on top of the asynchronous request code. It's important to note that if you use this method the calling thread will block until the data is loaded or the request times out. If the calling thread is the main thread of your application, your application will freeze while the request is being made. This is generally considered not a good thing from a UI perspective; I strongly encourage you to use the asynchronous connection and associated delegate methods.

Asynchronous Requests

Most of the time when you use the NSURLConnection class, you'll make asynchronous requests this way:

```
NSString *string = [NSString stringWithFormat:@"http://www.apple.com/];
NSURL *url = [[NSURL URLWithString:string] retain];
NSURLRequest *request = [NSURLRequest requestWithURL:url];
[[NSURLConnection alloc]
  initWithRequest:request delegate:self];❶
```

❶ Here we make the asynchronous call and set the delegate class to be self.

For this to work, you need to implement the following methods at a minimum. We'll take a closer look at NSURLConnection in "Using Web Services" on page 168:

```
- (NSURLRequest *)connection:(NSURLConnection *)connection
  willSendRequest:(NSURLRequest *)request
  redirectResponse:(NSURLResponse *)redirectResponse
{
    return request;
}

- (void)connection:(NSURLConnection *)connection
  didReceiveResponse:(NSURLResponse *)response
{
    [responseData setLength:0];❶
}

- (void)connection:(NSURLConnection *)connection
  didReceiveData:(NSData *)data
{
    [responseData appendData:data];❷
}

- (void)connection:(NSURLConnection *)
  connection didFailWithError:(NSError *)error
{
    ... implementation code would go here ...
}❸
```

```
- (void)connectionDidFinishLoading:(NSURLConnection *)connection {
    ... implementation code would go here ...
}❹
```

❶ You need to declare an `NSMutableData` variable (`responseData` in this example) in the interface file of your delegate class to hold the response data. As a stylistic choice, you may prefer to `alloc` and `init` your `NSMutableData` object, rather than calling the `setLength:` method as we have done here.

❷ This appends the data as it is received to the response data variable. There may be multiple calls to this delegate method as data comes in from the response.

❸ This method is called if an error occurs during the connection.

❹ This method is called if the connection completes successfully.

Using Web Services

With the (re)emergence of REpresentational State Transfer (REST) as the dominant paradigm for modern web service architectures, chiefly championed by emerging Web 2.0 companies and platforms, the number of available services has grown significantly over the past few years.

 If you are interested in learning more about RESTful web services, I recommend the book *RESTful Web Services (http://oreilly.com/catalog/9780596529260/)* by Leonard Richardson and Sam Ruby (O'Reilly).

The Google Weather Service

To illustrate the `NSURLConnection` class, we're going to look at one of these RESTful services, the (mostly undocumented, as far as I can tell) Google Weather Service. A request to the Google Weather API of the form *http://www.google.com/ig/api?weather=QUERY_STRING* will return forecasts with temperatures in Fahrenheit; the same request to *www.google.co.uk* will return a forecast with temperatures in Centigrade.

 While the Google Weather Service is a simple little service that has been around for some time in its current form, there is very little documentation surrounding it. As such, Google may not regard it as an "officially supported" API and the service may be subject to change without much notice.

So, for instance, if we made a request of the Google Weather API for the current conditions and forecast in London, the request would look like *http://www.google.com/ig/api?weather=London,UK*. If we do that, the service will return an XML document containing the current and forecasted conditions:

```xml
<?xml version="1.0"?>
<xml_api_reply version="1">
   <weather module_id="0" tab_id="0"
        mobile_row="0"
        mobile_zipped="1"
        row="0"
        section="0" >
      <forecast_information>
         <city data="London,  England"/>
         <postal_code data="London,UK"/>
         <latitude_e6 data=""/>❶
         <longitude_e6 data=""/>
         <forecast_date data="2009-08-29"/>
         <current_date_time data="2009-08-29 17:50:00 +0000"/>
         <unit_system data="US"/>
      </forecast_information>

      <current_conditions>
         <condition data="Clear"/>
         <temp_f data="64"/>
         <temp_c data="18"/>
         <humidity data="Humidity: 40%"/>
         <icon data="/ig/images/weather/sunny.gif"/>
         <wind_condition data="Wind: W at 17 mph"/>
      </current_conditions>

      <forecast_conditions>
         <day_of_week data="Sat"/>
         <low data="55"/>
         <high data="71"/>
         <icon data="/ig/images/weather/chance_of_rain.gif"/>
         <condition data="Chance of Rain"/>
      </forecast_conditions>
      <forecast_conditions>
         <day_of_week data="Sun"/>
         <low data="64"/>
         <high data="69"/>
         <icon data="/ig/images/weather/chance_of_rain.gif"/>
         <condition data="Chance of Rain"/>
      </forecast_conditions>
      <forecast_conditions>
         <day_of_week data="Mon"/>
         <low data="62"/>
         <high data="77"/>
         <icon data="/ig/images/weather/chance_of_rain.gif"/>
         <condition data="Chance of Rain"/>
      </forecast_conditions>
      <forecast_conditions>
         <day_of_week data="Tue"/>
         <low data="59"/>
         <high data="73"/>
         <icon data="/ig/images/weather/chance_of_rain.gif"/>
         <condition data="Chance of Rain"/>
      </forecast_conditions>
```

```
        </weather>
    </xml_api_reply>
```

❶ As far as I can tell, this is unimplemented, and Google does not do reverse geocoding to populate the latitude and longitude fields of the XML document with the values for the town or city concerned.

If we make a request about a nonexistent location—for instance, *http://www.google .com/ig/api?weather=Foo*—we'll get the following (rather unhelpful) XML error document returned:

```
<?xml version="1.0"?>
<xml_api_reply version="1">
    <weather module_id="0" tab_id="0" mobile_row="0"
            mobile_zipped="1" row="0" section="0" >
        <problem_cause data=""/>❶
    </weather>
</xml_api_reply>
```

❶ A far as I can tell this is unimplemented, and Google doesn't populate this field.

Building an application

Much like Apple's own Weather application, the application we're going to wrap around the Google Weather Service will be a utility application. So, open Xcode and start a new project. Select the Utility Application template from the iPhone OS category, and name the project "Weather" when prompted for a filename.

> The UI for this application will be pretty complicated, and will have a lot more elements than interfaces we've looked at before. So, I'll briefly mention an alternative. I could easily have implemented the Weather application as a table view; in fact, programmatically this is probably the easiest way, but it's not the prettiest.
>
> Pretty is important, both to people developing applications for Apple products and to the typical customer base. If you intend to sell your application on the App Store, you should think seriously about how your application looks. First impressions are important, and with so many applications available, both the UI and the application's icon are tools you can use to make your application stand out from the others.

While we're going to be spending some time putting together the interface for the application, that isn't the main focus of this chapter. However, most of the time you'll be using the `NSURLConnection` class asynchronously, so it's important for you to pay attention to the way it fits into the UI and your application's overall structure.

First we need to add a number of `IBOutlet`s to our *MainViewController.h* interface file. We're going to populate our GUI by querying the Google Weather Service and then parsing the XML we get back. If you compare the following to the XML file shown earlier, you should see a more or less one-to-one correspondence between XML elements and UI elements:

```objc
#import "FlipsideViewController.h"

@interface MainViewController : UIViewController
    <FlipsideViewControllerDelegate> {

    IBOutlet UIActivityIndicatorView *loadingActivityIndicator;

    IBOutlet UILabel *nameLabel;
    IBOutlet UILabel *dateLabel;

    IBOutlet UIImageView *nowImage;
    IBOutlet UILabel *nowTempLabel;
    IBOutlet UILabel *nowHumidityLabel;
    IBOutlet UILabel *nowWindLabel;
    IBOutlet UILabel *nowConditionLabel;

    IBOutlet UILabel *dayOneLabel;
    IBOutlet UIImageView *dayOneImage;
    IBOutlet UILabel *dayOneTempLabel;
    IBOutlet UILabel *dayOneChanceLabel;

    IBOutlet UILabel *dayTwoLabel;
    IBOutlet UIImageView *dayTwoImage;
    IBOutlet UILabel *dayTwoTempLabel;
    IBOutlet UILabel *dayTwoChanceLabel;

    IBOutlet UILabel *dayThreeLabel;
    IBOutlet UIImageView *dayThreeImage;
    IBOutlet UILabel *dayThreeTempLabel;
    IBOutlet UILabel *dayThreeChanceLabel;

    IBOutlet UILabel *dayFourLabel;
    IBOutlet UIImageView *dayFourImage;
    IBOutlet UILabel *dayFourTempLabel;
    IBOutlet UILabel *dayFourChanceLabel;

    IBOutlet UIButton *refreshButton;

}

- (IBAction)showInfo;
- (IBAction)refreshView:(id) sender; ❶
- (void)updateView; ❷

@end
```

❶ This method is called when the user taps the Refresh button. It starts the loading activity indicator spinning, and makes the call to query the Google Weather Service.

❷ We're going to use this function as a callback when we have successfully retrieved the XML document from the Google Weather Service. It will update the current view.

Now let's open *MainView.xib* in Interface Builder and put together the UI. I'm not going to walk you through the steps for building the interface this time. You've built enough UIs by this point that you should be familiar with how to go about it. Look at Figure 7-10 to see my final interface. You need to place 35 UI elements: 28 labels (UILabel), 5 images (UIImageView), 1 activity indicator (UIActivityIndicatorView), and 1 button (UIButton). However, don't be put off; it's really not going to take as long as you think it will.

 Remember: to change the font color, minimum size, and other settings, use the Attribute Inspector (⌘-1). You can change the attributes of several elements at once by dragging to select them, and then using the Attribute Inspector.

Figure 7-10. Building the UI for the main view

There are a few points to note:

- Each UIImage element must be resized to 40×40 pixels, the size of the GIF weather icons provided by the Google Weather Service.

- I set the style of the UIActivityIndicatorViewer to Large White in the Attributes Inspector and ticked the Hide When Stopped checkbox. We'll use this indicator to show network or other activity.

- I added a custom PNG icon for the Refresh button to the project, setting the UIButton type to Custom and the image to point at my refresh icon (you will need to drag your icon into your Xcode project before it will be available as a custom image). I resized the Refresh button to be the same size as the Info button provided by the template, setting the View Mode to "Scale to Fill" in the Attributes tab of the Inspector window.

- When connecting the UIButtons to the received actions—for example, when dragging the refreshView: action to the Refresh button—choose Touch Up Inside from the drop-down menu of events that Interface Builder will present to you when you make the connection.

With this number of UI elements to play with, it's going to be easy to get confused. What's more, we are not going to connect all of the labels to our code, as some of them aren't going to be updated (e.g., section headers and the "Temp:", "Humidity:", and "Wind:" labels).

So, for the elements you will connect to an IBOutlet, use the Identity Inspector's (⌘-4) Interface Builder Identity section to change the Name attribute of the element to be the same as the variable in the MainViewController interface file. Figure 7-11 shows the assignments.

While this doesn't make it easier to connect the outlets to the UI elements, it does make it easier to check whether we've made an incorrect connection. If you click on File's Owner and switch to the Connections tab of the Inspector window, as Figure 7-12 shows, you can quickly check that each outlet is connected to the correct UI element since the name on each side of the connection should be the same.

Although we've written the interface for the view controller and built and connected our view to the interface, we haven't implemented it yet. Let's hold off on that until we've built our data model.

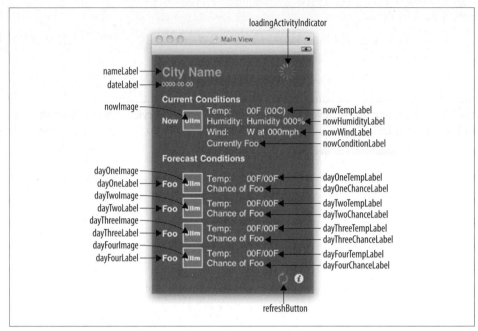

Figure 7-11. Associating names and variables with individual UI elements

Figure 7-12. Connecting the IBOutlets declared in the MainViewController.h file to the appropriate UI elements

Our model class needs to query the weather service, parse the response, and populate the data model. Right-click on the Other Sources group in the Groups & Files pane in Xcode and select Add→New File, select the Objective-C class from the iPhone OS Cocoa Touch category, and select NSObject from the "Subclass of" pop up. Click Next. Name the new class `WeatherForecast` when prompted, and open the *WeatherForecast.h* interface file in the Xcode editor. Like our UI, the interface file reflects the structure of the XML document we retrieved from the Google Weather Service. Add the lines shown in bold to the file:

```
#import <Foundation/Foundation.h>

@class MainViewController;

@interface WeatherForecast : NSObject {

    // Parent View Controller❶
    MainViewController *viewController;

    // Google Weather Service❷
    NSMutableData *responseData;
    NSURL *theURL;

    // Information❸
    NSString *location;
    NSString *date;

    // Current Conditions❹
    UIImage *icon;
    NSString *temp;
    NSString *humidity;
    NSString *wind;
    NSString *condition;

    // Forecast Conditions❺
    NSMutableArray *days;
    NSMutableArray *icons;
    NSMutableArray *temps;
    NSMutableArray *conditions;

}

@property (nonatomic, retain) NSString *location;
@property (nonatomic, retain) NSString *date;

@property (nonatomic, retain) UIImage *icon;
@property (nonatomic, retain) NSString *temp;
@property (nonatomic, retain) NSString *humidity;
@property (nonatomic, retain) NSString *wind;
@property (nonatomic, retain) NSString *condition;

@property (nonatomic, retain) NSMutableArray *days;
@property (nonatomic, retain) NSMutableArray *icons;
@property (nonatomic, retain) NSMutableArray *temps;
@property (nonatomic, retain) NSMutableArray *conditions;
```

```
- (void)queryService:(NSString *)city
  withParent:(UIViewController *)controller;❻

@end
```

❶ This is the variable used to hold the parent view controller. We're going to pass this in to the `Forecast` object when we call the `queryService:withParent` method.

❷ These are the variables used by the `NSURLConnection` class during its asynchronous request.

❸ These are the variables to hold the data from the `<forecast_information>` XML elements.

❹ These are the variables to hold the data from the `<current_conditions>` XML elements.

❺ These are the arrays to hold the data from the four `<forecast_conditions>` XML elements.

❻ This is the method we're going to use to trigger the asynchronous `NSURLConnection` request. We pass as arguments the name of the city we're interested in and the parent view controller. This allows us to substitute the city name into a partially formed REST request to the Google Weather Service.

Now open the implementation file (*WeatherForecast.m*) in the Xcode editor. We need to synthesize our properties and write our `queryService:withParent:` method that will start the asynchronous `NSURLConnection` process. Add the lines shown in bold to this file:

```
#import "WeatherForecast.h"
#import "MainViewController.h"

@implementation WeatherForecast


@synthesize location;
@synthesize date;

@synthesize icon;
@synthesize temp;
@synthesize humidity;
@synthesize wind;
@synthesize condition;

@synthesize days;
@synthesize icons;
@synthesize temps;
@synthesize conditions;

#pragma mark Instance Methods

- (void)queryService:(NSString *)city
  withParent:(UIViewController *)controller
```

```
{
    viewController = (MainViewController *)controller;
    responseData = [[NSMutableData data] retain];

    NSString *url = [NSString
      stringWithFormat:@"http://www.google.com/ig/api?weather=%@",
      city];❶
    theURL = [[NSURL URLWithString:url] retain];
    NSURLRequest *request = [NSURLRequest requestWithURL:theURL];❷
    [[NSURLConnection alloc] initWithRequest:request delegate:self];❸

}

-(void)dealloc {
    [viewController release];
    [responseData release];
    [theURL release];
    [location release];
    [date release];
    [icon release];
    [temp release];
    [humidity release];
    [wind release];
    [condition release];
    [days release];
    [icons release];
    [temps release];
    [conditions release];
    [super dealloc];
}

@end
```

❶ This builds the URL from the base URL and the city string that was passed to the queryService:withParent: method.

❷ This builds the NSURLRequest from the URL string.

❸ This makes the call to the Google Weather Service using an asynchronous call to NSURLConnection.

We declared our WeatherForecast class as the delegate for the NSURLConnection class. Now we need to add the necessary delegate methods. For now let's just implement the delegate methods; we'll get around to parsing the response later. Add the following lines to *WeatherForecast.m* just before the @end directive:

```
#pragma mark NSURLConnection Delegate Methods

- (NSURLRequest *)connection:(NSURLConnection *)connection
  willSendRequest:(NSURLRequest *)request
  redirectResponse:(NSURLResponse *)redirectResponse
{
    [theURL autorelease];
    theURL = [[request URL] retain];
    return request;
```

```
}

- (void)connection:(NSURLConnection *)connection
  didReceiveResponse:(NSURLResponse *)response
{
    [responseData setLength:0];
}

- (void)connection:(NSURLConnection *)connection
  didReceiveData:(NSData *)data
{
    [responseData appendData:data];
}

- (void)connection:(NSURLConnection *)connection
  didFailWithError:(NSError *)error
{

}

- (void)connectionDidFinishLoading:(NSURLConnection *)connection {

    NSString *content = [[NSString alloc]
      initWithBytes:[responseData bytes]
      length:[responseData length]
      encoding:NSUTF8StringEncoding];❶
    NSLog( @"Data = %@", content );❷

    // Insert code to parse the content here

    [viewController updateView];❸
}
```

❶ This converts the binary response data into an NSString object.

❷ Here we print the response to the console log.

❸ This is where we call the updateView: method in our parent view controller to take
the parsed response and display it in the view.

We're going to use the application delegate to create the WeatherForecast object and
to pass it to our MainViewController object. Add the lines shown in bold to *Weather-
AppDelegate.m*:

```
- (void)applicationDidFinishLaunching:(UIApplication *)application {

    MainViewController *aController =
      [[MainViewController alloc] initWithNibName:@"MainView" bundle:nil];
    self.mainViewController = aController;
    [aController release];

    WeatherForecast *forecast = [[WeatherForecast alloc] init];❶
    self.mainViewController.forecast = forecast;❷
    [forecast release];

    mainViewController.view.frame = [UIScreen mainScreen].applicationFrame;
```

```
        [window addSubview:[mainViewController view]];
        [window makeKeyAndVisible];
    }
```

❶ We're creating an instance of this class, which we're going to store inside the app delegate. You'll need to also add #import "WeatherForecast.h" to the top of *WeatherAppDelegate.m*.

❷ We pass the forecast object to the view controller, and then release it in the app delegate. There is no need to store an instance here, as we won't be using it from the delegate.

We have the view, model, and interface for the view controller. Now we know how the model works, and how we're going to push it into the view controller. So, let's implement the controller and tie up those loose ends. Add the following code to *MainViewController.m*:

```
    - (void)viewDidLoad {❶
        [super viewDidLoad];
        [self refreshView:self];
    }

    - (IBAction)refreshView:(id)sender {❷
        [loadingActivityIndicator startAnimating];
        [forecast queryService:@"London,UK" withParent:self];

    }

    - (void)updateView {❸

        // Add code to update view here

        [loadingActivityIndicator stopAnimating];

    }
```

❶ This is called when the view loads. This calls the viewDidLoad: method in the superclass and then calls the refreshView: method.

❷ This method is called when the Refresh button is tapped, and also from the view DidLoad: method. This starts the UIActivityViewIndicator spinning and then calls the queryService:withParent: method in the WeatherForecast object.

❸ This method is called from the WeatherForecast object when it finishes loading the XML from the remote service. This method will contain the code to update the view using the newly populated WeatherForecast object. For now all it does is stop the UIActivityView from spinning and hides it.

Additionally, we also need to make sure we do the following:

1. Import the *WeatherForecast.h* interface file inside *MainViewController.h*.

2. Declare the forecast, mark it as a property, and synthesize it.

3. Release all of the variables we declared in the class's interface file in *MainViewController.m*'s `dealloc:` method.

To do this, add the following line to the top of *MainViewController.h*:

```
#import "WeatherForecast.h"
```

Next, make the changes shown in bold to the end of *MainViewController.h*:

```
    IBOutlet UIButton *refreshButton;
    WeatherForecast *forecast;
}

- (IBAction)showInfo;
- (IBAction)refreshView:(id) sender;
- (void)updateView;

@property (nonatomic, retain) WeatherForecast *forecast;

@end
```

Then make the change shown in bold to the top of *MainViewController.h*:

```
#import "MainViewController.h"
#import "MainView.h"

@implementation MainViewController

@synthesize forecast;
```

Finally, add the lines shown in bold to *MainViewController.m*'s `dealloc:` method:

```
- (void)dealloc {

    [loadingActivityIndicator dealloc];

    [nameLabel dealloc];
    [dateLabel dealloc];

    [nowImage dealloc];
    [nowTempLabel dealloc];
    [nowHumidityLabel dealloc];
    [nowWindLabel dealloc];
    [nowConditionLabel dealloc];

    [dayOneLabel dealloc];
    [dayOneImage dealloc];
    [dayOneTempLabel dealloc];
    [dayOneChanceLabel dealloc];

    [dayTwoLabel dealloc];
    [dayTwoImage dealloc];
    [dayTwoTempLabel dealloc];
    [dayTwoChanceLabel dealloc];

    [dayThreeLabel dealloc];
    [dayThreeImage dealloc];
```

```
    [dayThreeTempLabel dealloc];
    [dayThreeChanceLabel dealloc];

    [dayFourLabel dealloc];
    [dayFourImage dealloc];
    [dayFourTempLabel dealloc];
    [dayFourChanceLabel dealloc];

    [refreshButton dealloc];
    [forecast dealloc];

    [super dealloc];
}
```

This is a good point to pause, take stock, and test the application. Click the Build and Run button in the Xcode toolbar. When the application opens you should see the UIActivityIndicator briefly appear in the top-lefthand corner of the view, and then disappear when the WeatherForecast object finishes loading the XML document from the Google Weather Service.

If you go to the Xcode Console, by selecting Run→Console from the Xcode menu bar, you should see something very much like Figure 7-13. This is the XML document retrieved from the weather service.

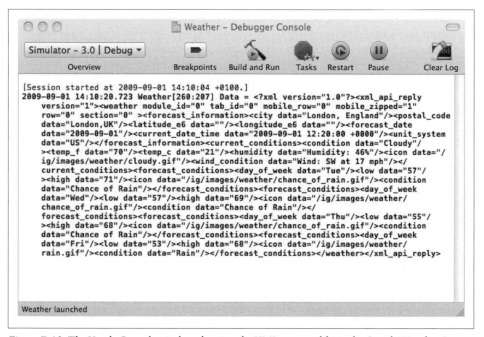

Figure 7-13. The Xcode Console window showing the XML retrieved from the Google Weather Service

At this point, all that is left to implement is the XML parsing code inside the Weather Forecast's connectionDidFinishLoading: method, and the code to take the data model from the forecast object and display it in the view inside the MainViewController's updateView: method.

Parsing the XML document

We're going to talk in detail about parsing data in the next chapter. This chapter is about networking, so I'm not going to discuss in depth how to parse the returned XML document here. If you're familiar with DOM-based XML parsers, the following should be familiar. If not, hang on until the next chapter.

 Making use of the NSXMLDocument class is the normal method for tree-based parsing of XML files on the Mac. However, despite being available in iPhone Simulator, this class is not available on the device itself.

However, for simple files, such as those returned by the Google Weather Service, I've never been a big fan of event-driven parsing. Since the NSXMLDocument class is not available on the iPhone, I generally use the *libxml2* library directly, via Matt Gallagher's excellent XPath wrappers for the library.

For more information about the XPath wrappers for the *libxml2* library, see Matt's blog post (*http://cocoawithlove.com/2008/10/using-libxml2-for-parsing-and-xpath.html*).

Using the XPath Wrappers

Download the wrappers from *http://cocoawithlove.googlepages.com/XPathQuery.zip*. Next, unzip the file and drag the *XPathQuery.h* and *XPathQuery.m* files into your project, remembering to tick the "Copy items into destination group's folder" checkbox. This will add the interface and implementation files for the wrappers to the project.

To use these wrappers, you need to add the *libxml2.dylib* library to the project. However, adding the *libxml2* library underlying these wrappers is slightly more involved than adding a normal framework:

1. Double-click on the Weather project icon in the Groups & Files pane in Xcode and go to the Build tab of the Project Info window.
2. Click on the Show drop-down menu and choose All Settings.
3. Go to the Search Paths subsection in this window, and in the Header Search Paths field double-click on the entry field.
4. Click the + button and add ${SDKROOT}/usr/include/libxml2 to the paths, as shown in Figure 7-14. Then click OK.
5. Then in the Linking subsection of this window, double-click on the Other Linker Flags field and click +. Add -lxml2 to the flags and then click OK.

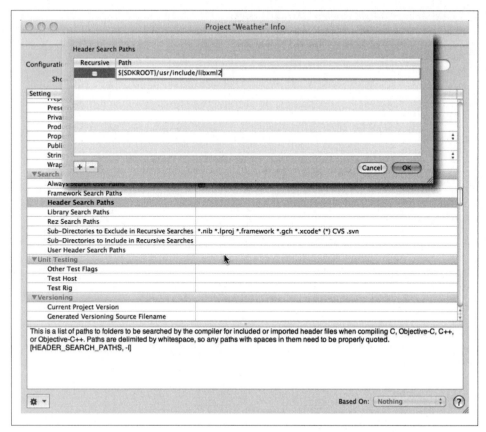

Figure 7-14. Adding the libxml2.dylib library in the Project Info window

Once we've done that, we can open the *WeatherForecast.m* implementation file and import the *XPathQuery.h* interface file. Add the following line to the top of *Weather-Forecast.m*:

```
#import "XPathQuery.h"
```

After importing the interface file, we now have everything in place to write our `connec tionDidFinishLoading:` method, using the XPath query language and *libxml2* to parse the XML document returned by the Google Weather Service. My intention here is not to teach you XPath, as several good books are available on that topic. However, if you examine the `xpathQueryString` variables in each XPath query, you will see how the data model maps onto the original XML document returned by the weather service. Here is the new `connectionDidFinishLoading:` method along with two methods (`fetchCon tent:` and `populateArray:fromNodes:`) to take care of some repetitive tasks:

```
// Retrieves the content of an XML node, such as the temperature, wind,
// or humidity in the weather report.
//
```

```objc
- (NSString *)fetchContent:(NSArray *)nodes {
    NSString *result = @"";
    for ( NSDictionary *node in nodes ) {
        for ( id key in node ) {
            if( [key isEqualToString:@"nodeContent"] ) {
                result = [node objectForKey:key];
            }
        }
    }
    return result;
}

// For nodes that contain more than one value we are interested in,
// this method fills an NSMutableArray with the values it finds.
// For example, the forecast returns four days, so there will be
// an array with four day names, an array with four forecast icons,
// and so forth.
//
- (void) populateArray:(NSMutableArray *)array fromNodes:(NSArray*)nodes {
    for ( NSDictionary *node in nodes ) {
        for ( id key in node ) {
            if( [key isEqualToString:@"nodeContent"] ) {
                [array addObject:[node objectForKey:key]];
            }
        }
    }
}

- (void)connectionDidFinishLoading:(NSURLConnection *)connection {

    days = [[NSMutableArray alloc] init];
    icons = [[NSMutableArray alloc] init];
    temps = [[NSMutableArray alloc] init];
    conditions = [[NSMutableArray alloc] init];

    NSString *xpathQueryString;
    NSArray *nodes;

    // Forecast Information ////////////////////////////////////////

    // Populate the location (an NSString object)
    //
    xpathQueryString = @"//forecast_information/city/@data";
    nodes = PerformXMLXPathQuery(responseData, xpathQueryString);
    location = [self fetchContent:nodes];
    NSLog(@"location = %@", location);

    // Populate the date (an NSString object)
    //
    xpathQueryString = @"//forecast_information/forecast_date/@data";
    nodes = PerformXMLXPathQuery(responseData, xpathQueryString);
    date = [self fetchContent:nodes];
    NSLog(@"date = %@", date);

    // Current Conditions ////////////////////////////////////////
```

```
// Populate the current day's weather icon (a UIImage object)
//
xpathQueryString = @"//current_conditions/icon/@data";
nodes = PerformXMLXPathQuery(responseData, xpathQueryString);
for ( NSDictionary *node in nodes ) {
    for ( id key in node ) {
        if( [ key isEqualToString:@"nodeContent"] ) {
            icon = [NSString
                stringWithFormat:@"http://www.google.com%@",
                [node objectForKey:key]];
        }
    }
}
NSLog(@"icon = %@", icon);

// Populate the temperature (an NSString object) in F and C
//
NSString *temp_f;
NSString *temp_c;
xpathQueryString = @"//current_conditions/temp_f/@data";
nodes = PerformXMLXPathQuery(responseData, xpathQueryString);
temp_f = [self fetchContent:nodes];

xpathQueryString = @"//current_conditions/temp_c/@data";
nodes = PerformXMLXPathQuery(responseData, xpathQueryString);
temp_c = [self fetchContent:nodes];

temp = [NSString stringWithFormat:@"%@F (%@C)", temp_f, temp_c];
NSLog(@"temp = %@", temp);

// Populate the humidity (an NSString object)
//
xpathQueryString = @"//current_conditions/humidity/@data";
nodes = PerformXMLXPathQuery(responseData, xpathQueryString);
humidity = [self fetchContent:nodes];
NSLog(@"humidity = %@", humidity);

// Populate the wind (an NSString object)
//
xpathQueryString = @"//current_conditions/wind_condition/@data";
nodes = PerformXMLXPathQuery(responseData, xpathQueryString);
wind = [self fetchContent:nodes];
NSLog(@"wind = %@", wind);

// Populate the condition (an NSString object)
//
xpathQueryString = @"//current_conditions/condition/@data";
nodes = PerformXMLXPathQuery(responseData, xpathQueryString);
condition = [self fetchContent:nodes];
NSLog(@"condition = %@", condition);

// Forecast Conditions /////////////////////////////////////////

// Fill the array (an NSMutableArray) of day names
```

```
    //
    xpathQueryString = @"//forecast_conditions/day_of_week/@data";
    nodes = PerformXMLXPathQuery(responseData, xpathQueryString);
    [self populateArray:days fromNodes:nodes];
    NSLog(@"days = %@", days);

    // Fill the array (an NSMutableArray) of day icons
    //
    xpathQueryString = @"//forecast_conditions/icon/@data";
    nodes = PerformXMLXPathQuery(responseData, xpathQueryString);
    for ( NSDictionary *node in nodes ) {
        for ( id key in node ) {
            if( [key isEqualToString:@"nodeContent"] ) {
              [icons addObject:
                  [NSString stringWithFormat:@"http://www.google.com%@",
                  [node objectForKey:key]]];
            }
        }
    }
    NSLog(@"icons = %@", icons);

    // Fill the array (an NSMutableArray) of daily highs/lows
    //
    NSMutableArray *highs = [[NSMutableArray alloc] init];
    NSMutableArray *lows = [[NSMutableArray alloc] init];

    xpathQueryString = @"//forecast_conditions/high/@data";
    nodes = PerformXMLXPathQuery(responseData, xpathQueryString);
    [self populateArray:highs fromNodes:nodes];
    xpathQueryString = @"//forecast_conditions/low/@data";
    nodes = PerformXMLXPathQuery(responseData, xpathQueryString);
    [self populateArray:lows fromNodes:nodes];
    for( int i = 0; i < highs.count; i++ ) {
        [temps
          addObject:[NSString stringWithFormat:@"%@F/%@F",
                      [highs objectAtIndex:i],
                      [lows objectAtIndex:i]]];
    }
    NSLog(@"temps = %@", temps);
    [highs release];
    [lows release];

    // Fill the array (an NSMutableArray) of daily conditions
    //
    xpathQueryString = @"//forecast_conditions/condition/@data";
    nodes = PerformXMLXPathQuery(responseData, xpathQueryString);
    [self populateArray:conditions fromNodes:nodes];
    NSLog(@"conditions = %@", conditions);

    [viewController updateView];
}
```

Populating the UI

Now that we've populated the data model, let's create the updateView: method in our view controller. This is where we take the data that we just parsed from the XML and push it into the current view. Replace the updateView: method in *MainViewController.m* with the following:

```
- (void)updateView {

    // City Info
    nameLabel.text = forecast.location;
    dateLabel.text = forecast.date;

    // Now
    nowTempLabel.text = forecast.temp;
    nowHumidityLabel.text = forecast.humidity;
    nowWindLabel.text = forecast.wind;
    nowConditionLabel.text = forecast.condition;
    NSURL *url = [NSURL URLWithString:(NSString *)forecast.icon];
    NSData *data = [NSData dataWithContentsOfURL:url];
    nowImage.image = [[UIImage alloc] initWithData:data];

    // Day 1
    dayOneLabel.text = [forecast.days objectAtIndex:0];
    dayOneTempLabel.text = [forecast.temps objectAtIndex:0];
    dayOneChanceLabel.text = [forecast.conditions objectAtIndex:0];
    url = [NSURL URLWithString:(NSString *)[forecast.icons objectAtIndex:0]];
    data = [NSData dataWithContentsOfURL:url];
    dayOneImage.image = [[UIImage alloc] initWithData:data];

    // Day 2
    dayTwoLabel.text = [forecast.days objectAtIndex:1];
    dayTwoTempLabel.text = [forecast.temps objectAtIndex:1];
    dayTwoChanceLabel.text = [forecast.conditions objectAtIndex:1];
    url = [NSURL URLWithString:(NSString *)[forecast.icons objectAtIndex:1]];
    data = [NSData dataWithContentsOfURL:url];
    dayTwoImage.image = [[UIImage alloc] initWithData:data];

    // Day 3
    dayThreeLabel.text = [forecast.days objectAtIndex:2];
    dayThreeTempLabel.text = [forecast.temps objectAtIndex:2];
    dayThreeChanceLabel.text = [forecast.conditions objectAtIndex:2];
    url = [NSURL URLWithString:(NSString *)[forecast.icons objectAtIndex:2]];
    data = [NSData dataWithContentsOfURL:url];
    dayThreeImage.image = [[UIImage alloc] initWithData:data];

    // Day 4
    dayFourLabel.text = [forecast.days objectAtIndex:3];
    dayFourTempLabel.text = [forecast.temps objectAtIndex:3];
    dayFourChanceLabel.text = [forecast.conditions objectAtIndex:3];
    url = [NSURL URLWithString:(NSString *)[forecast.icons objectAtIndex:3]];
    data = [NSData dataWithContentsOfURL:url];
    dayFourImage.image = [[UIImage alloc] initWithData:data];
```

```
        [loadingActivityIndicator stopAnimating];

    }
```

We're done. Click the Build and Run button on the Xcode toolbar to build and start the application in iPhone Simulator.

Once the application starts up, if all goes well you should get something that looks similar to Figure 7-15. There is, after all, almost always a chance of rain in London.

Figure 7-15. The Weather application running in iPhone Simulator

Tidying up

There are several things you can do to tidy up this bare-bones application. First you should clean up the UI, as it's pretty untidy when the application opens. The easiest way to do this is to have all your labels start as blank, and then populate the text when the view finishes loading the information from the Google Weather Service.

You might also want to add reachability checks when the application opens, and add some error handling in the `connection:didFailWithError:` delegate method inside the `WeatherForecast` class. You should also allow the user to choose which city to use by adding a text entry box on the flipside view, or perhaps even a map view.

In Chapter 11, we'll come back to this example when we discuss using device sensors. Most people are usually more concerned with the weather where they are now than the weather somewhere else, so we'll use the Core Location framework and the iPhone's GPS to locate users and provide them with a weather forecast for where they are right now.

CHAPTER 8

Handling Data

Most applications on the iPhone platform will make a network connection to retrieve data at some point. This data will usually be formatted so that it can be easily parsed, either as XML or, more frequently these days, as JSON.

In this chapter, we're going to look at how to get data directly from the user via the UI, and then how to parse data we've retrieved from the network. Finally, we'll look at how to store that data on the device.

Data Entry

The Cocoa Touch framework offers a number of UI elements, ranging from text entry fields to switches and segmented controls. Any of these can be used for data entry, but often when we talk about data entry we're talking about getting textual information into an application.

The two main UI elements that allow you to enter text are the UITextField and UIText View classes. While they may sound similar, they are actually quite different. The most noticeable difference between the two is that the UITextView allows you to enter (and display) a multiline text field, while UITextField doesn't.

The most annoying difference between the two is the issue of the *resigning first responder*. When tapped, both display a keyboard to allow the user to enter text. However, while the UITextField class allows the user to dismiss the keyboard (at which time the text field resigns as first responder) when the user taps the Done button, the UIText View class does not. Though there are multiple ways around this problem, as we'll find later on, it's still one of the more annoying quirks in the Cocoa Touch framework.

UITextField and Its Delegate

In Chapter 5, we used a UITextField as part of our AddCityController view. However, we didn't really exploit the full power of this class. We were simply polling the text field to see if the user had entered any text when the Save button was tapped, and perhaps more important, we weren't dismissing the keyboard when the user pressed the Return key. Here's the `saveCity:sender` method from that example:

```
- (void)saveCity:(id)sender {
    CityGuideDelegate *delegate =
     (CityGuideDelegate *)[[UIApplication sharedApplication] delegate];
    NSMutableArray *cities = delegate.cities;

    UITextField *nameEntry = (UITextField *)[nameCell viewWithTag:777];
    UITextView *descriptionEntry =
                    (UITextView *)[descriptionCell viewWithTag:777];

    if ( nameEntry.text.length > 0 ) {
        City *newCity = [[City alloc] init];
        newCity.cityName = nameEntry.text;
        newCity.cityDescription = descriptionEntry.text;
        newCity.cityPicture = cityPicture;
        [cities addObject:newCity];

        RootController *viewController = delegate.viewController;
        [viewController.tableView reloadData];
    }
    [delegate.navController popViewControllerAnimated:YES];

}
```

However, the `UITextFieldDelegate` protocol offers a rich set of delegate methods. To use them, you must declare your class as implementing that delegate protocol (lines with changes are shown in bold):

```
@interface AddCityController : UIViewController
  <UITableViewDataSource, UITableViewDelegate, UITextFieldDelegate>
{
  UITextField *activeTextField; ❶

  ... remainder of example code not shown ...
}
```

❶ If your application has more than one text field in the view, it's useful to keep track of which is currently the active field by using an instance variable.

 After implementing the delegate protocol, open the NIB that contains the `UITextField` (*AddCityController.xib* in the case of `CityGuide`). Next, Ctrl-drag from the `UITextField` to the controller (File's Owner in *Add-CityController.xib*) and select delegates from the pop up that appears. Save the NIB when you're done.

When the user taps the text field, the `textFieldShouldBeginEditing:` method is called in the delegate to ascertain whether the text field should enter edit mode and become the first responder. To implement this, you'd add the following to your controller's implementation (such as *AddCityController.m*):

```
- (BOOL)textFieldShouldBeginEditing:(UITextField *)textField {
    activeTextField = textField;❶
    return YES;
}
```

❶ If your application has more than one text field in the view, here's where you'd set the currently active field.

If this method returns NO, the text field will not become editable. Only if this method returns YES will the text field enter edit mode. At this point, the keyboard will be presented to the user; the text field will become the first responder; and the textFieldDid BeginEditing: delegate method will be called.

The easiest way to hide the keyboard is to implement the textFieldShouldReturn: delegate method and explicitly resign as the first responder. This method is called in the delegate when the Return key on the keyboard is pressed. To dismiss the text field when you tapped on the Return button, you'd add the following to your controller's implementation:

```
- (BOOL)textFieldShouldReturn:(UITextField *)textField {
    activeTextField = nil;❶
    [textField resignFirstResponder];
    return YES;
}
```

❶ If your application is keeping track of the currently active text field, this is where you should set the active field to nil before it resigns as first responder.

This method is usually used to make the text field resign as first responder, at which point the delegate methods textFieldShouldEndEditing: and textFieldDidEndEdit ing: will be triggered.

These methods can be used to update the data model with new content if required, or after parsing the input, to make other appropriate changes to the UI such as adding or removing additional elements.

UITextView and Its Delegate

As with the UITextField we used as part of our AddCityController view in Chapter 5, we didn't exploit the full power of the UITextView class in that example. Like the UITextField, the UITextView class has an associated delegate protocol that opens up its many capabilities.

Dismissing the UITextView

The UITextViewDelegate protocol lacks the equivalent to the textFieldShouldReturn: method, presumably since we shouldn't expect the Return key to be a signal that the user wishes to stop editing the text in a multiline text entry dialog (after all, the user may want to insert line breaks by pressing Return).

However, there are several ways around the inability of the `UITextView` to resign as first responder using the keyboard. The usual method is to place a Done button in the navigation bar when the `UITextView` presents the pop-up keyboard. When tapped, this button asks the text view to resign as first responder, which will then dismiss the keyboard.

However, depending on how you've planned out your interface, you might want the `UITextView` to resign when the user taps outside the `UITextView` itself.

To do this, you'd subclass `UIView` to accept touches, and then instruct the text view to resign when the user taps outside the view itself. Right-click on the Classes group in the Groups & Files pane in the Xcode interface, select Add→New File, and choose Cocoa Touch Class from the iPhone OS section. Next, select "Objective-C class" and choose UIView from the "Subclass of" menu. Click Next and name the class "CustomView".

In the interface (*CustomView.h*), add an `IBOutlet` for a `UITextView`:

```
#import <UIKit/UIKit.h>

@interface CustomView : UIView {
    IBOutlet UITextView *textView;
}

@end
```

Then, in the implementation (*CustomView.m*), implement the `touchesEn ded:withEvent:` method and ask the `UITextView` to resign as first responder. Here's what the implementation should look like (added lines are shown in bold):

```
#import "CustomView.h"

@implementation CustomView

- (id)initWithFrame:(CGRect)frame {
    if (self = [super initWithFrame:frame]) {
        // Initialization code
    }
    return self;
}

- (void)dealloc {
    [super dealloc];
}

- (void) awakeFromNib {
    self.multipleTouchEnabled = YES;
}

- (void)touchesEnded:(NSSet *)touches withEvent:(UIEvent *)event {
    NSLog(@"touches began count %d, %@", [touches count], touches);

    [textView resignFirstResponder];
```

```
    [self.nextResponder touchesEnded:touches withEvent:event];
}

@end
```

Once you've added the class, you need to save all your changes, then go into Interface Builder and click on your view. Open the Identity Inspector (⌘-4) and change the type of the view in your NIB file to be your `CustomView` rather than the default `UIView` class. Then in the Connections Inspector (⌘-2), drag the `textView` outlet to the `UITextView`. After doing so, and once you rebuild your application, touches outside the active UI elements will now dismiss the keyboard.

> If the `UIView` you are subclassing is "behind" other UI elements, these elements will intercept the touches before they reach the `UIView` layer.
>
> For instance, in the case of the *CityGuide3* application from Chapter 6 and its Add City interface, you would have to declare your custom view to be a subclass of the `UITableViewCell` class rather than a `UIView`. You would then need to change the class of the three table view cells in the *AddCityController.xib* main window to be `CustomView` rather than the default `UITableViewCell` (don't change the class of the view).
>
> You'd then need to connect the `textView` outlet of all three table view cells to the `UITextView` in the table view cell used to enter the long description.

While this solution is elegant, it can be used in only some situations. In many cases, you'll have to resort to the brute force method of adding a Done button to the navigation bar to dismiss the keyboard.

Parsing XML

The two widely used methods for parsing an XML document are SAX and DOM. A SAX (Simple API for XML) parser is event-driven. It reads the XML document incrementally and calls a delegate method whenever it recognizes a token. Events are generated at the beginning and end of the document, and the beginning and end of each element. A DOM (Document Object Model) parser reads the entire document and forms a tree-like corresponding structure in memory. You can then use the XPath query language to select individual nodes of the XML document using a variety of criteria.

Most programmers find the DOM method more familiar and easier to use; however, SAX-based applications are generally more efficient, run faster, and use less memory. So, unless you are constrained by system requirements, the only real factor when deciding to use SAX or DOM parsers comes down to preference.

If you want to know more about XML, I recommend *Learning XML*, Second Edition (*http://oreilly.com/catalog/9780596004200/*) by Erik T. Ray (O'Reilly) as a good place to start.

Parsing XML with libxml2

We met the *libxml2* parser and Matt Gallagher's XPath wrappers in the preceding chapter, and my advice is to use these wrappers if you want to do DOM-based parsing of XML on the iPhone or iPod touch.

See the sidebar "Using the XPath Wrappers" on page 182 in Chapter 7 for instructions on adding the `XPathQuery` wrappers to your project.

The wrappers offer two methods. The only difference between the two is that one expects an HTML document and is therefore less strict about what constitutes a "proper" document than the other, which expects a valid XML document:

```
NSArray *PerformHTMLXPathQuery(NSData *document, NSString *query);
NSArray *PerformXMLXPathQuery(NSData *document, NSString *query);
```

If you want to return the entire document as a single data structure, the following will do that. Be warned that except for the simplest of XML documents, this will normally generate a heavily nested structure of array and dictionary elements, which isn't particularly useful:

```
NSString *xpathQueryString;
NSArray *nodes;

xpathQueryString = @"/*";
nodes = PerformXMLXPathQuery(responseData, xpathQueryString);
NSLog(@"nodes = %@", nodes );
```

Let's take a quick look at the XML document returned by the Google Weather Service that we parsed in Chapter 7's Weather application. The XML document had a structure that looked like the following snippet:

```
<forecast_conditions>
    ...
    <icon data="/ig/images/weather/chance_of_rain.gif"/>
</forecast_conditions>
<forecast_conditions>
    ...
    <icon data="/ig/images/weather/chance_of_rain.gif"/>
</forecast_conditions>
<forecast_conditions>
    ...
    <icon data="/ig/images/weather/chance_of_rain.gif"/>
</forecast_conditions>
<forecast_conditions>
    ...
    <icon data="/ig/images/weather/chance_of_rain.gif"/>
</forecast_conditions>
```

To extract the URL of the icons, we carried out an XPath query:

```
xpathQueryString = @"//forecast_conditions/icon/@data";❶
nodes = PerformXMLXPathQuery(responseData, xpathQueryString);
```

❶ Here we're looking for the data attributes as part of an `<icon>` element, nested inside a `<forecast_conditions>` element. An array of all such occurrences will be returned.

The `nodes` array returned by the `PerformXMLXPathQuery` method looked like this:

```
(   {
        nodeContent = "/ig/images/weather/mostly_sunny.gif";
        nodeName = data;
    },
        {
        nodeContent = "/ig/images/weather/chance_of_rain.gif";
        nodeName = data;
    },
        {
        nodeContent = "/ig/images/weather/mostly_sunny.gif";
        nodeName = data;
    },
        {
        nodeContent = "/ig/images/weather/mostly_sunny.gif";
        nodeName = data;
    }
)
```

This structure is an `NSArray` of `NSDictionary` objects, and we parsed this by iterating through each array entry and extracting the dictionary value for the key `nodeContent`, adding each occurrence to the `icons` array:

```
for ( NSDictionary *node in nodes ) {
    for ( id key in node ) {
        if( [key isEqualToString:@"nodeContent"] ) {
            [icons addObject:
                [NSString stringWithFormat:@"http://www.google.com%@",
                [node objectForKey:key]]];
        }
    }
}
```

Parsing XML with NSXMLParser

The official way to parse XML on the iPhone is to use the SAX-based `NSXMLParser` class. However, the parser is strict and cannot take HTML documents:

```
NSString *url = @"http://feeds.feedburner.com/oreilly/news";
NSURL *theURL = [[NSURL URLWithString:url] retain];

NSXMLParser *parser = [[NSXMLParser alloc] initWithContentsOfURL:theURL];
[parser setDelegate:self];
[parser setShouldResolveExternalEntities:YES];
BOOL success = [parser parse];
NSLog(@"Success = %d", success);
```

We use the parser by passing it an XML document and then implementing its delegate methods. The `NSXMLParser` class offers the following delegate methods:

```
parserDidStartDocument:
parserDidEndDocument:
parser:didStartElement:namespaceURI:qualifiedName:attributes:
parser:didEndElement:namespaceURI:qualifiedName:
parser:didStartMappingPrefix:toURI:
parser:didEndMappingPrefix:
parser:resolveExternalEntityName:systemID:
parser:parseErrorOccurred:
parser:validationErrorOccurred:
parser:foundCharacters:
parser:foundIgnorableWhitespace:
parser:foundProcessingInstructionWithTarget:data:
parser:foundComment:
parser:foundCDATA:
```

The most heavily used delegate methods out of all of those available methods are the `parser:didStartElement:namespaceURI:qualifiedName:attributes:` method and the `parser:didEndElement:namespaceURI:qualifiedName:` method. These two methods, along with the `parser:foundCharacters:` method, will allow you to detect the start and end of a selected element and retrieve its contents. When the `NSXMLParser` object traverses an element in an XML document, it sends three separate messages to its delegate, in the following order:

```
parser:didStartElement:namespaceURI:qualifiedName:attributes:
parser:foundCharacters:
parser:didEndElement:namespaceURI:qualifiedName:
```

Returning to the Weather application: to replace our XPath- and DOM-based solution with an `NSXMLParser`-based solution, we would substitute the following code for the existing `queryService:withParent:` method:

```
- (void)queryService:(NSString *)city
  withParent:(UIViewController *)controller {
    viewController = (MainViewController *)controller;
    responseData = [[NSMutableData data] retain];

    NSString *url =
    [NSString stringWithFormat: @"http://www.google.com/ig/api?weather=%@",
    city];
    theURL = [[NSURL URLWithString:url] retain];
    NSXMLParser *parser = [[NSXMLParser alloc] initWithContentsOfURL:theURL];
    [parser setDelegate:self];
    [parser setShouldResolveExternalEntities:YES];
    BOOL success = [parser parse];
}
```

We would then need to delete all of the `NSURLConnection` delegate methods, substituting the following `NSXMLParser` delegate method to handle populating our arrays:

```
- (void)parser:(NSXMLParser *)parser
  didStartElement:(NSString *)elementName
  namespaceURI:(NSString *)namespaceURI
  qualifiedName:(NSString *)qName
  attributes:(NSDictionary *)attributeDict {
```

```
// Parsing code to retrieve icon path
if([elementName isEqualToString:@"icon"]) {
    NSString *imagePath = [attributeDict objectForKey:@"data"];
    [icons addObject:
        [NSString stringWithFormat:@"http://www.google.com%@", imagePath]];
}

// ... add remaining parsing code for other elements here

[viewController updateView];
}
```

This example parses only the icon element; if you wanted to use NSXMLParser here, you'd need to look at connectionDidFinishLoading: in the original Weather app, and add parsing code for each of those elements before you call [viewController updateView] in this method (otherwise, it will throw an exception and crash the app because none of the data structures are populated).

Unless you're familiar with SAX-based parsers, I suggest that XPath and DOM are conceptually easier to deal with than the event-driven model of SAX. This is especially true if you're dealing with HTML, as an HTML document would have to be cleaned up before being passed to the NSXMLParser class.

Parsing JSON

JSON (*http://www.json.org/*) is a lightweight data-interchange format, which is more or less human-readable but still easily machine-parsable. While XML is document-oriented, JSON is data-oriented. If you need to transmit a highly structured piece of data, you should probably render it in XML. However, if your data exchange needs are somewhat less demanding, JSON might be a good option.

The obvious advantage JSON has over XML is that since it is data-oriented and (almost) parsable as a hash map, there is no requirement for heavyweight parsing libraries. Additionally, JSON documents are much smaller than the equivalent XML documents. In bandwidth-limited situations, such as you might find on the iPhone, this can be important. JSON documents normally consume around half of the bandwidth as an equivalent XML document for transferring the same data.

While there is no native support for JSON in the Cocoa Touch framework, Stig Brautaset's *json-framework* library implements both a JSON parser and a generator and can be integrated into your project fairly simply.

Consuming Ruby on Rails

If you are dealing exclusively with Rails-based services, the ObjectiveResource framework (see *http://iphoneonrails.com/* for more details) is a port of the ActiveResource framework of Ruby on Rails. It provides a way to serialize Rails objects to and from Rails' standard RESTful web services via either XML or JSON. ObjectiveResource adds methods to NSObject using the category extension mechanism, so any Objective-C class can be treated as a remote resource.

Download the disk image with the latest version of the *json-framework* library from *http://code.google.com/p/json-framework/*. Open the disk image and drag and drop the JSON folder into the Classes group in the Groups & Files pane of your project. Remember to tick the "Copy items into destination group's folder" checkbox before adding the files. This will add the JSON source files to your project; you will still need to import the *JSON.h* file into your class to use it.

Linking to the JSON Framework

Since dynamic linking to third-party embedded frameworks is not allowed on the iPhone platform, copying the JSON source files into your project is probably the simplest way to make the parser available to your application. However, there is a slightly more elegant approach if you don't want to add the entire JSON source tree to every project where you use it.

Open the Finder and create an SDKs subfolder inside your home directory's Library folder, and copy the JSON folder located inside the SDKs folder in the disk image into the newly created *~/Library/SDKs* directory.

Back in Xcode, open your project and double-click on the project icon at the top of the Groups & Files pane to open the Project Info window. In the Architectures section in the Build tab, double-click on the Additional SDKs field and add *$HOME/Library/ SDKs/JSON/${PLATFORM_NAME}.sdk* to the list of additional SDKs in the pop-up window. Now go to the Linking subsection of the Build tab, double-click on the Other Linker Flags field, and add `-ObjC -all_load -ljson` to the flags using the pop-up window.

Now you just have to add the following inside your source file:

```
#import <JSON/JSON.h>
```

Note the use of angle brackets rather than double quotes around the imported header file, denoting that it is located in the standard include path rather than in your project.

The Twitter Search Service

To let you get familiar with the *json-framework* library, let's implement a bare-bones application to retrieve the trending topics on Twitter by making use of their RESTful Search API.

 If you're interested in the Twitter API, you should definitely look at Twitter's documentation (*http://apiwiki.twitter.com/*) for more details regarding the available methods. However, if you're serious about using the Twitter API, you should probably look into using the *MGTwitterEngine* library written by Matt Gemmell. You can download it from *http://mattgemmell.com/source*.

Making a request to the Twitter Search API of the form *http://search.twitter.com/trends.json* will return a JSON document containing the top 10 topics that are currently trending on Twitter. The response includes the time of the request, the name of each trend, and the URL to the Twitter Search results page for that topic:

```
{
    "trends":[
        {
            "name":"#musicmonday",
            "url":"http:\/\/search.twitter.com\/search?q=%23musicmonday"
        },
        {
            "name":"Spotify",
            "url":"http:\/\/search.twitter.com\/search?q=Spotify+OR+%23Spotify"
        },
        {
            "name":"Happy Labor Day",
            "url":"http:\/\/search.twitter.com\/search?q=%22Happy+Labor+Day%22"
        },
        {
            "name":"District 9",
            "url":"http:\/\/search.twitter.com\/search?q=%22District+9%22"
        },
        {
            "name":"Goodnight",
            "url":"http:\/\/search.twitter.com\/search?q=Goodnight"
        },
        {
            "name":"Chris Evans",
            "url":"http:\/\/search.twitter.com\/search?q=%22Chris+Evans%22"
        },
        {
            "name":"iPhone",
            "url":"http:\/\/search.twitter.com\/search?q=iPhone+OR+%23Iphone"
        },
        {
            "name":"Jay-Z",
            "url":"http:\/\/search.twitter.com\/search?q=Jay-Z"
```

```
    },
    {
        "name":"Dual-Screen E-Reader",
        "url":"http:\/\/search.twitter.com\/search?q=%22E-Reader%22"
    },
    {
        "name":"Cadbury",
        "url":"http:\/\/search.twitter.com\/search?q=Cadbury"
    }
  ],
  "as_of":"Mon, 07 Sep 2009 09:18:34 +0000"
}
```

The Twitter Trends Application

Open Xcode and start a new iPhone Application project. Select the View-based Application template, and name the project "TwitterTrends" when prompted for a filename.

We're going to need the JSON parser, so drag and drop the JSON source folder into the Classes group in the Groups & Files pane of your new project. Since the returned JSON document provides a URL, we're also going to reuse the `WebViewController` class we wrote in Chapter 7. Open the *Prototype* project from Chapter 7, and drag and drop the *WebViewController.m*, *WebViewController.h*, and *WebView.xib* files from there into your new project.

 Remember to select the "Copy items into destination group's folder" checkbox in the pop-up window when copying the files in both cases.

Refactoring

While we're here, let's do some refactoring. Open the *TwitterTrendsAppDelegate.h* file, right-click on the `TwitterTrendsAppDelegate` class name in the interface declaration, and select Refactor. This will bring up the Refactoring window. Let's change the name of the main application delegate class from `TwitterTrendsAppDelegate` to `TrendsDele gate`. Entering the new class name and clicking Preview shows that three files will be affected by the change. Click Apply and Xcode will propagate changes throughout the project. Remember to save all the affected files (⌘-Option-S) before you go on to refactor the next set of classes.

Next, let's refactor the `TwitterTrendsViewController` class, changing the class name from `TwitterTrendsViewController` to the more sensible `RootController`.

Open the *TwitterTrendsViewController.h* file, right-click on the `TwitterTrendsViewCon troller` class name, and choose Refactor again. Set the name to `RootController`. Click Preview, then Apply, and the changes will again propagate throughout the project. However, you'll notice that Xcode has not changed the *TwitterTrendsViewControl-*

ler.xib file to be more sensibly named, so you'll have to make this change by hand. Click once on this file in the Groups & Files pane, wait a second, and click again; on the second click you'll be able to rename it. Change its name to "RootView.xib".

Unfortunately, since we had to make this change by hand, it hasn't been propagated throughout the project. We'll have to make some more manual changes. Double-click the *MainWindow.xib* file to open it in Interface Builder. Click on the Root Controller icon in the main NIB window and open the Attributes Inspector (⌘-1). The NIB name associated with the root controller is still set to `TwitterTrendsViewController`, so set this to `RootView`. You can either type the name of the controller into the window and Xcode will automatically carry out name completion as you type, or use the control on the right of the text entry box to get a drop-down panel where you'll find the `Root View` NIB listed. Save and close the *MainWindow.xib* file.

We're done refactoring, and your Xcode main window should now closely resemble Figure 8-1.

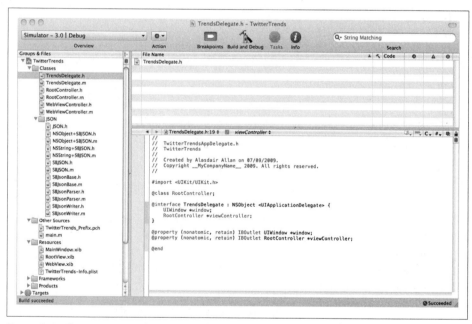

Figure 8-1. The Twitter Trends application after refactoring

Retrieving the trends

Let's start by writing a class to retrieve the trends using the Twitter API and the `NSURL Connection` class. Right-click (or Ctrl-click) on the Other Sources group in the Groups & Files pane in Xcode, select Add→New File, and select the Objective-C class, making it a subclass of `NSObject`. Name the new class "TwitterTrends" when prompted and click Finish.

Except for the contents of the connectionDidFinishLoading: method, this new class is going to be almost identical in structure to the Weather Forecast class we wrote in Chapter 7.

Open the *TwitterTrends.h* interface file in the Xcode editor. We're going to need a method to allow us to make the request to the Search Service. We're going to trigger the request from the RootViewController class. We'll need a reference back to the view controller so that we can update the view, so we'll pass that in as an argument. Add the lines shown in bold:

```
#import <Foundation/Foundation.h>

@class RootController;

@interface TwitterTrends : NSObject {
    RootController *viewController;
    NSMutableData *responseData;
    NSURL *theURL;
}

- (void)queryServiceWithParent:(UIViewController *)controller;

@end
```

Now open the *TwitterTrends.m* implementation file in the Xcode editor. If you compare the following code with the code in the WeatherForecast class from Chapter 7, you'll see that the code is virtually identical:

```
#import "TwitterTrends.h"
#import "RootController.h"

@implementation TwitterTrends

- (void)queryServiceWithParent:(UIViewController *)controller {
    viewController = (RootController *)controller;
    responseData = [[NSMutableData data] retain];

    NSString *url =
      [NSString stringWithFormat:@"http://search.twitter.com/trends.json"];
    theURL = [[NSURL URLWithString:url] retain];
    NSURLRequest *request = [NSURLRequest requestWithURL:theURL];
    [[NSURLConnection alloc] initWithRequest:request delegate:self];
}
- (NSURLRequest *)connection:(NSURLConnection *)connection
  willSendRequest:(NSURLRequest *)request
  redirectResponse:(NSURLResponse *)redirectResponse
{
    [theURL autorelease];
    theURL = [[request URL] retain];
    return request;
}
- (void)connection:(NSURLConnection *)connection
```

```
      didReceiveResponse:(NSURLResponse *)response
{
    [responseData setLength:0];
}

- (void)connection:(NSURLConnection *)connection
      didReceiveData:(NSData *)data
{
    [responseData appendData:data];
}

- (void)connection:(NSURLConnection *)connection
      didFailWithError:(NSError *)error {
        // Handle Error
}

- (void)connectionDidFinishLoading:(NSURLConnection *)connection {
    NSString *content = [[NSString alloc] initWithBytes:[responseData bytes]
                                          length:[responseData length]
                                          encoding:NSUTF8StringEncoding];
    NSLog( @"Data = %@", content );

}

-(void)dealloc {
    [viewController release];
    [responseData release];
    [theURL release];
    [super dealloc];
}

@end
```

OK, now that we have a class that can query the Twitter Search Service, let's use it. Inside the viewDidLoad: method of the *RootController.m* file add the following two lines of code (you must also uncomment the method by removing the /* before it and the */ after it):

```
TwitterTrends *trends = [[TwitterTrends alloc] init];
[trends queryServiceWithParent:self];
```

We also have to import the *TwitterTrends.h* header file once these have been added, so add the following line to the top of the file:

```
#import "TwitterTrends.h"
```

This is a good point to check our code. Make sure you've saved your changes and click the Build and Run button in the Xcode toolbar to compile and deploy your application in iPhone Simulator. We started the asynchronous query of the Search service from the viewDidLoad: method, printing the results to the console log when the query completes. So, once the application has started and you see the gray screen of the default view, open the Debugger Console (Run→Console) from the Xcode menu bar. You should see something similar to Figure 8-2. You've successfully retrieved the JSON trends file from the Twitter Search Service.

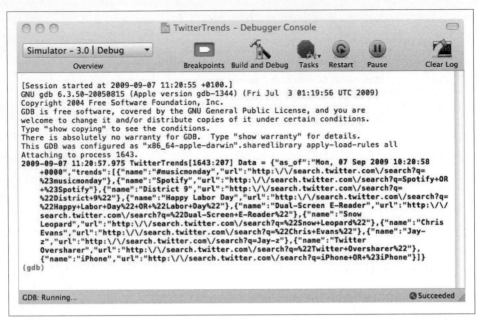

```
[Session started at 2009-09-07 11:20:55 +0100.]
GNU gdb 6.3.50-20050815 (Apple version gdb-1344) (Fri Jul  3 01:19:56 UTC 2009)
Copyright 2004 Free Software Foundation, Inc.
GDB is free software, covered by the GNU General Public License, and you are
welcome to change it and/or distribute copies of it under certain conditions.
Type "show copying" to see the conditions.
There is absolutely no warranty for GDB.  Type "show warranty" for details.
This GDB was configured as "x86_64-apple-darwin".sharedlibrary apply-load-rules all
Attaching to process 1643.
2009-09-07 11:20:57.975 TwitterTrends[1643:207] Data = {"as_of":"Mon, 07 Sep 2009 10:20:58
    +0000","trends":[{"name":"#musicmonday","url":"http:\/\/search.twitter.com\/search?q=
    %23musicmonday"},{"name":"Spotify","url":"http:\/\/search.twitter.com\/search?q=Spotify+OR
    +%23Spotify"},{"name":"District 9","url":"http:\/\/search.twitter.com\/search?q=
    %22District+9%22"},{"name":"Happy Labor Day","url":"http:\/\/search.twitter.com\/search?q=
    %22Happy+Labor+Day%22+OR+%22Labor+Day%22"},{"name":"Dual-Screen E-Reader","url":"http:\/\/
    search.twitter.com\/search?q=%22Dual-Screen+E-Reader%22"},{"name":"Snow
    Leopard","url":"http:\/\/search.twitter.com\/search?q=%22Snow+Leopard%22"},{"name":"Chris
    Evans","url":"http:\/\/search.twitter.com\/search?q=%22Chris+Evans%22"},{"name":"Jay-
    z","url":"http:\/\/search.twitter.com\/search?q=Jay-z"},{"name":"Twitter
    Oversharer","url":"http:\/\/search.twitter.com\/search?q=%22Twitter+Oversharer%22"},
    {"name":"iPhone","url":"http:\/\/search.twitter.com\/search?q=iPhone+OR+%23iPhone"}]}
(gdb)
```

Figure 8-2. The console log showing the retrieved JSON document

Building a UI

Now that we've managed to successfully retrieve the trends data, let's build a UI for the application. Looking at the JSON file, the obvious UI to implement here is a `UITableView`. The text in each cell will be the trend name, and when the user clicks on the cell we can open the associated Search Service URL using our `WebControllerView`.

Let's start by modifying the `RootController` class; since this is a simple bare-bones application, we're going to use the view controller class to both control our view and hold our data model. Open the *RootController.h* interface file in the Xcode editor and add the code shown in bold:

```
#import <UIKit/UIKit.h>

@interface RootController : UIViewController
  <UITableViewDataSource, UITableViewDelegate>
{
    UITableView *serviceView;
    NSMutableArray *names;
    NSMutableArray *urls;
}

@property (nonatomic, retain) IBOutlet UITableView *serviceView;
@property (nonatomic, retain) NSMutableArray *names;
@property (nonatomic, retain) NSMutableArray *urls;

@end
```

Make sure you've saved your changes, and double-click on the *RootView.xib* file to open it in Interface Builder. You'll initially be presented with a blank view (if you don't see it, double-click on the View icon). Drag and drop a navigation bar (`UINavigation Bar`) from the Library window into the View window and position it at the top of the view. Double-click on the title and change it from "Title" to "Twitter Trends". Now drag and drop a table view (`UITableView`) into the View window, and resize it to fill the remaining part of the view.

Click on File's Owner in the main RootView NIB window and change to the Connections Inspector (⌘-2). Click on the `serviceView` outlet and connect it to your `UITable View`. Now click on the `UITableView` and, again in the Connections Inspector, click and connect both the `dataSource` and `delegate` outlets to File's Owner.

That's it; you're done in Interface Builder, and you should be looking at something similar to Figure 8-3.

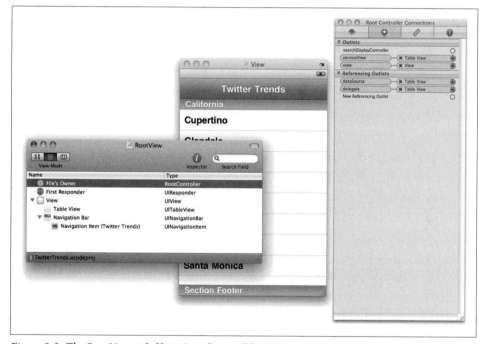

Figure 8-3. The RootView.xib file in Interface Builder

After making sure you've saved your changes to the *RootView.xib* NIB file, return to Xcode, open the *RootController.m* implementation file in the Xcode editor, and edit the code so that it looks like this:

```
#import "RootController.h"
#import "TwitterTrends.h"

@implementation RootController
```

```
@synthesize serviceView;
@synthesize names;
@synthesize urls;

- (void)viewDidLoad {
    names = [[NSMutableArray alloc] init];❶
    urls = [[NSMutableArray alloc] init];

    [UIApplication
        sharedApplication].networkActivityIndicatorVisible = YES;❷
    TwitterTrends *trends = [[TwitterTrends alloc] init];
    [trends queryServiceWithParent:self];❸

    [super viewDidLoad];
}

- (void)didReceiveMemoryWarning {
    [super didReceiveMemoryWarning];
}


- (void)dealloc {
    [names dealloc];
    [urls dealloc];
    [super dealloc];
}

@end
```

❶ Here we initialize the `names` and `urls` arrays we declared in the interface file. These will be populated by the `TwitterTrends` class.

❷ This is where we start the network activity indicator in the iPhone status bar spinning. We'll stop it from the `TwitterTrends connectionDidFinishLoading:` method.

❸ Here is where we start the asynchronous query to the Twitter Search API.

Now we need to implement the `UITableViewDelegate` methods; we need to implement only three of the delegate methods. Add the following methods to *RootController.m*:

```
- (NSInteger)tableView:(UITableView *)tableView
  numberOfRowsInSection:(NSInteger)section
{
    return names.count;❶
}

- (UITableViewCell *)tableView:(UITableView *)tableView
  cellForRowAtIndexPath:(NSIndexPath *)indexPath
{
    static NSString *CellIdentifier = @"Cell";
    UITableViewCell *cell =
    [tableView dequeueReusableCellWithIdentifier:CellIdentifier];
    if (cell == nil) {
        cell = [[[UITableViewCell alloc]
                    initWithFrame:CGRectZero
```

```
                reuseIdentifier:CellIdentifier]
            autorelease];
    }

    cell.textLabel.text = [names objectAtIndex:indexPath.row];❷
    return cell;
}


- (void)tableView:(UITableView *)tableView
  didSelectRowAtIndexPath:(NSIndexPath *)indexPath
{
    // Add code to handle selection here.
    [tableView deselectRowAtIndexPath:indexPath animated:YES];
}
```

❶ We're going to display a number of cells (equal to `names.count`) to the user. The names array will be filled from the `TwitterTrends` instance we created in the `viewDid Load:` method.

❷ This is where we set the cell label text to be the name of the trending topic.

Click the Build and Run button to test your code. If all goes well, you should still get the JSON document in the Console, but now your view should be a blank table view. Why is it blank? Well, we haven't parsed the JSON and populated our data model yet. Let's do that now.

You may also have noticed that the activity indicator keeps spinning. We'll take care of that, too.

Parsing the JSON document

We need to modify the `connectionDidFinishLoading:` method to parse the passed JSON document, populate the view controller's data model, and then request it to reload the table view with the new data.

Parsing JSON is relatively simple, as you will have to work with only one of two structures: either a single object or a list of objects. These map onto an `NSDictionary` (a key-value pair) or an `NSArray`, respectively. Replace the implementation of `connectionDid FinishLoading:` in *TwitterTrends.m* with the following:

```
- (void)connectionDidFinishLoading:(NSURLConnection *)connection {

    NSString *content = [[NSString alloc]
      initWithBytes:[responseData bytes]
      length:[responseData length]
      encoding:NSUTF8StringEncoding];❶

    SBJSON *parser = [[SBJSON alloc] init];❷
    NSDictionary *json = [parser objectWithString:content];❸
```

```
    NSArray *trends = [json objectForKey:@"trends"]; ❹

    for (NSDictionary *trend in trends) { ❺
        [viewController.names addObject:[trend objectForKey:@"name"]];
        [viewController.urls addObject:[trend objectForKey:@"url"]];
    }
    [parser release];
    [UIApplication
        sharedApplication].networkActivityIndicatorVisible = NO; ❻
    [viewController.serviceView reloadData]; ❼

}
```

❶ Here we take the returned response data and create a string representation.

❷ Here we allocate a parser instance.

❸ This is where we use the parser to build an NSDictionary (a hash map) of the JSON document.

❹ Here is where we extract an array of trend entries from the dictionary, extracting the object for key "trends".

❺ Here we extract the NSDictionary object at each array index, and grab the trend name and URL and populate the view controller using the accessor methods.

❻ This is where we stop the network activity indicator spinning.

❼ Here we ask the view controller to reload its view.

At the top of *TwitterTrends.m*, add the following:

```
#import "JSON/JSON.h"
```

If you rebuild your application in Xcode and run it, you should get something similar to Figure 8-4. The table view is now populated with the current trending topics on Twitter.

However, clicking on individual cells doesn't do anything yet, so we need to modify the tableView:didSelectRowAtIndexPath: method to use our WebViewController class. Replace the tableView:didSelectRowAtIndexPath: method in *RootController.m* with the following:

```
- (void)tableView:(UITableView *)tableView
  didSelectRowAtIndexPath:(NSIndexPath *)indexPath
{
    NSString *title = [names objectAtIndex:indexPath.row];
    NSURL *url = [NSURL URLWithString:[urls objectAtIndex:indexPath.row]];
    WebViewController *webViewController =
        [[WebViewController alloc] initWithURL:url andTitle:title];
    [self presentModalViewController:webViewController animated:YES];
    [webViewController release];
    [tableView deselectRowAtIndexPath:indexPath animated:YES];
}
```

Figure 8-4. The Twitter Trends application running in iPhone Simulator

Now that you're using the `WebViewController` class, you need to import it into the view controller, so add the following to the top of *RootController.m*:

```
#import "WebViewController.h"
```

If you rebuild the application again and click on one of the trending topics, the web view should open modally and you should see something similar to Figure 8-5.

Normally, when the JSON parser fails, it will return a nil value. However, we can add error handling when parsing the JSON file relatively simply by passing an `NSError` object to the parser's `objectWithString:error:` method. To do this, locate the `connectionDid FinishLoading:` method in *TwitterTrends.m* and find the following code:

```
NSDictionary *json = [parser objectWithString:content];
NSArray *trends = [json objectForKey:@"trends"];

for (NSDictionary *trend in trends) {
    [viewController.names addObject:[trend objectForKey:@"name"]];
    [viewController.urls addObject:[trend objectForKey:@"url"]];
}
```

Replace that code with the following:

```
NSError *error;
NSDictionary *json = [parser objectWithString:content error:&error];
```

```
if ( json == nil ) {
    UIAlertView *errorAlert = [[UIAlertView alloc]
      initWithTitle:@"Error"
      message:[error localizedDescription]
      delegate:self cancelButtonTitle:nil otherButtonTitles:@"OK", nil];
    [errorAlert show];
    [errorAlert autorelease];
} else {
    NSArray *trends = [json objectForKey:@"trends"];

    for (NSDictionary *trend in trends) {
        [viewController.names addObject:[trend objectForKey:@"name"]];
        [viewController.urls addObject:[trend objectForKey:@"url"]];
    }
}
```

Figure 8-5. The Twitter Trends web view

 You can verify that this error handler is working by replacing *http://search.twitter.com/trends.json* in the `queryServiceWithParent:` method in *TwitterTrends.m* with a URL that does not return a JSON-formatted response.

Tidying up

There are a few bits and pieces that I haven't added to this application but that you really should add if you are going to release it. Most of it has to do with error handling; for instance, you should do a reachability check before trying to retrieve the JSON document. However, this example illustrated that retrieving and parsing JSON documents is a relatively simple task. See "Apple's Reachability Class" on page 145 in Chapter 7 for details on implementing this.

Regular Expressions

Regular expressions, commonly known as *regexes*, are a pattern-matching standard for text processing, and are a powerful tool when dealing with strings. With regular expressions, an expression serves as a pattern to compare with the text being searched. You can use regular expressions to search for patterns in a string, replace text, and extract substrings from the original string.

Introduction to Regular Expressions

In its simplest form, you can use a regular expression to match a literal string; for example, the regular expression "string" will match the string "this is a **string**". Each character in the expression will match itself, unless it is one of the special characters +, ?, ., *, ^, $, (,), [, {, |, or \. The special meaning of these characters can be *escaped* by prepending a backslash character, \.

We can also tie our expression to the start of a string (^string) or the end of a string (string$). For the string "this is a string", ^string will not match the string, while string$ will.

We can also use quantified patterns. Here, * matches *zero or more* times, ? matches *zero or one* time, and + matches *one or more* times. So, the regular expression "23*4" would match "1245", "12345", and "123345", but the expression "23?4" would match "1245" and also "12345". Finally, the expression "23+4" would match "12345" and "123345" but not "1245".

Unless told otherwise, regular expressions are always greedy; they will normally match the longest string possible.

While a backslash escapes the meaning of the special characters in an expression, it turns most alphanumeric characters into special characters. Many special characters are available; however, the main ones are:

\d

    Matches a numeric character

\D

    Matches a nonnumeric character

\s

Matches a whitespace character

\S

Matches a nonwhitespace character

\w

Matches an alphanumeric (or the underscore) character

\W

Matches the inverse of \w

All of these special character expressions can be modified by the quantifier modifiers.

Many other bits of more complicated and advanced syntax are available. If you find yourself making heavy use of regexes, I recommend the books *Regular Expressions Cookbook* (*http://oreilly.com/catalog/9780596520694/*) by Jan Goyvaerts and Steven Levithan and *Mastering Regular Expressions*, Third Edition (*http://oreilly.com/catalog/9780596528126/*) by Jeffrey E. F. Friedl (both from O'Reilly).

RegexKitLite

Unfortunately, there is no built-in support for regular expressions in Objective-C, or as part of the Cocoa Touch framework. However, the RegexKit*Lite* library adds regular expression support to the base NSString class. See *http://regexkit.sourceforge.net/Regex KitLite/*.

 RegexKit*Lite* uses the regular expression engine provided by the ICU library. Apple does not officially support linking directly to the *libicucore.dylib* library. Despite this, many iPhone applications are available on the App Store that use this library, and it is unlikely that Apple will reject your application during the App Store review process for making use of it. However, if you're worried about using the ICU library, there are alternatives, such as the *libregex* wrapper GTMRegex provided as part of the Google Toolbox for Mac.

To add RegexKit*Lite* to your own project, download the *RegexKitLite-<X.X>.tar.bz2* compressed tarball (*X.X* will be the current version, such as 3.3), and uncompress and double-click it to extract it. Open the directory and drag and drop the two files, *RegexKitLite.h* and *RegexKitLite.m*, into your project. Remember to select the "Copy items into destination group's folder" checkbox before adding the files.

We're not done yet; we still need to add the *libicucore.dylib* library to our project. Double-click on the project icon in the Groups & Files pane in Xcode and go to the Build tab of the Project Info window. In the Linking subsection of the tab, double-click on the Other Linker Flags field and add -licucore to the flags using the pop-up window.

You'll want to use regular expressions to perform three main tasks: matching strings, replacing strings, and extracting strings. RegexKit*Lite* allows you to do all of these, but remember that when you want to use it, you need to import the *RegexKitLite.h* file into your class.

 Regular expressions use the backslash (\) character to escape characters that have special meaning inside the regular expression. However, since the backslash character is the C escape character, these in turn have to escape any uses of this character inside your regular expression by prepending it with another backslash character. For example, to match a literal ampersand (&) character, you must first prepend it with a backslash to escape it for the regular expression engine, and then prepend it with another backslash to escape this in turn for the compiler—that is, \\&. To match a single literal backslash (\) character with a regular expression therefore requires four backslashes: \\\\.

The RegexKit*Lite* library operates by extending the `NSString` class via an Objective-C category extension mechanism, making it very easy to use. If you want to match a string, you simply operate directly on the string you want to match. You can create a view-based project and add the following code into the `applicationDidFinishLaunching:` method. Just be sure to add `#import "RegexKitLite.h"` to the top of the app delegate's *.m* (implementation) file.

```
NSString *string = @"This is a string";
NSString *match = [string stringByMatching:@"a string$" capture:0];❶
NSLog(@"%@", match);
```

❶ This will return the first occurrence of the matched string.

If the match fails, the `match` variable will be set to `nil`, and if you want to replace a string, it's almost as easy:

```
NSString *string2 = @"This is a string";
NSString *regexString = @"a string$";
NSString *replacementString = @"another string";

NSString *newString = nil;
newString = [string2
  stringByReplacingOccurrencesOfRegex:regexString
  withString:replacementString];
NSLog(@"%@", newString);
```

If you run the application, you'll just get a gray window. Return to Xcode and choose Run→Console to see the output of the `NSLog` calls.

This will match "**a string**" in the variable `string2`, replacing it and creating the string "This is another string" in the variable `newString`.

While I've provided some examples to get you started, it would be impossible to cover regular expressions in detail here, and whole books have been written about this subject. Additionally, the RegexKit*Lite* library provides many other methods on top of those I've covered here, so if you need to perform regular expression tasks I haven't talked about, you might want to look at the documentation, which you can find at *http://regexkit.sourceforge.net/RegexKitLite/*.

Faking regex support with the built-in NSPredicate

While Cocoa Touch does not provide "real" regular expression support, Core Data does provide the NSPredicate class that allows you to carry out some operations that would normally be done via regular expressions in other languages. For those familiar with SQL, the NSPredicate class operates in a very similar manner to the SQL WHERE statement.

Let's assume we have an NSArray of NSDictionary objects, structured like this:

```
NSArray *arrayOfDictionaries = [NSArray arrayWithObjects:
  [NSDictionary dictionaryWithObjectsAndKeys:
     @"Learning iPhone Programming", @"title", @"2010", @"year", nil],
  [NSDictionary dictionaryWithObjectsAndKeys:
     @"Arduino Orbital Lasers", @"title", @"2012", @"year", nil],
  nil];
```

We can test whether a given object in the array matches the criteria foo = "bar" AND baz = "qux" as follows:

```
NSPredicate *predicate =
  [NSPredicate predicateWithFormat:@"year = '2012'"];
for (NSDictionary *dictionary in arrayOfDictionaries) {
    BOOL match = [predicate evaluateWithObject:dictionary];
    if (match) {
      NSLog(@"Found a match!");
    }
}
```

Alternatively, we can extract all entries in the array that match the predicate:

```
NSPredicate *predicate2 =
  [NSPredicate predicateWithFormat:@"year = '2012'"];
NSArray *matches =
  [arrayOfDictionaries filteredArrayUsingPredicate:predicate2];
for (NSDictionary *dictionary in matches) {
    NSLog(@"%@", [dictionary objectForKey: @"title"]);
}
```

However, we can also use predicates to test strings against regular expressions. For instance, the following code will test the email string against the regex we provided, returning YES if it is a valid email address:

```
NSString *email = @"alasdair@babilim.co.uk";
NSString *regex = @"^\\b[a-zA-Z0-9._%+-]+@[a-zA-Z0-9.-]+\\.[a-zA-Z]{2,4}\\b$";
NSPredicate *predicate3 =
  [NSPredicate predicateWithFormat:@"SELF MATCHES %@", regex];
BOOL match = [predicate3 evaluateWithObject:email];
if (match) {
    NSLog(@"Found a match!");
}
```

While the NSPredicate class is actually defined as part of the Foundation framework, it is intended (and used extensively) as part of the Core Data framework. We're not going to cover Core Data in this book. If you're interested in this framework, I recommend you look at *Core Data: Apple's API for Persisting Data on Mac OS X* by Marcus S. Zarra (Pragmatic Programmers).

Storing Data

If the user creates data while running your application, you may need a place to store the data so that it's there the next time the user runs it. You'll also want to store user preferences, passwords, and many other forms of data. You could store data online somewhere, but then your application won't function unless it's online. The iPhone can store data in lots of ways.

Using Flat Files

So-called *flat files* are files that contain data, but are typically not backed by the power of a full-featured database system. They are useful for storing small bits of text data, but they lack the performance and organizational advantages that a database provides.

Applications running on the iPhone or iPod touch are *sandboxed*; you can access only a limited subset of the filesystem from your application. If you want to save files from your application, you should save them into the application's Document directory.

Here's the code you need to locate the application's Document directory:

```
NSArray *arrayPaths = NSSearchPathForDirectoriesInDomains(
    NSDocumentDirectory,   NSUserDomainMask, YES);
NSString *docDirectory = [arrayPaths objectAtIndex:0];❶
```

❶ The first entry in the array will contain the file path to the application's Document directory.

Reading and writing text content

The NSFileManager methods generally deal with NSData objects.

For writing to a file, you can use the writeToFile:atomically:encoding:error: method:

```
NSString *string = @"Hello, World";
NSString *filePath = [docDirectory stringByAppendingString:@"/File.txt"];
[string writeToFile:filePath
        atomically:YES
        encoding:NSUTF8StringEncoding
        error:nil];
```

If you want to simply read a plain-text file, you can use the NSString class method stringWithContentsOfFile:encoding:error: to read from the file:

```
NSString *fileContents = [NSString stringWithContentsOfFile:filePath
                         encoding:NSUTF8StringEncoding error:nil];
NSLog(@"%@", fileContents);
```

Creating temporary files

To obtain the path to the default location to store temporary files, you can use the
NSTemporaryDirectory method:

```
NSString *tempDir = NSTemporaryDirectory();
```

Other file manipulation

The NSFileManager class can be used for moving, copying, creating, and deleting files.

Storing Information in an SQL Database

The public domain SQLite library (*http://www.sqlite.org*) is a lightweight transactional
database. The library is included in the iPhone SDK and will probably do most of the
heavy lifting you need for your application to store data. The SQLite engine powers
several large applications on Mac OS X, including the Apple Mail application, and is
extensively used by the latest generation of browsers to support HTML5 database features. Despite the "Lite" name, the library should not be underestimated.

Interestingly, unlike most SQL database engines, the SQLite engine makes use of dynamic typing. Most other SQL databases implement static typing: the column in which
a value is stored determines the type of a value. Using SQLite the column type specifies
only the type affinity (the recommended type) for the data stored in that column.
However, any column may still store data of any type.

Each value stored in an SQLite database has one of the storage types shown in Table 8-1.

Table 8-1. SQLite storage types

Storage type	Description
NULL	The value is a NULL value.
INTEGER	The value is a signed integer.
REAL	The value is a floating-point value.
TEXT	The value is a text string.
BLOB	The value is a blob of data, stored exactly as it was input.

If you're not familiar with SQL, I recommend you read *Learning SQL*, Second Edition (*http://oreilly.com/catalog/9780596520847/*) by Alan Beaulieu (O'Reilly). If you
want more information about SQLite specifically, I also recommend *SQLite* by Chris
Newman (Sams).

Adding a database to your project

Let's create a database for the City Guide application. Open the *CityGuide* project in Xcode and take a look at the application delegate implementation where we added four starter cities to the application's data model. Each city has three bits of interesting information associated with it: its name, description, and an associated image. We need to put this information into a database table.

 If you don't want to create the database for the City Guide application yourself, you can download a prebuilt copy containing the starter cities from this book's website (*http://learningiphoneprogramming.com/*).

Open a Terminal window, and at the command prompt type the code shown in bold:

```
$ sqlite3 cities.sqlite
```

This will create a cities database and start SQLite in interactive mode. At the SQL prompt, we need to create our database tables to store our information. Type the code shown in bold (`sqlite>` and `...>` are the SQLite command prompts):

```
SQLite version 3.4.0
Enter ".help" for instructions
sqlite> CREATE TABLE cities(id INTEGER PRIMARY KEY AUTOINCREMENT,
   ...> name TEXT, description TEXT, image BLOB);
sqlite> .quit
```

At this stage, we have an empty database and associated table. We need to add image data to the table as BLOB (*binary large object*) data; the easiest way to do this is to use Mike Chirico's *eatblob.c* program available from *http://souptonuts.sourceforge.net/code/eatblob.c.html*.

 The *eatblob.c* code will not compile out of the box on Mac OS X, as it makes use of the `getdelim` and `getline` functions. Both of these are GNU-specific and are not made available by the Mac's *stdlib* library. However, you can download the necessary source code from *http://learningiphoneprogramming.com/*.

Once you have downloaded the *eatblob.c* source file along with the associated *getdelim.[h,c]* and *getline[h,c]* source files, you can compile the *eatblob* program from the command line:

```
% gcc -o eatblob * -lsqlite3
```

So, for each of our four original cities defined inside the app delegate, we need to run the *eatblob* code:

```
% ./eatblob cities.sqlite ./London.jpg "INSERT INTO cities (id, name,
description, image) VALUES (NULL, 'London', 'London is the capital of the
United Kingdom and England.', ?)"
```

to populate the database file with our "starter cities."

 It's arguable whether including the images inside the database using a BLOB is a good idea, except for small images. It's a normal practice to include images as a file and include only metadata inside the database itself; for example, the path to the included image. However, if you want to bundle a single file (with starter data) into your application, it's a good trick.

We're now going to add the cities database to the City Guide application. However, you might want to make a copy of the City Guide application before modifying it. Navigate to where you saved the project and make a copy of the project folder, and then rename it, perhaps to *CityGuideWithDatabase*. Then open the new (duplicate) project inside Xcode and use the Project→Rename tool to rename the project itself.

After you've done this, open the Finder again and navigate to the directory where you created the *cities.sqlite* database file. Open the *CityGuide* project in Xcode, then drag and drop it into the Resources folder of the *CityGuide* project in Xcode. Remember to check the box to indicate that Xcode should "Copy items into destination group's folder."

To use the SQLite library, you'll need to add it to your project. Double-click on the project icon in the Groups & Files pane in Xcode and go to the Build tab of the Project Info window. In the Linking subsection of the tab, double-click on the Other Linker Flags field and add -lsqlite3 to the flags using the pop-up window.

Data persistence for the City Guide application

We've now copied our database into our project, so let's add some data persistence to the City Guide application.

Since our images are now inside the database, you can delete the images from the Resources group in the Groups & Files pane in Xcode. Remember not to delete the *QuestionMark.jpg* file because our add city view controller will need that file.

 SQLite runs much slower on the iPhone than it does in iPhone Simulator. Queries that run instantly on the simulator may take several seconds to run on the iPhone. You need to take this into account in your testing.

If you're just going to be querying the database, you can leave *cities.sqlite* in place and refer to it via the application bundle's resource path. However, files in the bundle are read-only. If you intend to modify the contents of the database as we do, your application must copy the database file to the application's document folder and modify it from there. One advantage to this approach is that the contents of this folder are preserved when the application is updated, and therefore cities that users add to your database are also preserved across application updates.

We're going to add two methods to the application delegate (*CityGuideDelegate.m*). The first copies the database we included inside our application bundle to the application's Document directory, which allows us to write to it. If the file already exists in that location, it won't overwrite it. If you need to replace the database file for any reason, the easiest way is to delete your application from the simulator and then redeploy it using Xcode. Add the following method to *CityGuideDelegate.m*:

```objc
- (NSString *)copyDatabaseToDocuments {
    NSFileManager *fileManager = [NSFileManager defaultManager];
    NSArray *paths =
      NSSearchPathForDirectoriesInDomains(NSDocumentDirectory,
                                          NSUserDomainMask, YES);
    NSString *documentsPath = [paths objectAtIndex:0];
    NSString *filePath = [documentsPath
                            stringByAppendingPathComponent:@"cities.sqlite"];

    if ( ![fileManager fileExistsAtPath:filePath] ) {
        NSString *bundlePath = [[[NSBundle mainBundle] resourcePath]
            stringByAppendingPathComponent:@"cities.sqlite"];
        [fileManager copyItemAtPath:bundlePath toPath:filePath error:nil];
    }
    return filePath;
}
```

The second method will take the path to the database passed back by the previous method and populate the `cities` array. Add this method to *CityGuideDelegate.m*:

```objc
-(void) readCitiesFromDatabaseWithPath:(NSString *)filePath {

    sqlite3 *database;

    if(sqlite3_open([filePath UTF8String], &database) == SQLITE_OK) {
        const char *sqlStatement = "select * from cities";
        sqlite3_stmt *compiledStatement;
        if(sqlite3_prepare_v2(database, sqlStatement,
                              -1, &compiledStatement, NULL) == SQLITE_OK) {
            while(sqlite3_step(compiledStatement) == SQLITE_ROW) {

                NSString *cityName =
                  [NSString stringWithUTF8String:(char *)
                  sqlite3_column_text(compiledStatement, 1)];
                NSString *cityDescription =
                  [NSString stringWithUTF8String:(char *)
                  sqlite3_column_text(compiledStatement, 2)];

                NSData *cityData = [[NSData alloc]
                 initWithBytes:sqlite3_column_blob(compiledStatement, 3)
                 length: sqlite3_column_bytes(compiledStatement, 3)];
                UIImage *cityImage = [UIImage imageWithData:cityData];

                City *newCity = [[City alloc] init];
                newCity.cityName = cityName;
                newCity.cityDescription = cityDescription;
                newCity.cityPicture = (UIImage *)cityImage;
```

```
                    [self.cities addObject:newCity];
                    [newCity release];
                }
            }
            sqlite3_finalize(compiledStatement);
        }
        sqlite3_close(database);
    }
```

You'll also have to declare the methods in *CityGuideDelegate.m*'s interface file, so add the following lines to *CityGuideDelegate.h* just before the @end directive:

```
-(NSString *)copyDatabaseToDocuments;
-(void) readCitiesFromDatabaseWithPath:(NSString *)filePath;
```

In addition, you need to import the *sqlite3.h* header file into the implementation, so add this line to the top of *CityGuideDelegate.m*:

```
#include <sqlite3.h>
```

After we add these routines to the delegate, we must modify the applicationDidFinish Launching: method, removing our hardcoded cities and instead populating the cities array using our database. Replace the applicationDidFinishLaunching: method in *CityGuideDelegate.m* with the following:

```
- (void)applicationDidFinishLaunching:(UIApplication *)application {

    cities = [[NSMutableArray alloc] init];
    NSString *filePath = [self copyDatabaseToDocuments];
    [self readCitiesFromDatabaseWithPath:filePath];

    navController.viewControllers = [NSArray arrayWithObject:viewController];
    [window addSubview:navController.view];
    [window makeKeyAndVisible];
}
```

We've reached a good point to take a break. Make sure you've saved your changes (⌘-Option-S), and click the Build and Run button on the Xcode toolbar. If all goes well, when your application starts it shouldn't look different from the City Guide application at the end of Chapter 5.

OK, we've read in our data in the application delegate. However, we still don't save newly created cities; we need to insert the new cities into the database when the user adds them from the AddCityController view. Add the following method to the view controller (*AddCityController.m*):

```
-(void) addCityToDatabase:(City *)newCity {
    NSArray *paths =
        NSSearchPathForDirectoriesInDomains(NSDocumentDirectory,
                                            NSUserDomainMask, YES);
    NSString *documentsPath = [paths objectAtIndex:0];
    NSString *filePath =
        [documentsPath stringByAppendingPathComponent:@"cities.sqlite"];

    sqlite3 *database;
```

```
if(sqlite3_open([filePath UTF8String], &database) == SQLITE_OK) {
    const char *sqlStatement =
      "insert into cities (name, description, image) VALUES (?, ?, ?)";
    sqlite3_stmt *compiledStatement;
    if(sqlite3_prepare_v2(database, sqlStatement,
                          -1, &compiledStatement, NULL) == SQLITE_OK)
    {
        sqlite3_bind_text(compiledStatement, 1,
                          [newCity.cityName UTF8String], -1,
                          SQLITE_TRANSIENT);
        sqlite3_bind_text(compiledStatement, 2,
                          [newCity.cityDescription UTF8String], -1,
                          SQLITE_TRANSIENT);
        NSData *dataForPicture =
          UIImagePNGRepresentation(newCity.cityPicture);
        sqlite3_bind_blob(compiledStatement, 3,
                          [dataForPicture bytes],
                          [dataForPicture length],
                          SQLITE_TRANSIENT);

    }
    if(sqlite3_step(compiledStatement) == SQLITE_DONE) {
        sqlite3_finalize(compiledStatement);
    }
  }
}
sqlite3_close(database);
}
```

We also need to import the *sqlite3.h* header file; add this line to the top of *AddCity-Controller.m*:

```
#include <sqlite3.h>
```

Then insert the call into the **saveCity:** method, directly after the line where you added the **newCity** to the **cities** array. The added line is shown in bold:

```
if ( nameEntry.text.length > 0 ) {
    City *newCity = [[City alloc] init];
    newCity.cityName = nameEntry.text;
    newCity.cityDescription = descriptionEntry.text;
    newCity.cityPicture = nil;
    [cities addObject:newCity];
    [self addCityToDatabase:newCity];

    RootController *viewController = delegate.viewController;
    [viewController.tableView reloadData];
}
```

We're done. Build and deploy the application by clicking the Build and Run button in the Xcode toolbar. When the application opens, tap the Edit button and add a new city. Make sure you tap Save, and leave edit mode.

Then tap the Home button in iPhone Simulator to quit the City Guide application. Tap the application again to restart it, and you should see that your new city is still in the list.

Congratulations, the City Guide application can now save its data.

Refactoring and rethinking

If we were going to add more functionality to the City Guide application, we should probably pause at this point and refactor. There are, of course, other ways we could have built this application, and you've probably already noticed that the database (our data model) is now exposed to the `AddCityViewController` class as well as the `CityGuideDelegate` class.

First, we'd change things so that the `cities` array is only accessed through the accessor methods in the application delegate, and then move all of the database routines into the delegate and wrap them inside those accessor methods. This would isolate our data model from our view controller. We could even do away with the `cities` array and keep the data model "on disk" and access it directly from the SQL database rather than preloading a separate in-memory array.

Although we could do this refactoring now, we won't do so in this chapter. However, in your own applications, I suggest that you don't access SQLite directly. Instead, use Core Data (discussed next) or be sure to move your SQLite calls into the delegate to abstract it from the view controller.

Core Data

Sitting above SQLite, and several other possible low-level data representations, is Core Data. The Core Data framework is an abstraction layer above the underlying data representation. Technically, Core Data is an object-graph management and persistence framework. Essentially, this means that Core Data organizes your application's model layer, keeping track of changes to objects. It allows you to reverse those changes on demand—for instance, if the user performs an undo command—and then allows you to serialize (archive) the application's data model directly into a persistent store.

Core Data is an ideal framework for building the model part of an MVC-based application, and if used correctly it is an extremely powerful tool. I'm not going to cover Core Data in this book, but if you're interested in exploring the Core Data framework, I've provided some pointers to further reading in Chapter 14.

CHAPTER 9

Distributing Your Application

At this point, you have several applications that are almost ready to distribute, and perhaps you have ideas for your own applications and you want to start writing your first application and publish it to the App Store. However, before you can do that, you have to do some more housekeeping.

Adding Missing Features

Two things have been missing from your iPhone applications, the first being the lack of a custom icon. This is crucial for the marketing of your application; you need to bring your application design together to present it to users. When a user scrolls through a long list of possible applications on the App Store, applications with strong icon design stand out. But remember that the user has to look at your application's icon every time he looks at the iPhone's home screen. The icon has to be distinctive to stand out, but it also has to be attractive so that the user is willing to keep your application around. I've uninstalled otherwise good applications because I couldn't put up with their icons, and I'm not alone.

Adding an Icon

The standard iPhone home screen icon used for your application is 57×57 pixels square in PNG format with no transparency or layers (*Icon.png*). You also must provide Apple with a 512×512-pixel version of your application icon for display on the App Store (*iTunesArtwork* with no extension; you will need to provide this when you upload your app). This larger image must be in TIFF or JPEG format, and again have no transparency or layers.

It's sensible to design your icon as 512×512 pixels and scale it down to the 57×57-pixel version supplied inside your application's bundle. Doing things the other way around usually means that an unattractive and often pixelated icon is shown on the App Store.

You can also provide a small icon, as a 29×29-pixel PNG file, in your application bundle called *Icon-Small.png*. Spotlight will use this icon on the device when the application name matches a term in the search query. Additionally, if your application includes a Settings Bundle (see Chapter 12 for more on Settings Bundles), this icon is displayed next to your application's name in the Settings application. If you do not provide this icon, your 57×57-pixel image is automatically scaled and used instead.

Both the iPhone and the iTunes store will, by default, apply some visual effects to the icon you provide. They will round the corners, and add both drop shadows and reflected shine.

You can prevent iTunes from adding visual effects by setting the `UIPrerenderedIcon` flag inside the application's *Info.plist* file. To do so, open the *<ApplicationName>-Info.plist* file for your project in the Xcode editor (it's in the Resources folder under Groups & Files) and click on the bottom entry, where a button with a plus sign on it will appear to the righthand side of the key-value pair table. Click on this button to add a new row to the table, and scroll down the list of possible options and select "Icon already includes gloss and bevel effects," as shown in Figure 9-1. When you've done so, check the box in the Value column to turn off the default visual effects added by both iTunes and the iPhone.

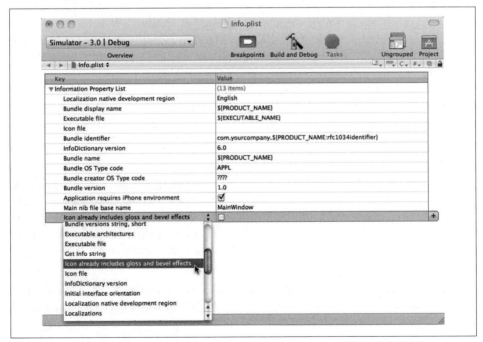

Figure 9-1. Adding the UIPrerenderedIcon flag to our application's Info.plist

Let's generate an icon for the City Guide application we built in Chapter 5. Figure 9-2 shows a sample image from the Tango Desktop Project, which was released into the public domain and is available from Wikimedia Commons (*http://commons .wikimedia.org*). You can find many public domain images at Wikimedia Commons. It's advisable for you to make modifications to the images you find there to avoid possible confusion—because the images are public domain, other people may use them in their own applications.

Figure 9-2. A simple icon for our City Guide application

You can download the icon shown in Figure 9-2 from *http://commons.wikimedia.org/ wiki/File:Applications-internet.svg* (right-click or Ctrl-click the link labeled `Applica tions-internet.svg` and choose Save Linked File). Open it in an image editor such as Adobe Illustrator or the free and open source Inkscape (*http://inkscape.org*).

Resize the file to 57×57 pixels and save it as a PNG file named *Icon.png*. (If you are using Inkscape, you will need to use File→Export Bitmap, choose the Page option, and set the width and height to 57 before you click Export.)

Next, open the City Guide application in Xcode. Drag and drop the *Icon.png* file into the Resources group in the Groups & Files pane, making sure to tick the box to indicate that Xcode should "Copy items into destination's group." Now double-click on the *CityGuide-Info.plist* file to open it in the Xcode editor, and set the Icon file to *Icon.png*, as shown in Figure 9-3.

If you build and deploy the application by clicking the Build and Run button in the Xcode toolbar, the application will start inside iPhone Simulator. If you quit the application by clicking the Home button, you will see that it now has a shiny new icon, as shown in Figure 9-4.

Adding a Launch Image

One of the ways in which the iPhone and the iPod touch cheat is by providing *launch images*. A launch image is immediately displayed on the screen when the application is started before the UI is displayed. Your application displays the launch image file while loading, which means there are no more blank screens while the application loads.

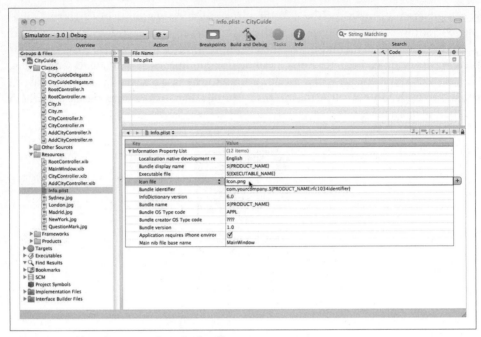

Figure 9-3. Adding the icon to the Info.plist file

Figure 9-4. The City Guide application with its new icon

Let's add one of these to the City Guide application. Build and deploy the City Guide application onto your iPhone or iPod touch. While your device is still connected and your application is still running, open the Organizer window by going to Window→Organizer in the Xcode menu bar. You will see a glowing green dot next to your device. Select your device, and in the Screenshots tab click the Capture button. Xcode will take a screen capture from your application, as shown in Figure 9-5.

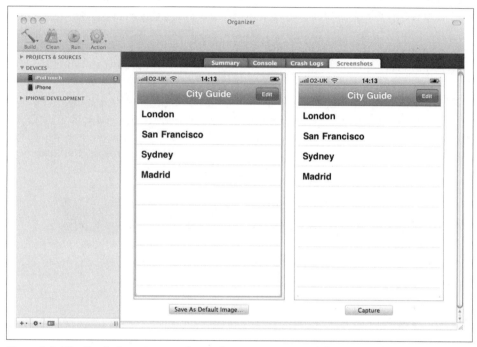

Figure 9-5. The Xcode Organizer window with a screen capture of the City Guide application's UI

Click the Save As Default Image button and select your project from the menu. When you return to the project in Xcode, you'll notice a *Default.png* image file appear in the Resources group in your project. If you rebuild the City Guide application at this point and redeploy it, the application will apparently now load instantly.

Although many developers have chosen to use the launch image as a splash screen, that's not how Apple intended this image to be used. Instead, it is intended to improve the user experience. Its presence adds to the user's perception that your application is quick to load and immediately ready for use when it does load.

Because this is a mobile platform, users will switch between applications frequently. Even more than on the Web, where users' attention spans are notoriously short, on the iPhone and iPod touch, users will become frustrated with applications that take a long time to launch (or shut down). You need to work to keep the launch time of your application to a minimum, and use the launch image to make a subtle transition into your application.

The launch image measures 320×480 pixels, and generally should be identical to the first screen of your application. However, since this is an image, the content is static, so you should not include any interface elements that may change from launch to launch. Therefore, avoid displaying elements that might look different between the launch image and your first screen. For instance, the *Default.png* image file we generated for our City Guide application includes a list of cities, but what happens if the user adds more cities? The list will change. We can't update the list of cities in the launch image, so it's probably best to remove them, leaving only the table view as shown in Figure 9-6. (This also has the benefit of hinting to the user that she can't interact with the app just yet.)

To do this, right-click on the *Default.png* image file in Xcode and select Reveal in Finder. This will open the Finder and highlight the image in your project folder. You can now open this image in your preferred image editor and make any changes you want. Remember, you need to save it back as a single-layer PNG file without transparency; otherwise, your application will have problems loading the file at launch.

Figure 9-6. A screen capture of the opening screen of the City Guide application (left), and the modified version (right) without the city entries

Most applications' launch images will be very plain; this is not a problem, as they are there solely to convince your users that your application is quick to load. If you interrupt the user experience with a splash screen, your users might ask themselves why you're wasting their time displaying such a screen, and why you don't just get on with it and load the application. If you make use of the launch image correctly, they'll know that you're doing your best to give them a seamless experience.

Changing the Display Name

The name displayed beneath your application icon on the iPhone home screen is, by default, the name of your Xcode project. However, only a limited number of characters are displayed before an ellipsis is inserted and your application name is truncated. This is fairly messy, and generally users don't like it. Fortunately, you can change your application's display name by editing the "Bundle display name" field in the application's *Info.plist* file.

If you look at our City Guide application, you'll notice that the display name is the same as our project name: "CityGuide". While the name is not long enough to be truncated when displayed on the iPhone's home screen, we might want it to be displayed as "City Guide" instead. Let's make that change now.

Open the *CityGuide* project in Xcode and click on the *CityGuide-Info.plist* file to open it in the Xcode editor. Double-click on the Value field in the "Bundle display name" field and change the `${PRODUCT_NAME}` macro to `City Guide`, as shown in Figure 9-7.

If you rebuild the application and deploy it in iPhone Simulator, you'll notice that the name displayed below the City Guide application icon has changed from "CityGuide" to "City Guide".

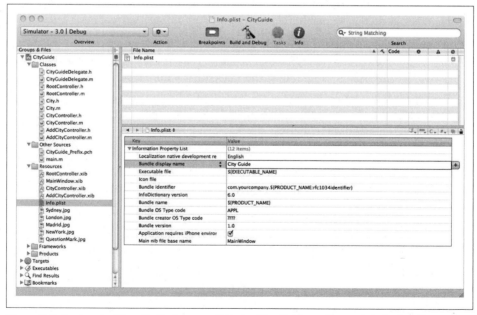

Figure 9-7. Setting the "Bundle display name" in the City Guide application's Info.plist file

Enabling Rotation

Until now, all of the applications we have built in the book have been in portrait mode and would not rotate into landscape mode, as many iPhone applications do when the user rotates the phone. Enabling this functionality is actually amazingly easy. In your view controller class, add the following method:

```
- (BOOL)shouldAutorotateToInterfaceOrientation:
  (UIInterfaceOrientation)interfaceOrientation {
    // Return YES for all supported orientations
    return YES;
}
```

If you rebuild your application and rotate your device, or if you select Hardware→Rotate Left or Hardware→Rotate Right in the simulator, your UI will rotate into landscape mode. If you have multiple view controllers (such as *RootController.m*, *CityController.m*, and *AddCityController.m*), you need to add this method to each of them.

> Although the shouldAutorotateToInterfaceOrientation: method was called in a timely fashion under the 2.0 SDK, this is not always the case under the 3.0 SDK. To ensure that you are (reliably) notified of changes in the device orientation, you should register for notification of orientation change messages.

However, the UI elements will also squash and stretch into the new orientation. You need to make sure that the individual UI elements can cope with their new sizes elegantly. You can do that in one of two ways:

- Be careful when using the Size tab in the Inspector window in Interface Builder to make sure they stretch in the correct fashion. The easiest way to do this is to make use of the Autosizing, Alignment, and Placement sections in the Size tab.

- Register for orientation change notifications and dynamically adapt your UI based on those events. For example, the built-in Calculator application has a different UI in portrait and landscape modes.

You can start generating orientation change notifications by calling this method of the UIDevice class (in the viewDidLoad: method of your view controller class):

```
[[UIDevice currentDevice] beginGeneratingDeviceOrientationNotifications];
```

When you are no longer concerned about orientation changes, you stop such notifications by calling this method:

```
[[UIDevice currentDevice] endGeneratingDeviceOrientationNotifications];
```

After starting notifications, you must also register your class to receive such messages using the NSNotificationCenter class:

```
NSNotificationCenter *notificationCenter =
  [NSNotificationCenter defaultCenter];
```

```
[notificationCenter addObserver:self
                    selector:@selector(handlerMethod:)
                    name:@"UIDeviceOrientationDidChangeNotification"
                    object:nil];
```

This would invoke the `handlerMethod:` selector (elsewhere in your view controller) in the current class when such a message was received:

```
-(void) handlerMethod:(NSNotification *)note {

    /* Deal with rotation of your UI here */
}
```

Building and Signing

The certificates we generated in Chapter 2 were intended only for development. If you want to distribute your application to end users, you'll need to return to the Developer Portal, generate a different set of profiles, and rebuild your application, signing it this time with your new distribution profile rather than the development profile you have used thus far.

> The different provisioning profiles are used for different purposes. The development profile you generated in Chapter 2 is intended for development and your own devices. The ad hoc distribution profile is intended for alpha and beta testing, while the App Store distribution profile is intended for distributing your final build to the iTunes App Store.

Ad Hoc Distribution

Ad hoc builds of your application are used to distribute your application outside your own development environment, and are intended to allow you to distribute your application to beta testers. In the same way you registered your iPhone or iPod touch for development, you must register all of the devices onto which you intend to distribute your application using an ad hoc build. You can register up to 100 devices per year in the iPhone Program Portal. This is a firm limit; deleting already registered devices will not allow you to add further devices.

> Normally when you distribute applications via the ad hoc method, no application artwork is displayed when the user looks at your application inside the iTunes interface. However, if you place a copy of the 512×512-pixel PNG of your icon in your application bundle and name it *iTunesArtwork* without any file extension, this will be used by iTunes.

To deploy your application to your users via the ad hoc method, you need to create a *distribution certificate*, register any devices you plan to use, and create an *ad hoc provisioning profile* in the iPhone Developer Program Portal.

Obtaining a distribution certificate

Just as in Chapter 2 when we dealt with development, the first thing you need is a distribution certificate, and to obtain that you need to generate a certificate-signing request (CSR) using the Keychain Access application:

1. As you did for the CSR you generated for the development certificate (see "Creating a Development Certificate" on page 12 in Chapter 2), launch the Keychain Access application.

2. Select Keychain Access→Preferences from the menu. Go to the Certificates preference pane to confirm that the Online Certificate Status Protocol (OCSP) and Certificate Revocation List (CRL) options are turned off.

3. Select Keychain Access→Certificate Assistant→Request a Certificate from a Certificate Authority from the Keychain Access menu, and enter the email address you selected as your Apple ID during the sign-up process and your name. Click the "Saved to disk" radio button, check the "Let me specify key pair information" checkbox, and click Continue. You'll be prompted for a filename for your certificate request.

4. Accept the defaults (a key size of 2,048 bits using the RSA algorithm) and click Continue.

The application will proceed to generate a CSR file and save it to disk.

In the iPhone Developer Program Portal (sign in to *http://developer.apple.com/iphone* and look for the program portal link), click on the Certificates link and in the Distribution tab click Request Certificate (if you already have a certificate, this option will be unavailable as you need only one). Follow the instructions that appear, and upload your CSR to the portal when asked.

If you joined the development program as an individual, you need to approve the signing request (in the Distribution tab of the Certificates section of the portal) before proceeding to download the new certificate. If you are part of a team, the nominated development team administrator needs to do this. After the request is approved, you may need to click on the Distribution tab to refresh the page. When you see a Download button, click it to save the certificate to disk.

Once the certificate file has downloaded, double-click it to install it into your Mac OS X login keychain, as shown in Figure 9-8.

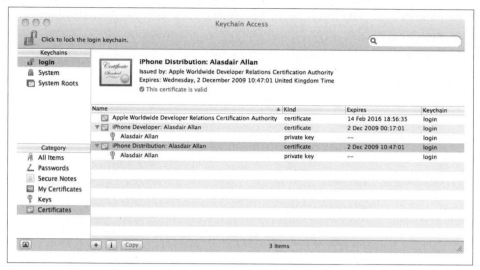

Figure 9-8. The Keychain Access application showing the newly installed distribution certificate needed by Xcode for ad hoc or App Store distribution

Registering devices

Before you create the provisioning profile, you'll need to register the devices you want the profile to support. To do this you'll need the unique device identifier (UDID) of all of these devices. Once you have the device identifiers, you need to add your users' devices in the same way you added your own development device in "Getting the UDID of Your Development Device" on page 14 in Chapter 2.

In the Program Portal, click Devices, select the Manage tab, and click Add Devices. Enter a device name in the appropriate box and the UDID in the box labeled Device ID, and click the Submit button. (You can click the + button to add more rows so that you can add several devices at once.) You have now registered the device; you need to do this for all of the devices to which you intend to distribute ad hoc builds.

Creating a provisioning profile

Now you're ready to create a mobile provisioning profile. Go to the Provisioning section of the iPhone Developer Program Portal, select the Distribution tab, and click New Profile.

Enter a profile name; you may be creating a number of ad hoc profiles, so naming your first distribution profile "Ad-hoc Distribution Profile" probably isn't a great idea. You may want to name it after the application you're distributing, so perhaps "City Guide Beta Test Profile" would be a good choice for distributing a beta of the City Guide application to testers.

Next, select the App ID you used for the application you're going to distribute, and then select all of the devices for which this profile will be valid, as shown in Figure 9-9.

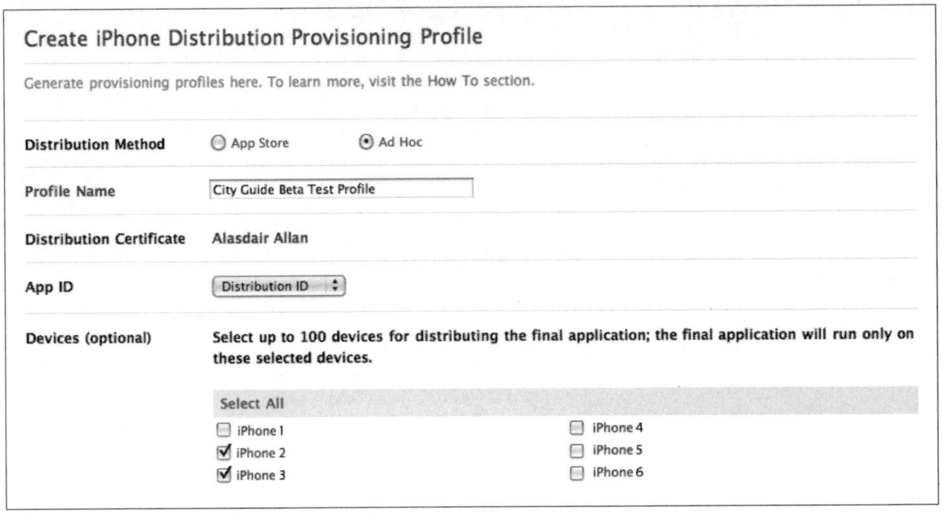

Create iPhone Distribution Provisioning Profile

Generate provisioning profiles here. To learn more, visit the How To section.

Distribution Method	○ App Store ⊙ Ad Hoc
Profile Name	City Guide Beta Test Profile
Distribution Certificate	Alasdair Allan
App ID	Distribution ID ⬍
Devices (optional)	**Select up to 100 devices for distributing the final application; the final application will run only on these selected devices.**

Select All

☐ iPhone 1   ☐ iPhone 4
☑ iPhone 2   ☐ iPhone 5
☑ iPhone 3   ☐ iPhone 6

Figure 9-9. Creating an ad hoc provisioning profile

Click Submit to generate the new mobile provisioning profile that you'll use to distribute the application to your beta testers. The status will appear as pending; click the Distribution tab to reload it until it is no longer pending. When the profile is ready, click the Download button and download the provisioning profile to your Mac. Now drag the provisioning file onto the Xcode icon in the dock to make it available to the development environment.

Building your application for ad hoc distribution

Let's make an ad hoc build of the City Guide application. Double-click the project icon at the top of the Group & Files pane and select the Configurations tab. Select the Release configuration in the main pane, and click the Duplicate button located at the bottom left of the configuration list. Name the duplicate configuration "Ad-hoc", as shown in Figure 9-10.

Return to the main Xcode window and use the Overview drop down to set the active configuration to be the new ad hoc configuration, and the active SDK to be the iPhone device rather than iPhone Simulator.

Now, in the Groups & Files pane of the Xcode interface, right-click on the Resources group and select Add→New File. Choose Code Signing and select an Entitlement (see Figure 9-11). Click Next, and name the file "dist.plist" when prompted. Click Finish.

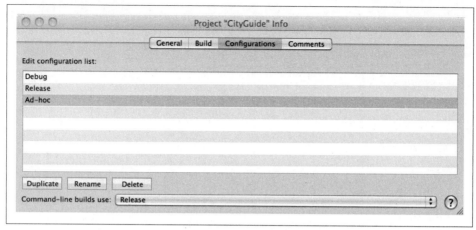

Figure 9-10. Creating an ad hoc configuration in the Xcode Project Info window

Figure 9-11. Adding the ad hoc distribution plist file to your project

In the Groups & Files pane, click on the *dist.plist* file and (very important) uncheck the `get-task-allow` Boolean property in the editor window, as shown in Figure 9-12. This step is necessary to turn off the ability for other processes (such as the debugger) to attach to your application, as this is disallowed by distribution profiles.

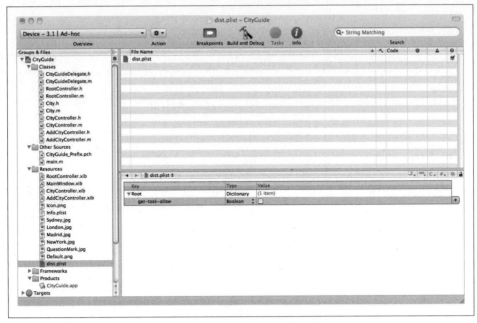

Figure 9-12. Unchecking the get-task-allow flag in the dist.plist file

Now, double-click on the project icon at the top of the Groups & Files pane to reopen the Project Info window. Click the Build tab and scroll down to the Code Signing section. Double-click on the Code Signing Entitlements value field, type **dist.plist** in the entitlements list, and click OK. Now click on the menu to the right of the Code Signing Identity→Any iPhone OS Device line and select the iPhone Distribution profile. Xcode should match this against the City Guide Beta Test profile we installed earlier, as shown in Figure 9-13.

Close the Project Info window. Before building your application, open the *CityGuide-Info.plist* file and make sure the Bundle Identifier in your *Info.plist* file matches the one used to create the ad hoc mobile provisioning profile. See "Putting the Application on Your iPhone" on page 37 in Chapter 3 if you're unsure about this part. If you've been able to deploy your application onto your iPhone or iPod touch and you generated a wildcard app ID earlier, you shouldn't have to change anything.

Now select Build→Build from the Xcode menu to build, but not to deploy, your application. You may be prompted to allow Xcode to access your private key by the Keychain application; you must permit the access to build the application.

Distributing an ad hoc build

Once you've made your build, go to the Products group in the Groups & Files pane in the Xcode interface and double-click to open the group if it is not already open. Inside you should find a single file called *CityGuide.app*. Right-click on this file and select

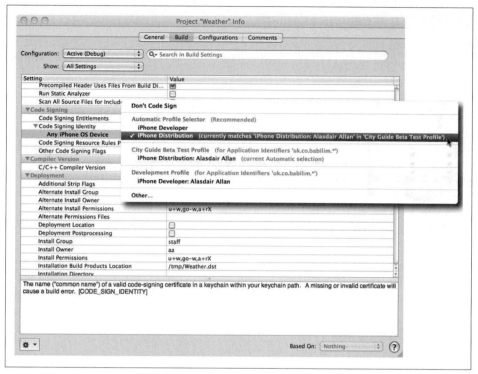

Figure 9-13. Choosing the iPhone Distribution profile

Reveal in Finder to open a Finder window in the directory containing the application bundle.

Copy the application bundle file onto your desktop and create a ZIP file containing both it and the ad hoc mobile provisioning profile you created earlier. This ZIP file is your ad hoc build and can be distributed directly to your users.

Users receiving an ad hoc build should follow these steps:

1. Plug their iPhone or iPod touch into their Mac.
2. Ensure that iTunes is running and can see their device.
3. Unzip the distribution archive file.
4. Drag the provisioning profile onto the iTunes icon in the dock.
5. Drag the application bundle file onto the iTunes icon in the dock.

If the user checks the Applications section of his iTunes library, he should now be able to see the new ("Ad-hoc") application, and he can install it onto his iPhone or iPod touch in the normal way by syncing his device with iTunes.

Developer-to-Developer Distribution

Apple intended ad hoc distribution to be a way for you to distribute your software to beta testers. However, developers have used it extensively for other purposes, including bypassing the App Store entirely and selling directly to the consumer (a somewhat torturous process).

If your intended end user is another developer, you can vastly simplify the ad hoc distribution process. Just create a normal development build, as though you were going to deploy the code to your own device, and send a copy of the binary to your colleague. He can then re-sign the binary with his own developer certificate using the Xcode command line `codesign` utility:

```
#! /bin/bash
export CODESIGN_ALLOCATE=/Developer/Platforms/iPhoneOS.platform\
/Developer/usr/bin/codesign_allocate
codesign -f -s "iPhone Developer" $1.app
```

Once he has re-signed the binary, he can use the Xcode Organizer window to install it onto his device. In the Applications section of the Summary tab, he should click the + symbol and select the binary. Xcode will then install it onto his iPhone or iPod touch.

App Store Distribution

Making a build of your application to submit to the App Store is similar to making an ad hoc build, and you'll use the same distribution certificate you created for the ad hoc build earlier in the chapter. However, you have to return to the iPhone Program Portal to generate a new distribution provisioning profile.

Open the iPhone Developer Program Portal in a browser (start at *http://developer.apple .com/iphone/* and follow the links to the Program Portal), and in the Provisioning section, select the Distribution tab and click New Profile. Enter a profile name; you'll need only one App Store profile, so unlike the ad hoc profile, a good choice might be "App Store Distribution Profile".

 Most developers use one (wildcarded) App Store distribution profile for all of their applications (see "Putting the Application on Your iPhone" on page 37 in Chapter 3). The only reason you would need to use a separate profile for your application is if it makes use of In-App Purchase or Push Notifications.

Finally, select the App ID you used for the application you're going to distribute; since this is an App Store provisioning profile, there is no need to select devices this time around.

Click Submit to generate the new mobile provisioning profile. The status will appear as pending; click the Distribution tab to reload it until it is no longer pending. When the profile is ready, click the Download button and download the provisioning profile to your Mac. Drag the provisioning file onto the Xcode icon in the dock to make it available to the development environment.

Building your application for App Store distribution

Let's make an App Store build of our City Guide application. Double-click on the project icon at the top of the Groups & Files pane and select the Configurations tab. Select the Release configuration in the main pane, and click the Duplicate button located at the bottom left of the configuration list, just as you did for the ad hoc build, but this time around name the duplicate configuration "Distribution".

Return to the main Xcode window and use the Overview drop down to set the active configuration to be the new distribution configuration, and the active SDK to be the iPhone device rather than iPhone Simulator.

Now double-click on the project icon at the top of the Groups & Files pane to reopen the Project Info window. Open the Build tab and scroll down to the Code Signing section. Click on the menu to the right of the Code Signing Identity→Any iPhone OS Device line and select the App Store distribution profile. Xcode will not automatically match this profile by default as it did with your developer profile. You must make this selection manually, as shown in Figure 9-14.

Close the Project Info window. Before building your application, check the *Info.plist* file for your app (such as *CityGuide-Info.plist*) and make sure the Bundle Identifier matches the one used to create the App Store provisioning profile. Now select Build→Build from the Xcode menu to build, but not to deploy, your application. Unless you've already clicked Always Allow on a previous build, you'll be prompted to grant access to your keychain. You must allow this access.

Once you've made your build, go to the Products group in the Groups & Files pane in the Xcode interface and double-click to open the group. Inside you should find a single file called *CityGuide.app*. Right-click on this file and select Reveal in Finder to open a Finder window in the directory containing the application bundle. Copy the application bundle file onto your desktop. It's this file that you'd upload to the iTunes Connect site to release it onto the App Store.

Submitting to the App Store

 While I've walked you through building a version of the City Guide application that is ready to be submitted to the App Store, you should not actually go ahead and submit it. The App Store might start to look a bit odd if every reader of this book did that.

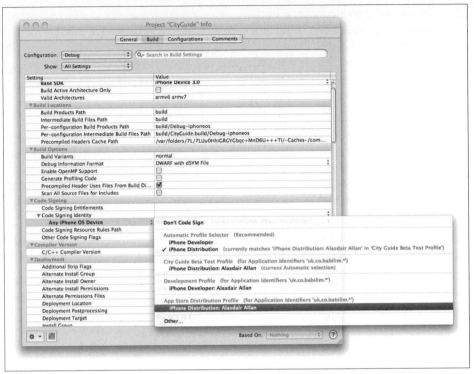

Figure 9-14. Choosing the App Store distribution profile manually

Log in to the iTunes Connect site (*http://itunesconnect.apple.com/*), and click the Manage Your Applications button and then the Add New Application button.

If this is the first time you've submitted an application to iTunes Connect, you'll be asked what primary language you will be using to enter your applications to the store. You'll then be asked what company or developer name you want displayed on the App Store for all your applications. Both your primary language and your company name cannot be changed, so choose carefully. You won't be asked these questions again the next time you submit an application to the store.

You'll then be asked whether your application uses encryption. If your application includes any encryption code, you may have to fill out some forms to comply with U.S. commercial encryption export controls.

Next, you'll be asked to provide information about your application:

Application name and application description
> The application display name and description will appear as is on the iTunes App Store. You do not have to use the same name for the application as you used for your project binary or bundle display name. However, it should be related to the display name, or this might form grounds for rejection by the review team. You should try to keep your description fairly short so that your application screenshots

---

will be "above the fold" (the part of the description the user will see without having to scroll) if the user is browsing the store from her iPhone or iPod touch.

Device requirements

At the time of this writing, the choices were iPhone only, iPhone & iPod touch (2nd Generation), and iPhone and iPod touch. It's best to select the least restrictive requirements you can to increase the number of possible users of your application.

Primary and secondary category

These are the App Store categories that best describe your application. You need only select the primary category.

Copyright, version, and SKU number

The copyright and version number entries are fairly self-explanatory. For copyright, you should list the copyright year and copyright holder's name. For the version, provide the version number of the app (1.0 is a good place to start). The SKU (or stock-keeping unit) number must be a unique alphanumeric identifier that you choose for this product. Bear in mind that this SKU cannot be changed at any point, even with the upload of a new binary (and version) of the application, so while you can choose just about anything, it should be fairly descriptive but not version-specific.

Keywords

Application keywords are associated with the application binary and can be edited only when uploading a new binary, so think carefully about your choice of keywords for your application. Separate multiple keywords with commas, not spaces.

Application and support URLs

Again, this is fairly self-explanatory. These are two URLs which can be identical; they point to support information about your application. Applications without associated URLs, or with URLs pointing to blank pages, will not be approved. Your support information should be in place before you upload your binary to iTunes Connect for review.

Support email address

This is the email address that will be published to iTunes as the support address when your application is approved. It would be a sensible move to create a separate email address for each of your applications, rather than use a personal address. If your application becomes popular, you will receive a lot of email.

Demo account

If your application needs an account on an online service to be fully operative, supply an account name and password here. If you don't, the review team will summarily reject your application.

After entering this metadata, you'll be asked to rate your application under certain categories: Cartoon or Fantasy Violence; Realistic Violence; Sexual Content or Nudity; Profanity or Crude Humor; Alcohol, Tobacco or Drug User or References; Mature/Suggestive Themes; Simulated Gambling; Horror/Fear Themes; Prolonged Graphic or

Sadistic Realistic Violence; and Graphic Sexual Content and Nudity. This will generate your App Rating (4+, 9+, 12+, or 17+) that will allow users to filter your application using the parental controls inside iTunes. If you don't rate your application realistically, the review team may reject it during the review process.

You'll then be asked to upload your application binary (which you must first compress into a ZIP file by right-clicking on your application bundle file and selecting Compress), your large 512×512-pixel icon image, and a number of screenshots. Your screenshots will be displayed on the App Store with your application, and each must be a JPEG or TIFF file that is 320×480, 480×320, 320×460, or 480×300 pixels in size.

Once you have uploaded all the requested files, you will be asked to set the price tier for your application, and the availability date. Your application will be made available on the store on this date, or whenever it leaves the review process and is approved by the App Store review team, whichever is later.

 The availability date, like all application metadata, applies to all versions of your application. If you later upload an update for your application and change the availability date to a date in the future, your current version will be removed from the App Store until that date arrives.

After setting the price, you will be offered the opportunity to localize all of the metadata you entered into several different languages, including Dutch, German, Italian, Japanese, Chinese, and several different dialects of English and French. You are not required to enter any localization for your application metadata, but if you are selling worldwide you may have better sales if both your application and its store entry are localized.

Finally, before posting your application for review by the App Store review team, you will be given the opportunity to review all of the information you have entered. If you find any mistakes, you can click on the tabs across the top to return to that stage of the process.

The App Store Resource Center

If you're confused about any aspect of distribution, you should make your way to the App Store Resource Center (*http://developer.apple.com/iphone/appstore/*). This site walks you through the process of preparing your application for submission, the App Store approval process itself, and how to manage your applications on the store once they're live.

Reasons for Rejection

The App Store review process is somewhat opaque, but generally, if your application is rejected, the review team will cite the specific section of the iPhone Developer Program License Agreement that it violates in the rejection email. If you're careful, you can avoid most of the common pitfalls and save yourself, and the review team, a lot of time.

 Copies of the iPhone Developer Program License Agreement, the agreement you signed with Apple to become an iPhone developer, and the iPhone Human Interface Guidelines are available for download from the App Store Resource Center in the App Store Approval Process section at *http://developer.apple.com/iphone/appstore*.

Some of the more common reasons for rejection concern the following:

Version number
Applications submitted with version numbers less than 1.0, or applications tagged as "beta" or "alpha," will be summarily rejected by the review team. Additionally, if there is any inconsistency in versioning—for instance, the version number in your application's About dialog does not match the version number in your *Info.plist* file (and the number you provided to iTunes Connect)—your application may be rejected.

Icons
The artwork for your 57×57-pixel icon must be identical to your 512×512 icon. Additionally, if you are uploading a free "lite" version of your application as well as a premium "pro" version, the application icons cannot be identical between the two versions.

Artwork
Using Apple's own graphics inside your application—for instance, logos or an image of an iPhone or iPod touch—is usually grounds for rejection.

Copyright material
Apple is extremely wary of allowing applications to make use of material (e.g., images, audio, and other media) that you do not have permission to use. Using material that might violate a trademark is similarly suspect.

Human Interface Guidelines
Violating the Human Interface Guidelines—for instance, using standard button icons for a nonstandard purpose, such as the Refresh, Organize, Trash, Reply, and Compose buttons—could be grounds for rejection.

Private frameworks
Applications published to the App Store are not allowed to link to private or third-party frameworks. Submitting applications for review that do link to such frameworks is an easy way to get your application rejected. Linking to third-party static libraries is a gray area, but is usually acceptable.

Existing functionality
A large number of applications have been rejected for duplicating existing functionality of a built-in app; applications that make extensive use of web browsers

are particularly vulnerable to this accusation. Other obvious candidates are email clients and music player applications.

Table views

Improper handling of table view cells when the application has a table view in edit mode can be grounds for rejection, as can not deselecting table view cells appropriately after selecting them to perform some action.

Network reachability

Not testing for the presence of a network connection or not handling the loss of network connectivity correctly (and informing the user) is a common cause for rejection.

Bandwidth limitations

If your application makes use of large amounts of bandwidth, you need to make sure your current network connection is over the cellular network. Transferring large amounts of data over the cellular network can (sometimes) be grounds for rejection. So, if your application does that, you should disable, or throttle, data transfer when the device is on the cellular network.

Keyboard type

You should ensure that you are using the correct keyboard type when prompting for user input; using an inappropriate keyboard is usually grounds for rejection (e.g., using the keyboard designed to enter phone numbers for other purposes).

OS compatibility

If you claim that your application will run on OS 3.0 and later, you must ensure that it really does so. Apple will test your application with all of the versions of the OS between your minimum specified version and the current release. If the review team discovers that your application does not function correctly with a specific version of the OS, they will normally reject it. Unfortunately, it's fairly rare for them to tell you in which version of the OS the bug manifested. This can lead to the unfortunate situation where you cannot duplicate the bug since you and the reviewer are testing the application under different OS revisions.

Description

Do not include the price in your application description, as part of your icon, or anywhere in the UI. According to Apple, this may "potentially confuse users" as the text cannot be localized to all markets.

Crippled functionality

If you provide a free "lite" version of your application, it cannot have crippled functionality (e.g., obviously disabled buttons or menu items). It also cannot directly refer to the paid "pro" version of the application. Free or "lite" versions of an application are acceptable, but the application must be a fully functional application in itself and cannot reference features that are not implemented.

Minimal user functionality

    If your application doesn't actually do very much, it might get rejected. However, there are numerous cases where applications that don't do very much have been accepted (e.g., flashlight applications).

Does not work as advertised

    Applications that do not work as described in their application descriptions will be summarily rejected. You should therefore be careful when writing your application description when submitting your application to iTunes Connect.

CHAPTER 10

Using Sensors

Mobile phones aren't just for making phone calls anymore. The iPhone, like a lot of high-end smartphones these days, comes with a number of sensors: camera, accelerometer, GPS module, and digital compass. We're entering a period of change: more and more users expect these sensors to be integrated into the "application experience." If your application can make use of them, it probably should.

Hardware Support

While the iPhone is almost unique among mobile platforms in guaranteeing that your code will run on all of the current devices, there is some variation in available hardware between the various models.

Determining Available Hardware Support

Table 10-1 lists the hardware differences between the devices. Because your app will likely support multiple devices, you'll need to write code to check which features are supported and adjust your application's behavior as appropriate.

Table 10-1. Hardware support in various iPhone and iPod touch models

Hardware features	Original iPhone	iPhone 3G	iPhone 3GS	First-generation iPod touch	Second-generation iPod touch	Third-generation iPod touch
Cellular	x	x	x			
WiFi	x	x	x	x	x	x
Bluetooth	x	x	x		x	x
Speaker	x	x	x		x	x
Audio-in	x	x	x		x	x
Accelerometer	x	x	x	x	x	x
Magnetometer			x			

Hardware features	Original iPhone	iPhone 3G	iPhone 3GS	First-generation iPod touch	Second-generation iPod touch	Third-generation iPod touch
GPS		X	X			
Proximity sensor	X	X	X			
Camera	X	X	X			
Video capture			X			
Vibration	X	X	X			

Network availability

We covered Apple's Reachability code in detail in "Apple's Reachability Class" on page 145 in Chapter 7. We can easily determine whether the network is reachable, and whether we are using the wireless or WWAN interface:

```
Reachability *reach = [
    [Reachability reachabilityForInternetConnection] retain];
NetworkStatus status = [reach currentReachabilityStatus];❶
```

❶ This call will return a network status: NotReachable, ReachableViaWiFi, or ReachableViaWWAN.

Camera availability

We cover the camera in detail later in this chapter. However, it is simple to determine whether a camera is present in the device:

```
BOOL available = [UIImagePickerController
    isSourceTypeAvailable:UIImagePickerControllerSourceTypeCamera];
```

Once you have determined that a camera is present, you can inquire whether it supports video by making a call to determine the available media types the camera supports:

```
NSArray *media = [UIImagePickerController availableMediaTypesForSourceType:
                    UIImagePickerControllerSourceTypeCamera];
```

If the kUTTypeMovie media type is returned as part of the array, the camera will support video recording.

Audio input availability

You can poll whether audio input is available using the AVAudioSession singleton class by checking the inputIsAvailable class property:

```
AVAudioSession *audioSession = [AVAudioSession sharedInstance];
BOOL audioAvailable = audioSession.inputIsAvailable;
```

You will need to add the *AVFoundation.Framework* (right-click or Ctrl-click on the Frameworks folder in Xcode and choose Add→Existing Frameworks). You'll also need to import the header (put this in your declaration if you plan to implement the `AVAudioSessionDelegate` protocol, discussed shortly):

```
#import <AVFoundation/AVFoundation.h>
```

You can also be notified of any changes in the availability of audio input (e.g., a second-generation iPod touch user has plugged in headphones with microphone capabilities). First, nominate your class as a delegate:

```
audioSession.delegate = self;
```

Declare it as implementing the `AVAudioSessionDelegate` protocol in the declaration:

```
@interface YourAppDelegate : NSObject <UIApplicationDelegate,
    AVAudioSessionDelegate >
```

Then implement `inputIsAvailableChanged:` in the implementation:

```
- (void)inputIsAvailableChanged:(BOOL)audioAvailable {
    NSLog(@"Audio availability has changed");
}
```

GPS availability

I'm going to cover the Core Location framework, and GPS, later in the chapter. However, the short answer to a fairly commonly asked question is that, unfortunately, the Core Location framework does not provide any way to get direct information about the availability of specific hardware.

While you cannot check for the availability of GPS using Core Location, you can require the presence of GPS hardware for your application to load. I will discuss this in the next section.

Setting Required Hardware Capabilities

If your application requires specific hardware features in order to run, you can add a list of required capabilities to your application's *Info.plist* file. Your application will not start unless those capabilities are present on the device.

Later in the chapter we'll modify the Weather application to make use of the Core Location framework to determine current position, so let's modify it now to make sure this capability is available.

You may want to make a copy of the Weather application before modifying, as we have done previously. Navigate to where you saved the project and make a copy of the project folder, and then rename it. Then open the new (duplicate) project inside Xcode and use the Project→Rename tool to rename the project.

Open the Weather application in Xcode, open the *Weather-Info.plist* file in the Xcode editor, and click on the bottommost entry. A button with a plus sign (+) on it will appear to the righthand side of the key-value pair table. Click on this button to add a new row to the table; then scroll down the list of possible options and select "Required device capabilities" (the UIRequiredDeviceCapabilities key) as shown Figure 10-1. This will add an (empty) array to the *.plist* file. If you add "location-services" (see Figure 10-2) as Item 0 of this array (some versions of Xcode may label the first item in the array Item 1), your application will no longer start if such services are unavailable. If you want to add further entries, select Item 0 and click the plus button to the righthand side of the table.

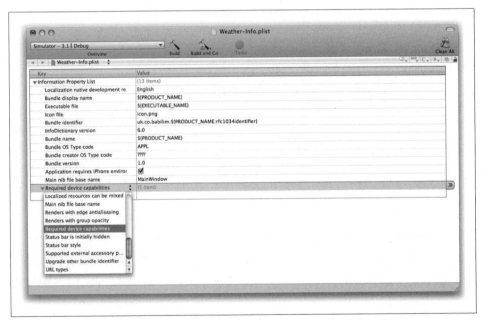

Figure 10-1. Setting the "Required device capabilities" key

The allowed values for the keys are *telephony*, *sms*, *still-camera*, *auto-focus-camera*, *video-camera*, *wifi*, *accelerometer*, *location-services*, *gps*, *magnetometer*, *microphone*, *opengles-1*, *opengles-2*, *armv6*, *armv7*, and *peer-peer*. A full description of the possible keys is available in the Device Support section of the iPhone Application Programming Guide available from the iPhone Dev Center.

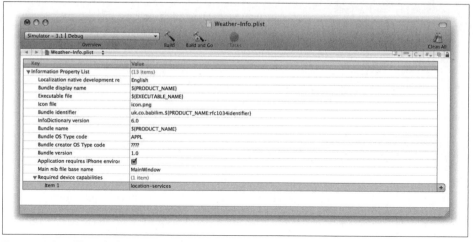

Figure 10-2. Adding the location-services item to "Required device capabilities"

Using the Camera

We looked at the image picker view controller in Chapter 6, where we used it to add pictures to our City Guide application using our `AddCityController` class. We have to change only one line in our code from Chapter 6 to make our City Guide application use the camera instead of the saved photo album.

If you open the *CityGuide* project in Xcode and look at the `viewDidLoad:` method in the `AddCityController` class, you'll see that we set the source of the image picker controller to be the photo album:

```
pickerController.sourceType =
    UIImagePickerControllerSourceTypeSavedPhotosAlbum;
```

Changing the source to `UIImagePickerControllerSourceTypeCamera` will mean that when you call `presentModalViewController:`, which presents the `UIImagePickerControl` `ler`, the camera interface rather than the photo album will be presented to the user, allowing him to take a new picture.

If you want to enable video, you need to add the relevant media type to the array indicating the media types to be accessed by the picker. By default, this array contains only the `image` media type. The following code should determine whether your device supports a camera, and if it does, it will add all of the available media types (including video on the iPhone 3GS) to the media types array. If there is no camera present, the source will be set to the photo album as before:

```
if ([UIImagePickerController
    isSourceTypeAvailable:UIImagePickerControllerSourceTypeCamera])
{
    pickerController.sourceType = UIImagePickerControllerSourceTypeCamera;
```

```
    NSArray* mediaTypes =
      [UIImagePickerController availableMediaTypesForSourceType:
                             UIImagePickerControllerSourceTypeCamera];
    pickerController.mediaTypes = mediaTypes;
  } else {
    pickerController.sourceType =
      UIImagePickerControllerSourceTypeSavedPhotosAlbum;
    pickerController.allowsEditing = YES;
  }
```

The Core Location Framework

The Core Location framework is an abstraction layer in front of several different methods to find the user's location (and, by extrapolation, her speed and course). It can provide the latitude, longitude, and altitude of the device (along with the level of accuracy to which this is known). There are three levels of accuracy:

- The least accurate level uses the cell network to locate the user (the process is similar to triangulation, but more complex). This can quickly provide a position to around 12 km accuracy, which can be reduced to 1–3 km after some time depending on the tower density at your current location.

- The next accuracy level is obtained by utilizing Skyhook Wireless's WiFi-based positioning system. This is much more precise, giving a position to approximately 100 m. However, it depends on the user being in range of a known wireless hotspot.

- The highest level of accuracy is obtained by using GPS hardware, which should provide a position to less than 40 m.

 On the iPod touch, the user's location is derived solely from WiFi positioning. The original iPhone will use WiFi and cell tower triangulation, and on the iPhone 3G and 3GS it will also make use of the built-in GPS hardware.

The actual method used to determine the user's location is abstracted away from both the user and the developer. The only control the developer has over the chosen method is by requesting a certain level of accuracy, although the actual accuracy achieved is not guaranteed. Further, the battery power consumed and the time to calculate the position increase with increasing accuracy.

 Some users may choose to explicitly disable reporting of their position. You should therefore always check to see whether location services are enabled before attempting to turn on these services. This will avoid unnecessary prompting from your application.

The Core Location framework is implemented using the `CLLocationManager` class. The following code will create an instance of this class, and from then on will send location update messages to the designated delegate class:

```
CLLocationManager *locationManager = [[CLLocationManager alloc] init];
locationManager.delegate = self;
if( locationManager.locationServicesEnabled ) {
    [locationManager startUpdatingLocation];
} else {
    NSLog(@"Location services not enabled.");
}
```

 To use this code, you will need to add the Core Location framework. In Groups & Files, right-click or Ctrl-click on Frameworks and select Add→Existing Frameworks. Add CoreLocation. You will also need to declare your class as implementing the `CLLocationManagerDelegate` protocol and import CoreLocation in your declaration or implementation with the following code:

```
#import <CoreLocation/CoreLocation.h>
```

We can filter these location update messages based on a distance filter. Changes in position of less than this amount will not generate an update message to the delegate:

```
locationManager.distanceFilter = 1000;  // 1km
```

We can also set a desired level of accuracy; this will determine the location method(s) used by the Core Location framework to determine the user's location:

```
locationManager.desiredAccuracy = kCLLocationAccuracyKilometer;
```

The `CLLocationManagerDelegate` protocol offers two methods. The first is called when a location update occurs:

```
- (void)locationManager:(CLLocationManager *)manager
  didUpdateToLocation:(CLLocation *)newLocation
  fromLocation:(CLLocation *)oldLocation
{
    NSLog(@"Moved from %@ to %@", oldLocation, newLocation);
}
```

The second is called when an error occurs:

```
- (void)locationManager:(CLLocationManager *)manager
  didFailWithError:(NSError *)error {
    NSLog(@"Received Core Location error %@", error);
    [manager stopUpdatingLocation];
}
```

If the location manager is not able to ascertain the user's location immediately, it reports a `kCLErrorLocationUnknown` error and keeps trying. In most cases, you can choose to ignore the error and wait for a new event. However, if the user denies your application access to the location service, the manager will report a `kCLErrorDenied` error. Upon receiving such an error, you should stop the location manager.

Location-Dependent Weather

In Chapter 7 we built a simple Weather application, but it would be much better if the application gave us weather information for our current location. We can use the Core Location framework to retrieve the user's latitude and longitude. However, the Google Weather Service, which we used to back our Weather application, takes only city names, not latitude or longitude arguments.

There are several ways around this problem. For instance, the MapKit framework, which we'll meet later in the book, offers *reverse geocoding* capabilities (which turn coordinates into postal addresses). However, for this example, I'm going to make use of one of the many web services offered by the GeoNames.org site to carry our reverse geocoding to retrieve the nearest city from the latitude and longitude returned by the Core Location framework.

Using the GeoNames reverse geocoding service

One of the RESTful web services offered by GeoNames.org will return an XML or JSON document listing the nearest populated place using reverse geocoding. Requests to the service take the form *http://ws.geonames.org/findNearbyPlaceName? lat=<XX.X>&lng=<XX.X>* if you want an XML document returned, or *http://ws.geo-names.org/findNearbyPlaceNameJSON?lat=<XX.X>&lng=<XX.X>* if you prefer a JSON document. There are several optional parameters: radius (in km), max (maximum number of rows returned), and style (SHORT, MEDIUM, LONG, and FULL).

Passing the longitude and latitude of Cupertino, California, which is the location returned by Core Location in all cases for iPhone Simulator, the JSON service would return the following JSON document:

```
{
    "geonames":[
        {
            "countryName":"United States",
            "adminCode1":"CA",
            "fclName":"city, village,...",
            "countryCode":"US",
            "lng":-122.0321823,
            "fcodeName":"populated place",
            "distance":"0.9749",
            "fcl":"P",
            "name":"Cupertino",
            "fcode":"PPL",
            "geonameId":5341145,
            "lat":37.3229978,
            "population":50934,
            "adminName1":"California"
        }
```

```
        ]
    }
```

Modifying the Weather application

Let's modify our Weather application to make use of Core Location and (optionally) give us the weather where we are, rather than just for a hardwired single location. Open the Weather project in Xcode and click on the *WeatherAppDelegate.h* interface file to open it in the Xcode editor.

We're going to use the application delegate to manage the `CLLocationManager`. I've highlighted the changes you need to make to this file in bold:

```
#import <CoreLocation/CoreLocation.h>

@class MainViewController;

@interface WeatherAppDelegate : NSObject
   <UIApplicationDelegate, CLLocationManagerDelegate>❶
{
    UIWindow *window;
    MainViewController *mainViewController;

    BOOL updateLocation;❷
    CLLocationManager *locationManager;❸
}

@property (nonatomic, retain) IBOutlet UIWindow *window;
@property (nonatomic, retain) MainViewController *mainViewController;
@property (nonatomic) BOOL updateLocation;
@property (nonatomic, retain) CLLocationManager *locationManager;

@end
```

❶ We declare that the application delegate is also a `CLLocationManager` delegate.

❷ We declare a Boolean variable to indicate whether we're currently supposed to be monitoring the device's location.

❸ We declare an instance of the `CLLocationManager`.

You will also need to add the Core Location framework to the project. In Groups & Files, right-click or Ctrl-click on Frameworks and select Add→Existing Frameworks. Select CoreLocation and click Add.

In the corresponding implementation file (*WeatherAppDelegate.m*), we first need to synthesize the new variables we declared in the interface file:

```
@synthesize updateLocation;
@synthesize locationManager;
```

After that, add the code shown in bold to the `applicationDidFinishLaunching:` method. This creates an instance of the `CLLocationManager` class and sets the delegate for the class to be the current class (the application delegate).

```
- (void)applicationDidFinishLaunching:(UIApplication *)application {

    // Create instance of Main View controller
    MainViewController *aController =
      [[MainViewController alloc]
       initWithNibName:@"MainView" bundle:nil];
    self.mainViewController = aController;
    [aController release];

    // Create instance of LocationManager object
    self.locationManager =
            [[[CLLocationManager alloc] init] autorelease];❶
    self.locationManager.delegate = self;❷

    // Create instance of WeatherForecast object
    WeatherForecast *forecast = [[WeatherForecast alloc] init];
    self.mainViewController.forecast = forecast;
    [forecast release];

    // Set the main view
    mainViewController.view.frame = [UIScreen mainScreen].applicationFrame;
    [window addSubview:[mainViewController view]];
    [window makeKeyAndVisible];
}
```

❶ This creates the `CLLocationManager` instance.

❷ This sets the delegate for the instance to the current class.

Finally, we have to make sure the `CLLocationManager` instance is released in the `dealloc:` method, and implement the two `CLLocationManagerDelegate` methods we're going to need. Make the changes shown in bold:

```
- (void)dealloc {
    [locationManager release];
    [mainViewController release];
    [window release];
    [super dealloc];
}

#pragma mark CLLocationManager Methods

- (void)locationManager:(CLLocationManager *)manager
  didUpdateToLocation:(CLLocation *)newLocation
  fromLocation:(CLLocation *)oldLocation {❶
    NSLog(@"Location: %@", [newLocation description]);
    if ( newLocation != oldLocation ) {
      // Add code here

    }
}

- (void)locationManager:(CLLocationManager *)manager
  didFailWithError:(NSError *)error {❷
    NSLog(@"Error: %@", [error description]);
}
```

❶ This is the delegate method to handle changes in location.

❷ This is the delegate method to handle any errors that occur.

We're going to modify the (currently unused) flip side of the Weather application and add a switch (UISwitch), similar to our Battery Monitor application from Chapter 6. This will toggle whether our application should be updating its location. However, let's modify the FlipSideViewController interface file before we go to the NIB file, adding both a switch and a switchThrown: interface builder action that we'll connect to the switch. I've also added a reference to the application delegate. Make the changes shown in bold to *FlipSideViewController.h*:

```
@protocol FlipsideViewControllerDelegate;

@class WeatherAppDelegate;

@interface FlipsideViewController : UIViewController {
    id <FlipsideViewControllerDelegate> delegate;
    IBOutlet UISwitch *toggleSwitch;
    WeatherAppDelegate *appDelegate;
}

@property (nonatomic, assign) id <FlipsideViewControllerDelegate> delegate;

- (IBAction)done;
- (IBAction)switchThrown;

@end
```

In the corresponding implementation (*FlipSideViewController.m*), import both the Core Location framework and the application delegate interface file:

```
#import <CoreLocation/CoreLocation.h>
#import "WeatherAppDelegate.h";
```

Then in the viewDidLoad: method, we need to populate the reference to the application delegate and use the value of the updateLocation Boolean declared earlier to set the state of the UISwitch. Add the lines shown in bold:

```
- (void)viewDidLoad {
    [super viewDidLoad];
    self.view.backgroundColor = [UIColor viewFlipsideBackgroundColor];

    appDelegate = (WeatherAppDelegate *)
      [[UIApplication sharedApplication] delegate];
    toggleSwitch.on = appDelegate.updateLocation;

}
```

In the done: method, which is called when the user clicks on the Done button to close the flipside view, we must set the same updateLocation Boolean variable in the application delegate to be that of the state of the switch. If the user has changed the switch state on the flip side, it will now be reflected in the application delegate. Add the line shown in bold:

```
- (IBAction)done {
    appDelegate.updateLocation = toggleSwitch.on;
    [self.delegate flipsideViewControllerDidFinish:self];
}
```

Next, provide an implementation of the `switchThrown:` method that you'll attach to the `UISwitch` in Interface Builder:

```
-(IBAction)switchThrown {
    NSLog(@"Switch thrown");
    if ( toggleSwitch.on ) {
        [appDelegate.locationManager startUpdatingLocation];
    } else {
        [appDelegate.locationManager stopUpdatingLocation];
    }
}
```

Finally, remember to release the `toggleSwitch` inside the `dealloc:` method:

```
- (void)dealloc {
    [toggleSwitch release];
    [super dealloc];
}
```

Now let's add that switch to the flipside view. Make sure you've saved all your changes and then double-click on the *FlipsideView.xib* file to open it in Interface Builder. Drag and drop a label (`UILabel`) and a switch (`UISwitch`) element from the Library window into the Flipside View window. Position them and adjust the attributes (⌘-1) of the label so that your layout looks like Figure 10-3.

Click File's Owner, open the Connections Inspector (⌘-2), and connect the `toggleSwitch` outlet to the `UISwitch`. Then connect the `switchThrown:` action to the `UISwitch`'s Value Changed event. While you're here, double-click on the navigation bar title and change the text to "Preferences". Save your changes; we're done here.

We've reached a natural point to take a break and test the application. Save *Flipside-View.xib* and return to Xcode. Then click the Build and Run button in the Xcode toolbar to compile and deploy the Weather application into the simulator. Once it's running, click the Info button to go to the flip side of the application and toggle the switch. If you look at the Debugger Console (Run→Console in the Xcode menu bar), you should (after a small amount of time) see something that looks a lot like Figure 10-4.

iPhone Simulator will always report its location as being at Lat. +37.33168900, Long. −122.03073100, corresponding to 1 Infinite Loop, Cupertino, CA.

Quit the simulator. Back in Xcode, click on the *MainViewController.h* interface file to open it in the editor. Since we're now going to have multiple locations, we need somewhere to store the name of the location that we'll get back from the reverse geocoder. So, add an `NSString` to *MainViewController.h* (somewhere inside the opening and closing curly braces after the `@interface` directive) to store the location:

```
NSString *location;
```

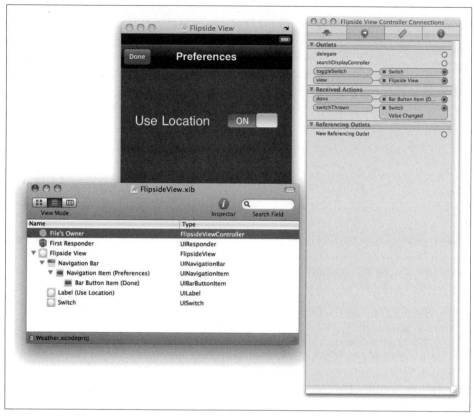

Figure 10-3. Adding the UISwitch to the FlipsideView controller

Then expose this and the `UIActivityIndicator` (we're going to use that shortly) as properties. Add the following just before the `@end` directive:

```
@property(nonatomic, retain) UIActivityIndicatorView *loadingActivityIndicator;
@property(nonatomic, retain) NSString *location;
```

Since we've declared `location` and `loadingActivityIndicator` as properties, go back to the implementation file (*MainViewController.m*) and add these lines to synthesize those properties:

```
@synthesize loadingActivityIndicator;
@synthesize location;
```

Then in the `viewDidLoad:` method, initialize the location string:

```
- (void)viewDidLoad {
    [super viewDidLoad];
    location = [[NSString alloc] init];
    [self refreshView:self];
}
```

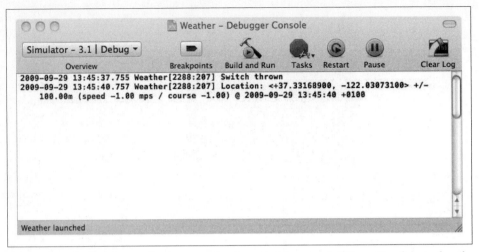

Figure 10-4. The Weather application reporting the current location (of iPhone Simulator) when the flipside switch is thrown

Make sure it is released in the `dealloc:` method:

```
- (void)dealloc {
    [location release];
    ... rest of the method not shown ...
}
```

Next, in the `refreshView:` method, check whether the app is monitoring the device's location so that you know whether to query the Google Weather Service with the default location (London, UK) or with the current location:

```
- (IBAction)refreshView:(id)sender {
    [loadingActivityIndicator startAnimating];

    WeatherAppDelegate *appDelegate =
        (WeatherAppDelegate *)[[UIApplication sharedApplication] delegate];
    if( appDelegate.updateLocation ) {
        NSLog( @"updating for location = %@", self.location );
        [forecast queryService:self.location withParent:self];

    } else {
        [forecast queryService:@"London,UK" withParent:self];
    }

}
```

Since we've made use of the application delegate, we need to make sure we import it into the `MainViewController` implementation. Add this line to the top of the file:

```
#import "WeatherAppDelegate.h"
```

Now we're done with the view controller.

What's left to do? First, we need to build a class to query the GeoNames reverse geocoder service, and then we need to pass the latitude and longitude to the reverse geocoder service from the `CLLocationManager` delegate method `locationManager:didUp dateToLocation:fromLocation:` in the application delegate.

 Since we're going to make use of the JSON service, we need to add the JSON parser to our project in the same way we did in Chapter 8 for the Twitter Trends application. See "Parsing JSON" on page 199 in Chapter 8 for details on how to add the *json-framework* library to your project.

Right-click on the Other Sources group in the Groups & Files pane of the Xcode interface and select Add→New Files. In the New File pop up, make sure Cocoa Touch Class (under iPhone OS) is selected. Next, choose "Objective-C class", a subclass of `NSObject`, and click the Next button. Name the new class "FindNearbyPlace" when prompted and click Finish.

Click on the *FindNearbyPlace.h* interface file and modify the template so that it looks like the following code:

```
#import <Foundation/Foundation.h>

@class WeatherAppDelegate;

@interface FindNearbyPlace : NSObject {
    WeatherAppDelegate *appDelegate;
    NSMutableData *responseData;
    NSURL *theURL;
}

- (void)queryServiceWithLat:(NSString *)latitude
  andLong:(NSString *)longitude;

@end
```

Modify the *FindNearbyPlace.m* implementation file so that it looks like the following code. You may recognize this code from Chapter 8; apart from the `connectionDidFinish Loading:` method, it's almost identical to the Trends API code we wrote for the Twitter Trends application:

```
#import "WeatherAppDelegate.h"
#import "MainViewController.h"
#import "FindNearbyPlace.h"
#import "JSON/JSON.h"

@implementation FindNearbyPlace

- (void)queryServiceWithLat:(NSString *)latitude
  andLong:(NSString *)longitude
{

    appDelegate = (WeatherAppDelegate *)
```

```
        [[UIApplication sharedApplication] delegate];
    responseData = [[NSMutableData data] retain];

    NSString *url = [NSString stringWithFormat:
      @"http://ws.geonames.org/findNearbyPlaceNameJSON?lat=%@&lng=%@",
      latitude, longitude];
    theURL = [[NSURL URLWithString:url] retain];
    NSURLRequest *request = [NSURLRequest requestWithURL:theURL];
    [[NSURLConnection alloc] initWithRequest:request delegate:self];

}

- (NSURLRequest *)connection:(NSURLConnection *)connection
  willSendRequest:(NSURLRequest *)request
  redirectResponse:(NSURLResponse *)redirectResponse
{
    [theURL autorelease];
    theURL = [[request URL] retain];
    return request;
}

- (void)connection:(NSURLConnection *)connection
  didReceiveResponse:(NSURLResponse *)response
{
    [responseData setLength:0];
}

- (void)connection:(NSURLConnection *)connection
  didReceiveData:(NSData *)data
{
    [responseData appendData:data];
}

- (void)connection:(NSURLConnection *)connection
  didFailWithError:(NSError *)error
{
    // Handle Error
}

- (void)connectionDidFinishLoading:(NSURLConnection *)connection {
    NSString *content =
      [[NSString alloc] initWithBytes:[responseData bytes]
                        length:[responseData length]
                        encoding:NSUTF8StringEncoding];
    NSLog(@"Content = %@", content);

    SBJSON *parser = [[SBJSON alloc] init];
    NSDictionary *json = [parser objectWithString:content];
    NSArray *geonames = [json objectForKey:@"geonames"];

    NSString *city = [[NSString alloc] init];
    NSString *state = [[NSString alloc] init];
    NSString *country = [[NSString alloc] init];
    for (NSDictionary *name in geonames) {
        city = [name objectForKey:@"name"];
```

```
        state = [name objectForKey:@"adminCode1"];
        country = [name objectForKey:@"countryName"];
    }
    [parser release];

    NSLog( @"Location = %@, %@, %@", city, state, country );

    NSString *string = [NSString stringWithFormat:@"%@,%@", city, state];
    appDelegate.mainViewController.location = string;❶
    [appDelegate.mainViewController.loadingActivityIndicator
        stopAnimating];❷
    [appDelegate.mainViewController refreshView: self];❸

}

-(void)dealloc {
    [appDelegate release];
    [responseData release];
    [theURL release];
    [super dealloc];
}

@end
```

❶ This sets the location string in our `MainViewController` class.

❷ This stops the loading indicator spinning in the `MainViewController` class.

❸ This refreshes the main view managed by the `MainViewController` class.

Now we have the class to query and parse the reverse geocoder service; we just need to write the code in the `locationManager:didUpdateToLocation:fromLocation:` delegate method.

Click on the application delegate implementation file (*WeatherAppDelegate.m*) to open it in the Xcode editor and import the geocoder class by adding this line at the top:

```
#import "FindNearbyPlace.h"
```

Next, in the `didUpdateToLocation:` method, add the code shown in bold:

```
- (void)locationManager:(CLLocationManager *)manager
  didUpdateToLocation:(CLLocation *)newLocation
  fromLocation:(CLLocation *)oldLocation
{
    NSLog(@"Location: %@", [newLocation description]);

    if ( newLocation != oldLocation ) {

        [self.mainViewController.loadingActivityIndicator
            startAnimating];❶
        FindNearbyPlace *find = [[FindNearbyPlace alloc] init];
        NSString *latitude = [NSString stringWithFormat:@"%f",
                                    newLocation.coordinate.latitude];
        NSString *longitude = [NSString stringWithFormat:@"%f",
                                    newLocation.coordinate.longitude];
```

```
            [find queryServiceWithLat:latitude andLong:longitude];
    }
}
```

❶ This starts the activity indicator spinning. We'll stop it when we've parsed the JSON returned by the GeoNames service and we're ready to refresh the view in the `con nectionDidFinishLoading:` method of the `FindNearbyPlace` class.

Here we simply retrieve the latitude and longitude from the `CLLocation` object, and we pass them to our `FindNearbyPlace` class to resolve. There the `connectionDidFinishLoad ing:` method takes care of updating the main view controller.

We're done. Save your changes and click Build and Run to compile and deploy the application in iPhone Simulator. Once it's running, click the Info button to go to the flip side of the application and toggle the switch. Click the Done button and return to the main view. After a little while the activity indicator in the top-righthand corner should start spinning and the weather information should change from being for London to being for Cupertino, California.

Tidying up

Don't be fooled. The application has many dangling loose ends to clean up before it can be considered "ready for release." For instance, in the `FindNearbyPlace` class we concatenate the city and state to create the location we pass to the Google Weather Service:

```
city = [name objectForKey:@"name"];
state = [name objectForKey:@"adminCode1"];
NSString *string = [NSString stringWithFormat:@"%@,%@", city, state];

appDelegate.mainViewController.location = string;
```

While this works for U.S. locations (`Cupertino, CA`), it fails for British locations where you end up with a string of the form `London,ENG`, which the Weather service can't understand.

However, as it stands, it's a nice starting point for integrating multiple web services into a single application.

Using the Accelerometer

The iPhone's accelerometer measures the linear acceleration of the device so that it can report its roll and pitch, but not its yaw.

Yaw, *pitch*, and *roll* refer to the rotation of the device in three axes. If you think about an aircraft in the sky, pushing the nose down or pulling it up modifies the pitch angle of the aircraft. However, if you keep the nose straight ahead, you can also modify the roll of the aircraft using the flaps; one wing will come up, the other will go down. Finally, keeping the wings level you can use the tail flap to change the heading (or yaw) of the aircraft (rotating it in a 2D plane).

If you are dealing with an iPhone 3GS, which has a digital compass, you can combine the accelerometer and magnetometer readings to have roll, pitch, and yaw measurements (see the following section for details on how to access the magnetometer).

The accelerometer reports three figures: X, Y, and Z (see Figure 10-5). Acceleration values for each axis are reported directly by the hardware as G-force values. Therefore, a value of 1.0 represents a load of approximately 1-gravity (Earth's gravity). X corresponds to roll, Y to pitch, and Z to whether the device is front side up or front side down, with a value of 0.0 being reported when the iPhone is edge-on.

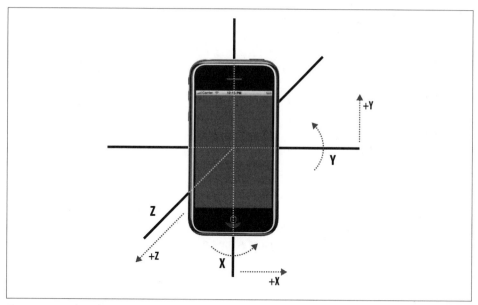

Figure 10-5. The iPhone accelerometer axes

When dealing with acceleration measurements, you must keep in mind that the accelerometer is measuring just that: the linear acceleration of the device. When at rest (in whatever orientation), the figures represent the force of gravity acting on the device, and correspond to the roll and pitch of the device (in the X and Y directions at least). But while in motion, the figures represent the acceleration due to gravity, plus the acceleration of the device itself relative to its rest frame.

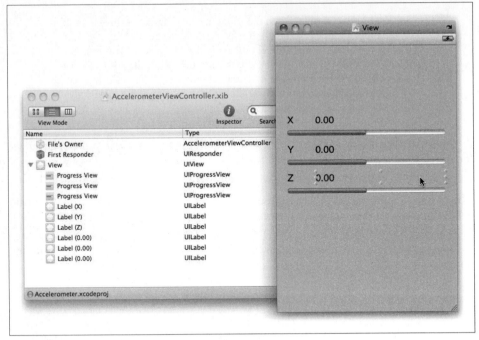

Figure 10-6. The Accelerometer application UI

Writing an Accelerometer Application

 You can follow along while I build this application in a screencast available on the book's website (*http://learningiphoneprogramming.com/pages/accelerometer.html*).

Let's implement a simple view-based application to illustrate how to approach the accelerometer. Open Xcode and start a new iPhone project, select a View-based Application template, and name the project "Accelerometer" when prompted for a name.

Before jumping back into Xcode to show you how to use the accelerometer, we're going to build the UI for the application. Double-click on the *AccelerometerViewController.xib* NIB file to open it in Interface Builder.

We're going to both report the raw figures from the accelerometer and display them using a UIProgressView element. So, drag and drop three progress bars along with labels for those bars into the View window. After you do that, it should look something like Figure 10-6. I've used two labels for each progress bar: one to hold the X, Y, or Z and the other to hold the accelerometer measurements.

Make sure you've saved your changes, and close Interface Builder and return to Xcode. Click on the *AccelerometerViewController.h* interface file to open it in the Xcode editor.

We're going to declare three **UILabel** and three **UIProgressView** variables as **IBOutlet**s. Since they aren't going to be used outside the class, there isn't much point in declaring them as class properties. We'll also declare a **UIAccelerometer** instance. Here's how the *AccelerometerViewController.h* interface file should look when you are done:

```
#import <UIKit/UIKit.h>

@interface AccelerometerViewController :
  UIViewController <UIAccelerometerDelegate> {❶
    IBOutlet UILabel *xLabel;
    IBOutlet UILabel *yLabel;
    IBOutlet UILabel *zLabel;

    IBOutlet UIProgressView *xBar;
    IBOutlet UIProgressView *yBar;
    IBOutlet UIProgressView *zBar;

    UIAccelerometer *accelerometer;

}

@end
```

❶ Here we declare that the class implements the **UIAccelerometer** delegate protocol.

Make sure you've saved your changes and click on the corresponding *Accelerometer-ViewController.m* implementation file to open it in the Xcode editor. We don't actually have to do very much here, as Interface Builder is going to handle most of the heavy lifting. Here's what the file should look like when you are done:

```
#import "AccelerometerViewController.h"

@implementation AccelerometerViewController

- (void)viewDidLoad {
    accelerometer = [UIAccelerometer sharedAccelerometer];❶
    accelerometer.updateInterval = 0.1;❷
    accelerometer.delegate = self;❸
    [super viewDidLoad];
}

- (void)didReceiveMemoryWarning {
    [super didReceiveMemoryWarning];
}

- (void)dealloc {
    [xLabel release];
    [yLabel release];
    [zLabel release];
    [xBar release];
    [yBar release];
    [zBar release];

    accelerometer.delegate = nil;
    [accelerometer release];
```

```
    [super dealloc];
}

#pragma mark UIAccelerometerDelegate Methods

- (void)accelerometer:(UIAccelerometer *)meter
  didAccelerate:(UIAcceleration *)acceleration❹
{
    xLabel.text = [NSString stringWithFormat:@"%f", acceleration.x];
    xBar.progress = ABS(acceleration.x);

    yLabel.text = [NSString stringWithFormat:@"%f", acceleration.y];
    yBar.progress = ABS(acceleration.y);

    zLabel.text = [NSString stringWithFormat:@"%f", acceleration.z];
    zBar.progress = ABS(acceleration.z);
}

@end
```

❶ The UIAccelerometer is a singleton object, so we grab a reference to the singleton rather than allocate and initialize a new instance of the class.

❷ We set the update interval to 0.1 s, hence the accelerometer:didAccelerate: method will be called 10 times every second.

❸ We declare that this class is the delegate for the UIAccelerometer.

❹ We implement the accelerometer:didAccelerate: delegate method and use it to set the X, Y, and Z labels to the raw accelerometer readings, and the progress bar values to the absolute value (the value without regard to sign) of the accelerometer reading, each time it is called.

All we need to do now is connect the outlets to the UI elements we created earlier and we're done. Make sure you've saved your changes to the code and double-click on the *AccelerometerViewController.xib* file to go back into Interface Builder.

Click on File's Owner, and go to the Connections Inspector (⌘-2) and connect the xLabel, yLabel, and zLabel outlets to the appropriate UILabel elements in the View window. Then connect the xBar, yBar, and zBar outlets to the corresponding UIProg ressBar elements, as shown in Figure 10-7.

OK, we're done. Save the NIB and return to Xcode. Before you click the Build and Run button, make sure you've configured the project to deploy onto your iPhone or iPod touch to test it. Since this application makes use of the accelerometer, and iPhone Simulator doesn't have one, we're going to have to test it directly on the device. We covered deploying applications onto your iPhone or iPod touch at the end of Chapter 3.

If all goes well, you should see something that looks a lot like Figure 10-8.

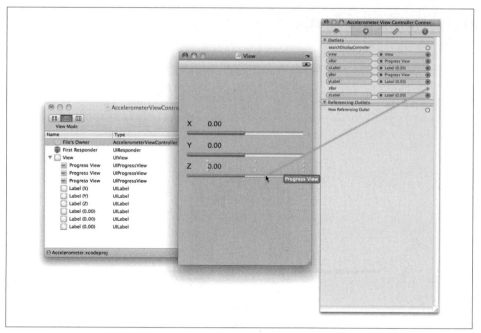

Figure 10-7. Connecting the outlets to the UI elements

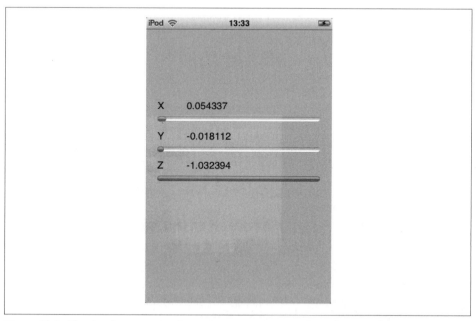

Figure 10-8. The Accelerometer application running on an iPod touch sitting face-up on my desk, measuring a 1-gravity acceleration straight down

Using the Digital Compass

In addition to the accelerometer, the iPhone 3GS has a magnetometer that acts as a digital compass. Combining the heading (yaw) information (see Figure 10-9) returned by this device with the roll and pitch information returned by the accelerometer will let you determine the true orientation of the iPhone in real time.

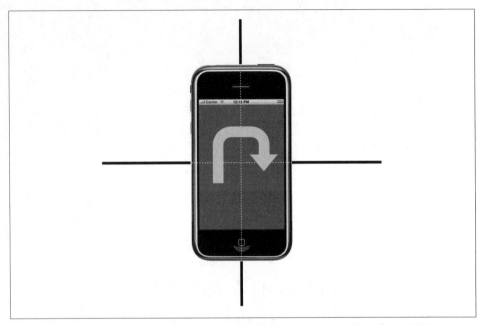

Figure 10-9. Using the magnetometer (a.k.a. the digital compass) in the iPhone 3GS, you can determine the heading (yaw) of the device

You should be aware that the magnetometer is measuring the strength of the magnetic field surrounding the device. In the absence of any strong local fields, these measurements will be of Earth's ambient magnetic field, allowing the device to determine its "heading" with respect to the geomagnetic North Pole. The geomagnetic heading and true heading, relative to the geographical North Pole, can vary widely (by several tens of degrees depending on your location).

As well as reporting the current location, the CLLocationManager class can, in the case where the device's hardware supports it, report the current heading of the device. The following code will create an instance of the class, and will send both location and heading update messages to the designated delegate class:

```
CLLocationManager *locationManager = [[CLLocationManager alloc] init];
locationManager.delegate = self;
if( locationManager.locationServicesEnabled &&
        locationManager.headingAvailable)❶
{
```

```
[locationManager startUpdatingLocation];
[locationManager startUpdatingHeading];
} else {
  NSLog(@"Can't report heading");
}
```

❶ It's even more important to check whether heading information is available than it is to check whether location services are available, as the availability of heading information is currently restricted to iPhone 3GS devices only.

We can filter these update messages based on an angular filter. Changes in heading of less than this amount will not generate an update message to the delegate:

```
locationManager.headingFilter = 5;  // 5 degrees
```

The default value of this property is kCLHeadingFilterNone. Use this value if you want to be notified of all heading updates.

The CLLocationManagerDelegate protocol offers a method that is called when the heading is updated:

```
- (void)locationManager:(CLLocationManager*)manager
  didUpdateHeading:(CLHeading*)newHeading
{
  // If the accuracy is valid, process the event.
  if (newHeading.headingAccuracy > 0)
  {
    CLLocationDirection theHeading = newHeading.magneticHeading;

    // Do something with the event data.
  }
}
```

If location updates are also enabled, the location manager returns both true heading and magnetic heading values. If location updates are not enabled, the location manager returns only the magnetic heading value:

```
CLLocationDirection trueHeading = newHeading.trueHeading;
```

As I mentioned previously, the magnetometer readings will be affected by local magnetic fields, so the CLLocationManager will attempt to calibrate its heading readings by displaying a heading calibration panel before it starts to issue update messages. However, before it does so, it will call the locationManagerShouldDisplayHeadingCalibration: delegate method:

```
- (BOOL)locationManagerShouldDisplayHeadingCalibration:
(CLLocationManager *)manager {
  ... code not shown ...
}
```

If you return YES from this method, the CLLocationManager will proceed to display the device calibration panel on top of the current window. The calibration panel prompts the user to move the device in a figure-eight pattern so that Core Location can distinguish between Earth's magnetic field and any local magnetic fields. The panel will

remain visible until calibration is complete or until you dismiss it by calling the
dismissHeadingCalibrationDisplay: method in the CLLocationManager class.

Accessing the Proximity Sensor

The proximity and ambient light sensors are two separate sensors. The ambient light
sensor is used to change the brightness level of the device's screen automatically, while
the proximity sensor is used by the device to turn the screen off when you put the phone
to your ear to make a call. Although it does have an ambient light sensor, the iPod touch
does not have a proximity sensor.

Unfortunately, there is no way to access the ambient light sensor in the official SDK.
However, developers can access the proximity sensor via the UIDevice class. This sensor
is an infrared LED emitter/detector pair positioned near the earpiece, as shown in
Figure 10-10. It measures the return reflection of the transmitted infrared beam to detect
(large) objects near the phone.

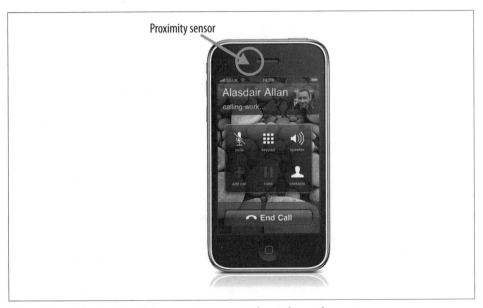

Figure 10-10. The IR LED of the proximity sensor is located near the earpiece

You can enable the sensor in your application by toggling the proximityMonitoringEn
abled Boolean:

```
UIDevice *device = [UIDevice currentDevice];
device.proximityMonitoringEnabled = YES;
```

You can query whether the proximity sensor is close to the user:

```
BOOL state = device.proximityState;
```

If proximity monitoring is enabled, a UIDeviceProximityStateDidChangeNotification notification will be posted by the UIDevice when the state of the proximity sensor changes; you can ask that your application is notified when this occurs by registering your class as an observer with the notification center:

```
[[NSNotificationCenter defaultCenter]
  addObserver:self selector:@selector(proximityChanged:)
  name:@"UIDeviceProximityStateDidChangeNotification" object:nil];
```

Notifications would then get received by the proximityChanged: method:

```
- (void) proximityChanged: (NSNotification *)note {
  UIDevice *device = [note object];
  NSLog(@"In proximity: %i", device.proximityState);
}
```

Using Vibration

The motor that controls vibration is not a sensor; technically, it's an actuator. Because sensors and actuators generally go hand in hand, we'll look at the capability here.

Making the iPhone vibrate is a simple system call. You first need to add the Audio-Toolbox framework to your project (right- or Ctrl-click on Frameworks, then use the Add Existing Frameworks option), and then import the AudioToolbox headers into the class where you intend to trigger the vibration:

```
#import <AudioToolbox/AudioToolbox.h>
```

At this point, you can make the device produce a short buzz by calling the following method:

```
AudioServicesPlaySystemSound(kSystemSoundID_Vibrate);
```

Unfortunately, despite the fact that the underlying (private) Telephony framework offers relatively subtle levels of control over the vibration pattern, the official support in the SDK is limited to this single call.

You need to be careful about using the vibration feature. Using continuous vibration, or using a timer to maintain the vibration, is a reason for rejection during the App Store review process.

CHAPTER 11

Geolocation and Mapping

The Core Location API is one of the great things about the iPhone and iPod touch platforms, but until the arrival of the MapKit Framework in the 3.0 SDK, it was actually quite hard to take that location-aware goodness and display it on a map. The arrival of the MapKit framework has simplified this enormously.

Let's work through a few example applications to get you familiar with the framework.

User Location

> You can follow along while I build this application in a screencast available on the book's website (*http://learningiphoneprogramming.com/pages/whereami.html*).

The first thing we're going to do is build a simple application to answer the question "Where am I?". Start a new iPhone project in Xcode, select a view-based template, and name the project "WhereAmI" when prompted.

Next, you need to add the MapKit and Core Location frameworks to your new project. You do not need the Core Location framework to work with MapKit, but we're going to use it later in the chapter, so we may as well add it now:

1. Right-click on the Frameworks group in the Groups & Files pane in Xcode and select Add→Existing Frameworks. In the pop-up window that appears, select the MapKit framework and click Add.

2. Do this a second time, but for the Core Location framework.

If you have upgraded your Xcode (and iPhone SDK) distribution in the middle of developing a project, *MapKit.framework* may not show up in the list of frameworks Xcode presents in the framework selection pop up. In this case, you may be able to resolve the problem by opening the Targets group in the Groups & Files pane in Xcode, right-clicking on the application's target, and selecting Get Info. Navigate to the Build pane of the Target Info window and set the Base SDK of your project to the SDK you currently have installed (rather than the SDK with which you initially developed the project).

If this doesn't resolve the problem, you may have to add the framework manually. Click on the Add Other button in the bottom left of the window. The *MapKit.framework* framework is located in the */Developer/ Platforms/iPhoneOS.platform/Developer/SDKs/<iPhoneOSX.X.sdk>/ System/Library/Frameworks/* directory and you should be able to add it manually. Replace *<iPhoneOSX.X.sdk>* with your current SDK version.

Once that's done, click on the *WhereAmIViewController.h* interface file to open it in the Xcode editor and add a map view instance to the class, along with the `imports` needed for Core Location and MapKit:

```
#import <UIKit/UIKit.h>
#import <MapKit/MapKit.h>
#import <CoreLocation/CoreLocation.h>

@interface WhereAmIViewController : UIViewController {
    MKMapView *mapView;
}

@property (nonatomic, retain) IBOutlet MKMapView *mapView;

@end
```

Then click on the corresponding implementation file (*WhereAmIViewController.m*) to open it in the Xcode editor. Make sure you synthesize the `mapView` property, remove the /* and */ comment delimiters from `viewDidLoad:`, and release the `mapView` property in the `dealloc:` method:

```
#import "WhereAmIViewController.h"

@implementation WhereAmIViewController

@synthesize mapView;

- (void)viewDidLoad {
    [super viewDidLoad];
}

- (void)didReceiveMemoryWarning {
    [super didReceiveMemoryWarning];
}

- (void)viewDidUnload {
```

```
    }

    - (void)dealloc {
        [mapView release];
        [super dealloc];
    }

    @end
```

Save your changes to the `WhereAmIViewController` class and double-click on the *Where-AmIViewController.xib* file to open it in Interface Builder. Drag and drop an `MKMap View` from the Library window into the View window. Now click on File's Owner, select the Attributes Inspector (⌘-2), and connect the `mapView` outlet to the `MKMapView`, as shown in Figure 11-1.

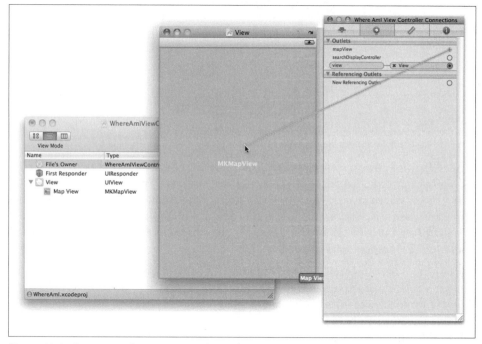

Figure 11-1. Connecting the mapView outlet to the MKMapView

We're done for now in Interface Builder. Save your changes to the NIB file and go back into Xcode and click the Build and Run button on the Xcode toolbar to build and deploy your application in iPhone Simulator. You should see something similar to Figure 11-2.

It's not amazingly interesting so far, so let's use Core Location to change that.

Figure 11-2. The default map view in iPhone Simulator

While MapKit knows the current user location and can mark it on the map (you'll see the property that enables this, `showsUserLocation`, in the `didUpdateToLoca tion:fromLocation:` method shortly), there is no way to monitor it or update the current map view when the location changes. So, we're going to implement an application that uses Core Location to determine and zoom to the current location and then display the standard user location marker using MapKit.

Click on the *WhereAmIAppDelegate.h* interface file to open it in the Xcode editor. We're going to declare that the application delegate also implements the `CLLocationManager Delegate` protocol, and add a `locationManager` property to the class declaration. Make the changes shown in bold to this interface file:

```
#import <UIKit/UIKit.h>
#import <CoreLocation/CoreLocation.h>

@class WhereAmIViewController;

@interface WhereAmIAppDelegate : NSObject
  <UIApplicationDelegate, CLLocationManagerDelegate>
{
    UIWindow *window;

    CLLocationManager *locationManager;
```

```
        WhereAmIViewController *viewController;
}

@property (nonatomic, retain) IBOutlet UIWindow *window;
@property (nonatomic, retain) IBOutlet CLLocationManager *locationManager;
@property (nonatomic, retain) IBOutlet WhereAmIViewController *viewController;

@end
```

In the implementation file (*WhereAmIAppDelegate.m*), we need to create an instance of the location manager and start updating our location (see "The Core Location Framework" on page 254 in Chapter 10 for an overview of the location manager):

```
#import "WhereAmIAppDelegate.h"
#import "WhereAmIViewController.h"

@implementation WhereAmIAppDelegate

@synthesize window;
@synthesize locationManager;
@synthesize viewController;

- (void)applicationDidFinishLaunching:(UIApplication *)application {
    self.locationManager = [[[CLLocationManager alloc] init] autorelease];
    if ( self.locationManager.locationServicesEnabled ) {
        self.locationManager.delegate = self;
        self.locationManager.distanceFilter = 1000;
        [self.locationManager startUpdatingLocation];
    }
    [window addSubview:viewController.view];
    [window makeKeyAndVisible];
}

- (void)dealloc {
    [viewController release];
    [window release];
    [super dealloc];
}

@end
```

Now we must implement the locationManager:didUpdateToLocation:fromLocation: delegate method. Add the following to *WhereAmIAppDelegate.m*:

```
- (void)locationManager:(CLLocationManager *)manager
  didUpdateToLocation:(CLLocation *)newLocation
  fromLocation:(CLLocation *)oldLocation {

    double miles = 12.0;
    double scalingFactor =
      ABS( cos(2 * M_PI * newLocation.coordinate.latitude /360.0) );

    MKCoordinateSpan span;
    span.latitudeDelta = miles/69.0;
    span.longitudeDelta = miles/( scalingFactor*69.0 );
```

```
        MKCoordinateRegion region;
        region.span = span;
        region.center = newLocation.coordinate;

        [viewController.mapView setRegion:region animated:YES];
        viewController.mapView.showsUserLocation = YES;
    }
```

Here we set the map region to be 12 miles square, centered on the current location. Then we zoom in and display the current user location.

The number of miles spanned by a degree of longitude range varies based on the current latitude. For example, one degree of longitude spans a distance of ~69 miles at the equator but shrinks to 0 at the poles. However, unlike longitudinal distances, which vary based on the latitude, one degree of latitude is always ~69 miles (ignoring variations due to the slightly ellipsoidal shape of Earth).

Length of 1 degree of Longitude (miles) = cosine (latitude) × 69 (miles)

Click the Build and Run button on the Xcode toolbar to build and deploy your application in iPhone Simulator. You should see something like Figure 11-3.

Figure 11-3. The map view showing the current user location

Before leaving this example, let's add one more feature to display the current latitude and longitude on top of the map. Open the *WhereAmIViewController.h* interface file and add two outlets to UILabel for the latitude and longitude values:

```
@interface WhereAmIViewController : UIViewController {

    MKMapView *mapView;
    UILabel *latitude;
    UILabel *longitude;

}

@property (nonatomic, retain) IBOutlet MKMapView *mapView;
@property (nonatomic, retain) IBOutlet UILabel *latitude;
@property (nonatomic, retain) IBOutlet UILabel *longitude;

@end
```

Since we've added these two properties, we need to synthesize them in the corresponding implementation file, and additionally remember to release them in the `dealloc:` method. Make the changes shown in bold to *WhereAmIViewController.m*:

```
@implementation WhereAmIViewController

@synthesize mapView;
@synthesize latitude;
@synthesize longitude;

... some code not shown ...

- (void)dealloc {
    [mapView release];
    [latitude release];
    [longitude release];
    [super dealloc];
}

@end
```

Make sure you've saved those changes and double-click on the *WhereAmIViewController.xib* file to open it in Interface Builder. Drag and drop a round rect button (UIButton) onto the view, resizing it roughly to the size shown in Figure 11-4.

We're going to use the button as a backdrop for latitude and longitude labels. It's actually a fairly common trick to do this as it gives a nice box with rounded corners, but you must uncheck the User Interaction Enabled box in the View section of the Attributes Inspector (⌘-1). This will disable the user's ability to select the button. If you're uncomfortable doing this, you could equally well use a UIImage as a backdrop, or simply set the UILabel backgrounds to white or another appropriate color.

Next, drag and drop two labels from the Library onto the button in the View window and change the label contents to be "Latitude" and "Longitude". Finally, drag and drop two more labels onto the button and position them next to the previous two and set

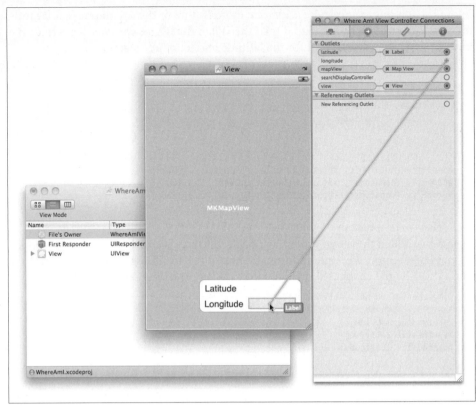

Figure 11-4. Connecting the label outlets in Interface Builder

the contents to be blank. Now click on File's Owner, go to the Attributes tab of the Inspector window, and connect the longitude and latitude outlets to your two blank labels, as shown in Figure 11-4.

Save your changes to the NIB file. Back in Xcode, click on the *WhereAmIAppDelegate.m* file to open it in the Xcode editor. Now all you have to do is populate the two labels you added. In the `locationManager:didUpdateToLocation:fromLocation:` method, add the lines shown in bold:

```
- (void)locationManager:(CLLocationManager *)manager
  didUpdateToLocation:(CLLocation *)newLocation
  fromLocation:(CLLocation *)oldLocation
{
    MKCoordinateSpan span;
    span.latitudeDelta = 0.2;
    span.longitudeDelta = 0.2;

    MKCoordinateRegion region;
    region.span = span;
    region.center = newLocation.coordinate;
```

```
        [viewController.mapView setRegion:region animated:YES];
        viewController.mapView.showsUserLocation = YES;
        viewController.latitude.text =
          [NSString stringWithFormat:@"%f", newLocation.coordinate.latitude];
        viewController.longitude.text =
          [NSString stringWithFormat:@"%f", newLocation.coordinate.longitude];
    }
```

Make sure you've saved your changes and click the Build and Run button in the Xcode toolbar. If all goes well, you should be presented with a view that looks similar to Figure 11-5.

Figure 11-5. The current user location

Annotating Maps

Like we did for the `UIWebView` in Chapter 7, here we're going to build some code that you'll be able to reuse in your own applications later. We're going to build a view controller that we can display modally, and which will display an `MKMapView` annotated with a marker pin and can then be dismissed, returning us to our application.

We can reuse the Prototype application code we built in Chapter 7, which I used to demonstrate how to use the web and mail composer views. Open the Finder and navigate to the location where you saved the *Prototype* project. Right-click on the folder containing the project files and select Duplicate; a folder called *Prototype copy* will be created containing a duplicate of our project. Rename the folder *Prototype3*, and just as we did when we rebuilt the Prototype application to demonstrate the mail composer, prune the application down to the stub with the Go! button and associated `pushedGo:` method we can use to trigger the display of our map view (see "Sending Email" on page 161 in Chapter 7 for details).

Now, right-click on the Classes group in the Groups & Files pane, select Add→New File, and select Cocoa Touch Class from the iPhone section. Create a `UIViewControl ler` subclass, leaving the "With XIB for user interface" checkbox ticked. Name the new class "MapViewController" when prompted.

> At this point, I normally rename the NIB file that Xcode automatically created, removing the "Controller" part of the filename and leaving it as *MapView.xib*, as I feel this is a neater naming scheme.

You'll need to add both the MapKit and the Core Location frameworks to your project, as you did in the preceding section, so that you can use the classes these frameworks offer.

> We're going to be using the Core Location and MapKit frameworks throughout this project; instead of having to include them every time we need them we can use the *Prototype_prefix.pch* header file to import them into all the source files in the project. Open this file (it's in the Other Sources group) and change it to read as follows:
>
> ```
> #ifdef OBJC__
>     #import <Foundation/Foundation.h>
>     #import <UIKit/UIKit.h>
>     #import <CoreLocation/CoreLocation.h>
>     #import <MapKit/MapKit.h>
> #endif
> ```
>
> This file is called a *prefix file* because it is prefixed to all of your source files. However, the compiler precompiles it separately; this means it does not have to reparse the file on each compile run, which can dramatically speed up your compile times on larger projects.

Let's start by creating the UI for the new map view. Double-click on the *MapView.xib* file to open the NIB file in Interface Builder. Drag and drop a navigation bar (`UINavigationBar`) from the Library window, positioning it at the top of the view. Then drag a map view (`MKMapView`) into the view and resize it to fill the remaining portion of the View window. Finally, drag a bar button item (`UIBarButtonItem`) onto the navigation bar, and in the Attributes Inspector (⌘-1) change its Style and Identifier to Done in the

Bar Button Item section of the tab. At this point, your view should look similar to Figure 11-6.

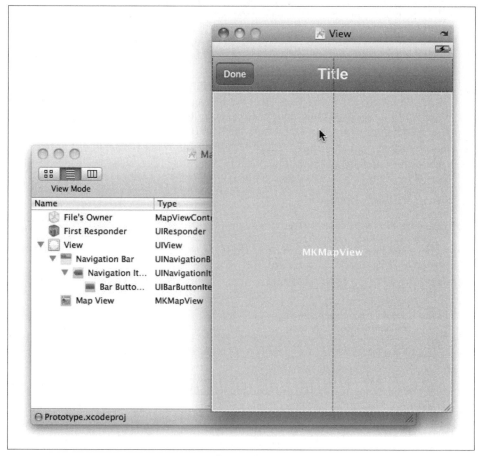

Figure 11-6. Creating our map view in Interface Builder

After saving the changes to the *MapView.xib* file, close it and return to Xcode. Open the *MapViewController.h* interface file. Just as we did for the web view, we want to make this class self-contained so that we can reuse it without any modifications. Therefore, override the `init:` function again to pass the information you need when instantiating the object:

```
#import <UIKit/UIKit.h>

@interface MapViewController : UIViewController <MKMapViewDelegate> {
    CLLocationCoordinate2D theCoords;
    NSString *theTitle;
    NSString *theSubTitle;
    IBOutlet MKMapView *mapView;
```

```
        IBOutlet UINavigationItem *mapTitle;
}

- (id) initWithCoordinates:(CLLocationCoordinate2D)coordinates;
- (id) initWithCoordinates:(CLLocationCoordinate2D)coordinates
  andTitle:(NSString *)title;
- (id) initWithCoordinates:(CLLocationCoordinate2D)coordinates
  andTitle:(NSString *)title andSubTitle:(NSString *)subtitle;
- (IBAction) done:(id)sender;

@end
```

I've actually provided three independent init methods; which one you use depends on how much metadata you want to pass to the MapViewController class. If you look at the corresponding implementation in the *MapViewController.m* file, you'll notice that I've really only coded one of them. The other two are simply convenience methods that are chained to the first:

```
#import "MapViewController.h"

@implementation MapViewController

- (id) initWithCoordinates:(CLLocationCoordinate2D)coordinates
  andTitle:(NSString *)title andSubTitle:(NSString *)subtitle
{
    if ( self = [super init] ) {
        theTitle = title;
        theSubTitle = subtitle;
        theCoords = coordinates;
    }
    return self;
}

- (id) initWithCoordinates:(CLLocationCoordinate2D)coordinates
  andTitle:(NSString *)title
{
    return [self initWithCoordinates:coordinates
                andTitle:title andSubTitle:nil];
}

- (id) initWithCoordinates:(CLLocationCoordinate2D)coordinates
{
    return [self initWithCoordinates:coordinates
                andTitle:nil andSubTitle:nil];
}

- (IBAction) done:(id)sender {
    [self dismissModalViewControllerAnimated:YES];
}

- (void)viewDidLoad {
    [super viewDidLoad];
    mapTitle.title = theTitle;

    // code to add annotations goes here later
```

```
    }

    - (void)didReceiveMemoryWarning {
        [super didReceiveMemoryWarning];
    }

    - (void)dealloc {
        [theTitle release];
        [theSubTitle release];
        [mapView release];
        [mapTitle release];
        [super dealloc];
    }

    @end
```

Save your changes and click on the *PrototypeViewController.m* implementation file to open it in the Xcode editor. Import the `MapViewController` class:

```
#import "MapViewController.h"
```

Then replace the `pushedGo:` method with the following:

```
-(IBAction) pushedGo:(id)sender {
    CLLocationCoordinate2D coord = {37.331689, -122.030731};
    MapViewController *mapView =
      [[MapViewController alloc] initWithCoordinates:coord
                                 andTitle:@"Apple"
                                 andSubTitle:@"1 Infinite Loop"];
    [self presentModalViewController:mapView animated:YES];
    [mapView release];
}
```

Now we have to go back into Interface Builder and connect the web view up to our controller code. Open the *MapView.xib* file in Interface Builder and make sure the view mode is in list mode (⌘-Option-2). Expand all the nodes by Option-clicking on the disclosure triangle to the left of the view. Next, click on File's Owner and follow these steps:

1. In the Connections Inspector (⌘-2), connect the `mapTitle` outlet to the `UINaviga tionItem` "Navigation Item (Title)".

2. Connect the `mapView` outlet to the `MKMapView`.

3. Connect the `done:` received action to the `UIBarButtonItem` "Bar Button Item (Done)".

4. Click on the map view and connect the `delegate` outlet back to File's Owner.

At this point, if you click on File's Owner in the main NIB window and check the Connections tab, you should see something very much like Figure 11-7.

It's time to stop and test our application. Save the NIB file, return to Xcode, and click on the Build and Run button to compile and start the application in iPhone Simulator.

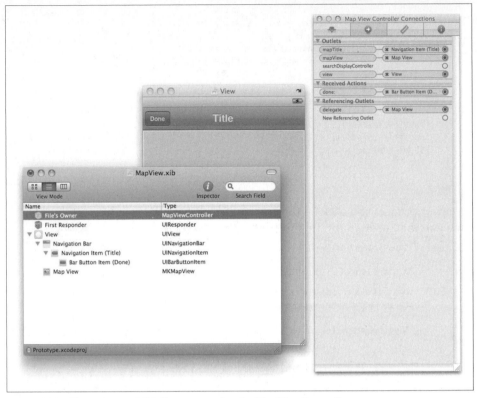

Figure 11-7. The map view NIB file connected to the MapViewController

Tap the Go! button and the map view should load. Right now we haven't specified any annotations, or a region, so you should just see a default world map (see Figure 11-8).

Let's change that. The first thing we need to do is create a class that implements the `MKAnnotation` protocol. Right-click on the Classes group in the Groups & Files pane, select Add→New File, and create a new Objective-C class (an `NSObject` subclass). Name the new class "SimpleAnnotation" when prompted.

Open the *SimpleAnnotation.h* interface file Xcode has just created in the editor and modify it as follows:

```
#import <Foundation/Foundation.h>

@interface SimpleAnnotation : NSObject
  <MKAnnotation>
{
    CLLocationCoordinate2D coordinate;
    NSString *title;
    NSString *subtitle;
}

@property (nonatomic, assign) CLLocationCoordinate2D coordinate;
```

```
@property (nonatomic, retain) NSString *title;
@property (nonatomic, retain) NSString *subtitle;

+ (id)annotationWithCoordinate:(CLLocationCoordinate2D)coord;
- (id)initWithCoordinate:(CLLocationCoordinate2D)coord;

@end
```

Figure 11-8. The initial main view (left) and the web view (right)

Then open the corresponding *SimpleAnnotation.m* implementation file, and make the changes shown here:

```
#import "SimpleAnnotation.h"

@implementation SimpleAnnotation

@synthesize coordinate;
@synthesize title;
@synthesize subtitle;

+ (id)annotationWithCoordinate:(CLLocationCoordinate2D)coord {
    return [[[[self class] alloc] initWithCoordinate:coord] autorelease];
}

- (id)initWithCoordinate:(CLLocationCoordinate2D)coord {
```

```
        if ( self = [super init] ) {
            self.coordinate = coord;
        }
        return self;
    }

    - (void)dealloc {
        [title release];
        [subtitle release];
        [super dealloc];
    }

    @end
```

The `SimpleAnnotation` class is just a container; it implements the `MKAnnotation` protocol to allow it to hold the coordinates and title (with subtitle) of our annotation.

Save your changes and click on the *MapViewController.m* implementation file to open it in the Xcode editor. Import the `SimpleAnnotation` class:

```
#import "SimpleAnnotation.h"
```

Edit the `viewDidLoad:` method to add the annotation using `theCoords`, `theTitle`, and `theSubTitle` passed to the `MapViewController` when it was initialized:

```
- (void)viewDidLoad {
    [super viewDidLoad];
    mapTitle.title = theTitle;

    SimpleAnnotation *annotation =
      [[SimpleAnnotation alloc] initWithCoordinate:theCoords];
    annotation.title = theTitle;
    annotation.subtitle = theSubTitle;

    MKCoordinateRegion region = { theCoords, {0.2, 0.2} };
    [mapView setRegion:region animated:NO];
    [mapView addAnnotation: annotation];
    [annotation release];
}
```

We're done. Make sure all your changes are saved, and click the Build and Run button in the Xcode toolbar to build and deploy your application in iPhone Simulator. If all goes well, clicking on the Go! button should give you a view that looks like Figure 11-9.

Figure 11-9. The finished MapViewController and its view

At this point, you have reusable `MapViewController` and `SimpleAnnotation` classes, along with an associated NIB file that you can drag and drop directly into your own projects.

You might want to think about some improvements if you do that, of course. For instance, you could easily expand the class to handle multiple annotations. While the annotations themselves can provide a much richer interface than a simple pushpin, look at the documentation for the `MKAnnotationView` class for some inspiration.

CHAPTER 12

Integrating Your Application

The iPhone offers standard view controllers for taking pictures with the camera and sending email from within your own application. The software ecosystem surrounding your application is extremely rich with such built-in services and applications. You should take advantage of these as much as possible. In this chapter, we'll look at how you can do that.

Application Preferences

Users look for application preferences in two main settings: in the application itself, and in the iPhone's Settings application. For simple applications, applications with few preferences, and applications with preferences that need to be modified regularly, you should keep the preferences within the application itself. However, for more complicated applications, applications with complicated or numerous different preferences, and applications with preferences that the user will rarely have to modify, it's preferable to use the Settings application.

 Despite it being done in some applications currently for sale on the App Store, Apple advises that you should never split your preferences between the Settings application and a custom settings screen inside your own application. According to Apple, "If you have preferences, pick one solution and use it exclusively." This is good advice; having multiple places to change settings is confusing not just for the user, but also for you as a developer.

Adding a preferences panel for your application to the main Settings application is easy. You do this by adding a special *Settings.bundle* file to your application and then configuring the *Root.plist* file contained inside the bundle in the Xcode editor.

When the built-in Settings application launches, it checks each third-party application for the presence of a Settings Bundle. For each bundle it finds, it displays the application's name and icon on the main page. When the user taps the row belonging to the application, Settings loads the *Root.plist* Settings Page file and uses that file to display your application's main page of preferences.

Let's add a Settings Bundle to the Where Am I? application we wrote in Chapter 11. Open the *WhereAmI* project in Xcode, right-click on the project's icon in the Groups & Files pane in Xcode, and select Add→New File. In the pop-up window that appears, click on the Resource category in the lefthand pane underneath iPhone OS, select Settings Bundle, as shown in Figure 12-1, and click Next. Accept the default suggested name of *Settings.bundle* when prompted.

You'll notice that the bundle appears in the Groups & Files pane in Xcode with an icon that looks a lot like a Lego brick. If you click on the arrow beside it to expand the bundle you'll see the *Root.plist* file that contains an XML description of the settings root page, and an *en.lproj* directory containing the localized string resource file (for English). You can add further localizations to your Settings Bundle if needed.

Figure 12-1. Adding a Settings Bundle to your application

The default Settings Bundle contains some example settings. Click on the Build and Run button in the Xcode toolbar to compile and deploy the application into iPhone Simulator. Tap the simulator's Home button to quit out of the application, and then find the Settings application on the Home screen. Tap the Settings application to open it, and you should see something similar to Figure 12-2.

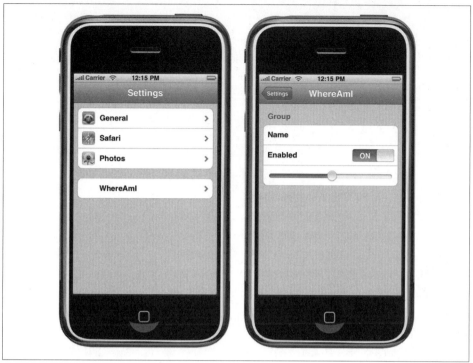

Figure 12-2. The simulator Settings application (left) with the default Settings Bundle we added to the Where Am I? application (right)

Since we haven't added an icon to the application (see "Adding an Icon" on page 225 in Chapter 9), the space to the left of the WhereAmI entry is blank; if we had added an icon it would be displayed next to our application name. If you now tap the WhereAmI entry, you'll be presented with the default preferences pane generated from the Settings Bundle, also shown in Figure 12-2.

 If a file called *Icon-Settings.png* (a 29×29-pixel image) is located at the top level of your application's bundle directory (drag it into the top level of your project under Groups & Files and check the box to copy the item), that icon is used to identify your application preferences in the Settings application. If no such image is present, the Settings application uses a scaled down version of your application's icon file instead.

Returning to Xcode, click on the *Root.plist* file inside *Settings.bundle* to open it in the Xcode editor, and you'll see the property list description of the Settings page. Option-click the disclosure triangle next to PreferencesSpecifiers, and you'll see all the settings, as shown in Figure 12-3.

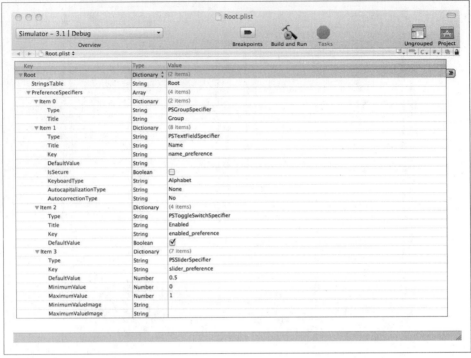

Figure 12-3. The Root.plist file in Settings.bundle

 Like any property list file, Xcode by default displays the *Root.plist* file as a key-value pair list. However, you can see the raw XML of the *Root.plist* property list by right-clicking on the Root key and selecting Open As→Source Code File.

If you compare Figures 12-2 and 12-3, you can see how the property list file (Figure 12-3) compares to the rendered user interface (Figure 12-2):

- Item 0 (`PSGroupSpecifier`) is a group label whose value is the string `Group`.
- Item 1 (`PSTextFieldSpecifier`) is a text label whose value is the string `Name`.
- Item 2 (`PSToggleSwitchSpecifier`) is a toggle switch labeled "Enabled" with a default value of YES.
- Item 3 (`PSSliderSpecifier`) is a slider bar with a minimum value of 0, a maximum value of 1, and a default value of 0.5.

Each UI element is an item described in the `PreferenceSpecifiers` array.

To make this easier to work with, you can tell Xcode explicitly that the *Root.plist* file is an iPhone Settings bundle. From the Xcode menu select View→Property List

Type→iPhone Settings plist (you may need to double-click on Root.plist before this option becomes available on the menu). This tells Xcode to format the contents of the property list a little differently, as shown in Figure 12-4, making it easier to understand and edit.

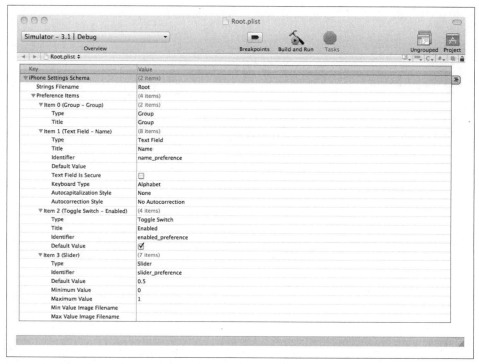

Figure 12-4. The Root.plist file formatted using the View→Property List Type→iPhone Settings plist from the Xcode menu bar

There are six possible property list keys:

- Group (`PSGroupSpecifier`)
- Title (`PSTitleValueSpecifier`)
- Text Field (`PSTextFieldSpecifier`)
- Toggle Switch (`PSToggleSwitchSpecifier`)
- Multi Value (`PSMultiValueSpecifier`)
- Slider (`PSSliderSpecifier`)

Additionally, although we won't go into it here, you can point to child preference panes (additional settings pages) using the Child Pane (`PSChildPaneSpecifier`) property list key.

Let's modify the default property key list provided by Xcode.

Click on Item 3 and press the Backspace key to delete it from the property list file; do the same for Item 1. You should be left with a Group and a Toggle Switch.

Rename the Group: under Item 0, double-click on the Title property's value and enter **Latitude & Longitude**.

Keep the Toggle Switch unmodified. After doing this, the *Root.plist* file should resemble Figure 12-5.

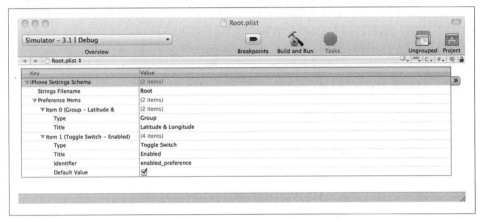

Figure 12-5. The edited property list pane in the Xcode editor

Make sure you've saved your changes to the *Root.plist* file and click the Build and Run button in the Xcode toolbar. Once the application has started, tap the Home button and make your way to the Settings application. Tap the WhereAmI preference entry, and you should now see something closely resembling Figure 12-6. We're going to use the preference pane to toggle whether we want the application to display the latitude and longitude on the screen when it displays our map.

 When you run your application in iPhone Simulator, it stores preference values in *~/Library/Application Support/iPhone Simulator/User/Applications/<APP_ID>/Library/Preferences*, where *<APP_ID>* is a randomly generated directory name. However, each time Xcode performs a clean install of your application, any previous version of the application's preferences will be deleted.

Return to Xcode and click on the *WhereAmIAppDelegate.m* file to open it in the Xcode editor. Now add the following class method, which initializes the default settings for the application:

```
+ (void)initialize {
    NSUserDefaults *defaults = [NSUserDefaults standardUserDefaults];
    NSDictionary *defaultsToRegister =
      [NSDictionary dictionaryWithObject:@"YES"
```

```
                    forKey:@"enabled_preference"];
    [defaults registerDefaults:defaultsToRegister];
}
```

Figure 12-6. The edited property list pane in the Settings application

If your user has already accessed the application's settings inside the iPhone Settings application, the default settings will already have been initialized. If this has not been done, the values will not exist and will be set to `nil` (or in the case of Booleans, to `NO`). As the application delegate is loaded, this method initializes the user defaults (the `initialize:` message is sent to each class before it receives any other messages).

Using this method to set the defaults has the unfortunate side effect that you have to specify your defaults in two places: in the *Root.plist* file, where they properly belong; and in your application delegate, where they don't.

The right way to deal with this problem is to read in the defaults from the *Settings.bundle* file which is stored as part of your application. To do this, replace the `initialize:` method with the following:

```
+ (void)initialize {

    NSUserDefaults *defaults = [NSUserDefaults standardUserDefaults];
    NSString *settingsBundle =
      [[NSBundle mainBundle] pathForResource:@"Settings" ofType:@"bundle"];
    NSDictionary *settings =
      [NSDictionary dictionaryWithContentsOfFile:
        [settingsBundle stringByAppendingPathComponent:@"Root.plist"]];

    NSArray *preferences = [settings objectForKey:@"PreferenceSpecifiers"];
    NSMutableDictionary *defaultsToRegister =
      [[NSMutableDictionary alloc] initWithCapacity:[preferences count]];

    [defaults registerDefaults:defaultsToRegister];
}
```

If your application preferences don't exist when your application is launched, you can therefore read the values directly from the *Settings.bundle* file rather than having to store the defaults in two places.

You can check that your preference bundle is working correctly by adding the following into the application delegate's `applicationDidFinishLaunching:` method and checking the Console (select Run→Console from the Xcode menu bar). Add the lines shown in bold:

```
- (void)applicationDidFinishLaunching:(UIApplication *)application {
    NSUserDefaults *defaults = [NSUserDefaults standardUserDefaults];
    BOOL enabled = [defaults boolForKey:@"enabled_preference"];
    NSLog(@"enabled = %d", enabled);

    self.locationManager = [[[CLLocationManager alloc] init] autorelease];

    ... other code not shown ...
}
```

We may have working preferences, but they don't do anything yet. Let's change that right now. Click on the *WhereAmIViewController.h* interface file to open it in the Xcode editor, and add the following outlets to the declaration (inside the curly braces of the `@interface` block):

```
IBOutlet UIButton *backgroundButton;
IBOutlet UILabel *latLabel;
IBOutlet UILabel *longLabel;
```

There is no need to make them properties.

Make sure you've saved all your changes (Option-⌘-S), and then double-click on the *WhereAmIViewController.xib* NIB file to open it in Interface Builder. Click on File's Owner, and in the Connections tab of the Inspector window connect the `background Button` outlet to the `UIButton` we used as a background for the labels, as shown in Figure 12-7; then connect the `latLabel` and `longLabel` outlets to the "Latitude" and "Longitude" `UILabel`s, respectively.

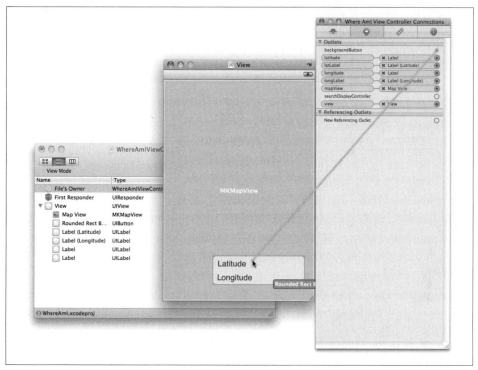

Figure 12-7. Connecting the new outlets to File's Owner

Save your changes to the NIB file and return to Xcode. Then click on the *WhereAmI-ViewController.m* implementation file to open it in the Xcode editor. Add the following `viewWillAppear:` method:

```
- (void)viewWillAppear:(BOOL)animated {

    NSUserDefaults *defaults = [NSUserDefaults standardUserDefaults];
    if ( [defaults boolForKey:@"enabled_preference"] ) {
        backgroundButton.hidden = NO;
        latLabel.text = @"Latitude";
        longLabel.text = @"Longitude";
    } else {
        backgroundButton.hidden = YES;
        latLabel.text = @"";
        longLabel.text = @"";
    }

    [super viewWillAppear:animated];
}
```

This method checks the application preferences to see if Latitude & Longitude are enabled. If they are, we set the text of the labels appropriately and make sure the button is visible. Correspondingly, if Latitude & Longitude are disabled, we hide the button and empty both strings.

Finally, we have to go back into the application delegate file and make a small modification to the `locationManager:didUpdateToLocation:fromLocation:` method. Here we have to stop the application from printing the current latitude and longitude to the screen if Latitude & Longitude are disabled via preferences. Add the lines shown in bold (wrapping the two existing assignments):

```
NSUserDefaults *defaults = [NSUserDefaults standardUserDefaults];
if ( [defaults boolForKey:@"enabled_preference"] ) {
  viewController.latitude.text =
    [NSString stringWithFormat:@"%f", newLocation.coordinate.latitude];
  viewController.longitude.text =
    [NSString stringWithFormat:@"%f", newLocation.coordinate.longitude];
}
```

This brackets the lines that set the text of the `UILabels` with an `if()` block; we set the text of the labels only if Latitude & Longitude are enabled in the preferences.

We're done here. Make sure all of your changes have been saved, and click the Build and Run button in the Xcode toolbar to compile and deploy your application into iPhone Simulator.

By default, the Latitude & Longitude display is enabled, so everything should appear as before. However, if you disable Latitude & Longitude in Settings, quit out of Settings, and relaunch the Where Am I? application, you'll see that Latitude & Longitude has disappeared, as shown in Figure 12-8.

Figure 12-8. With Latitude & Longitude enabled in the preferences (left) and disabled (right)

Accessing Global Preferences

As well as your own application preferences, you can programmatically access the device's global preferences from your own application:

```
NSString *path = [NSHomeDirectory()
  stringByAppendingPathComponent:
  @"Library/Preferences/.GlobalPreferences.plist"];
NSDictionary *dict = [NSDictionary dictionaryWithContentsOfFile:path];
NSLog(@"Phone number: %@", [dict objectForKey:@"SBFormattedPhoneNumber"]);
```

While there are a number of entries, the two keys that are probably going to be of most interest to you as a developer are `AppleLocale` and `SBFormattedPhoneNumber`. These are the current localizations used by the device; as I am based in the United Kingdom my `AppleLocale` is `en_GB`, and my phone number is formatted to the current locale.

You can also retrieve the phone number directly from the global preferences:

```
NSString *phoneNumber = [[NSUserDefaults standardUserDefaults]
  objectForKey:@"SBFormattedPhoneNumber"];
NSLog(@"Phone number: %@", phoneNumber);
```

You should be aware that the phone number might not always be available unless the number has been set in the Phone→My Number preference panel in the Settings application on the device. This is not guaranteed to be the case for all devices, as some carriers don't set this automatically.

Custom URL Schemes

One of the more interesting features provided by the SDK is the ability for your application to use custom URL schemes to launch other applications, and in turn, to register custom URL schemes of its own. These schemes can be used to launch your application, either from the browser or from another application on the device. Additionally, such schemes are not just limited to launching the application; you can pass additional information to your application via the URL.

Using Custom Schemes

Most of the built-in applications Apple provides respond to custom URL schemes; for example, the Maps, Mail, YouTube, iTunes, and App Store applications will all open in response to custom URLs. However, there are also many established third-party applications with published URL schemes that you can use in your own application.

 At the time of this writing, a fairly extensive list of URL schemes for third-party iPhone applications was available at *http://handleopenurl .com/scheme*.

Making a telephone call

You can easily trigger a telephone call from your application by using the `tel:` URL scheme:

```
NSString *string = @"tel:+19995551234"; ❶
NSURL *url = [NSURL URLWithString:string];
[[UIApplication sharedApplication] openURL:url];
```

❶ The phone number must not contain spaces or square brackets, although it can contain dashes and a leading + sign indicating that the international call prefix should be prepended.

Sending an SMS message

Unfortunately, Apple has not provided either a standard view controller as it did with email or an API for sending SMS messages from your application. This is regrettable, but if you consider the abuses that programmatic access might allow, you can probably follow the company's reasoning as to why this is not available.

However, you can use the custom URL scheme `sms:[phone number]` to open the SMS application and allow your users to send SMS messages:

```
NSString *string = @"sms:+19995551234"; ❶
NSURL *url = [NSURL URLWithString:string];
[[UIApplication sharedApplication] openURL:url];
```

❶ As for `tel:` URLs, the phone number must not contain spaces or square brackets.

As this will cause your application to exit and you cannot prepopulate the body of the SMS message, it's not generally very useful.

Registering Custom Schemes

Regardless of what you intend to do after a custom URL launches your application, you must first register your custom scheme using your application's *Info.plist* file. Let's do that for our City Guide application. You can choose any of the versions of the City Guide application we've worked on so far for this addition.

Open the project in Xcode and click on its *Info.plist* file to open it in the Xcode editor. Right-click the top row's Information Property List and select Add Row. A row will be added and you'll be prompted to select a key from a drop-down menu. Scroll to the bottom and select "URL types." This will create an array key item, so click the disclosure triangle next to "URL types" to expand it.

Click on Item 0 to expand it to show the URL identifier line. The value for this can actually be anything, but it's normal to use the Bundle Identifier, so double-click on the Bundle Identifier value to select it and then copy the identifier string. Then double-click on the field to the right of the URL identifier and paste it into the box.

Now right-click on Item 0, and select Add Row. You'll be presented with a shorter drop down of possible values; this time select URL Schemes. This will create an array key item. Expand it, double-click on the value box for its Item 0, and enter `cityguide`.

If you've followed the procedure correctly, your *Info.plist* file should now look like mine does in Figure 12-9. We're done; adding a custom URL scheme to your application really is that easy.

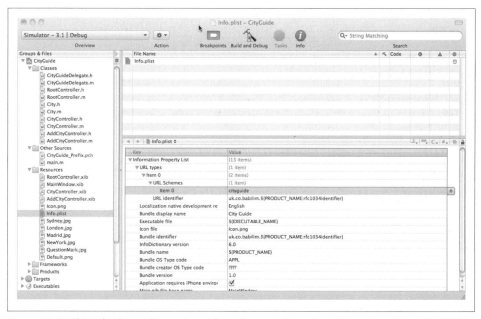

Figure 12-9. The Info.plist with our cityguide:// scheme registered

Of course, now that we've added the custom URL scheme we need to modify our application code so that it knows what to do with it. We're going to modify the City Guide application to take URLs of the form *cityguide://<City Name>* and open the relevant city page (e.g., the London page for *cityguide://London*).

If two different applications register with the same URL scheme, the most recently installed application will be the one that responds to custom URLs conforming to the URL scheme.

We really need to make only a few changes to the City Guide application to implement handling custom URL schemes. When the application is opened in response to a *cityguide://* URL, the `application:handleOpenURL:` method is called in the application delegate class.

Click on the *CityGuideDelegate.m* implementation file to open it in the Xcode editor, and add the following method:

```
- (BOOL)application:(UIApplication *)application
  handleOpenURL:(NSURL *)url
{
    // URL of the form cityguide://London
    viewController.placeFromURL = [url host];
    return YES;
}
```

Save your changes and then click on the *RootController.h* interface file. Here we need to declare an instance variable (put this inside the @implementation block's curly braces):

```
NSString *placeFromURL;
```

Now declare it as a property:

```
@property (nonatomic, retain) NSString *placeFromURL;
```

In the corresponding *RootController.m* implementation file, synthesize the new property:

```
@synthesize placeFromURL;
```

Now modify the viewDidLoad: method to do the actual work. I've highlighted the code that you need to add to deal with the custom URL scheme:

```
- (void)viewDidLoad {
    self.title = @"City Guide";
    self.navigationItem.rightBarButtonItem = self.editButtonItem;
    CityGuideDelegate *delegate =
      (CityGuideDelegate *)[[UIApplication sharedApplication] delegate];
    cities = delegate.cities;

    if ( self.placeFromURL ) {
        NSIndexPath *indexPath;
        for( int i = 0; i < cities.count; i++ ) {
            City *thisCity = [cities objectAtIndex:i];
            if( [thisCity.cityName isEqualToString:self.placeFromURL] ) {
                indexPath = [NSIndexPath indexPathForRow:i inSection:0];
            }
        }

        // Begin debugging code
        UIAlertView *alert = [[UIAlertView alloc]
          initWithTitle:self.placeFromURL
          message:[NSString stringWithFormat:@"indexPath = %@", indexPath]
          delegate:self
          cancelButtonTitle:nil
          otherButtonTitles:@"OK", nil];❶
        [alert show];
        [alert autorelease];
        // End debugging code

        CityController *city =
          [[CityController alloc] initWithIndexPath:indexPath];
        [delegate.navController pushViewController:city animated:NO];
        [city release];
```

```
        }
    }
```

❶ Displaying the UIAlertView is purely for debugging purposes to give some feedback. We're using it because the Debugger Console is unavailable, since the application is started by clicking a URL rather than by running under Xcode. It's not integral to handling the custom URL scheme, and once you understand what's going on, you can delete this section of the code.

We're done. Click the Build and Run button to compile and deploy the application into iPhone Simulator. Once the application is launched, quit again by clicking the Home button and navigate to Safari. Click on the address bar, enter **cityguide://London**, and click the Go button (or tap the Return key).

If all goes well, Safari should quit and the City Guide application will launch. Soon afterward, you should see something similar to Figure 12-10.

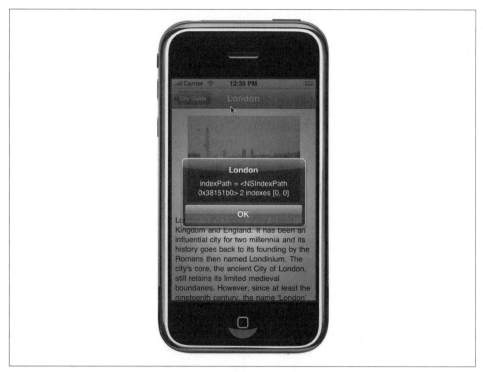

Figure 12-10. Opening the City Guide application from Safari

This doesn't work only in Safari; we can now open the City Guide application from other applications using the following snippet of code:

```
NSString *string = @"cityguide://London";❶
NSURL *url = [NSURL URLWithString:string];
[[UIApplication sharedApplication] openURL:url];
```

➊ This will open the London city guide in the City Guide application.

Media Playback

Just as it has done for images with the `UIImagePickerController` class (see "The Image Picker View Controller" on page 133 in Chapter 6) and for email with the `MFMailCom poseViewController` class (see "Sending Email" on page 161 in Chapter 7), Apple has provided a standard way to select and play back iPod media inside your own application.

 The `MPMediaPickerController` and associated classes make use of the iPod library; this is not present in iPhone Simulator and will work correctly only on the device itself.

However, things are a little bit more complicated than the two previous cases; here we use an `MPMediaPickerController` that, via the `MPMediaPickerControllerDelegate` protocol, returns an `MPMediaItemCollection` object containing the media items the user has selected, and that can be played using an `MPMusicPlayerController` object.

These classes are provided by the Media Player framework; if you want to use them, you must add the Media Player framework to your project by right-clicking the Frameworks group in Groups & Files and selecting Add→Existing Frameworks.

Let's reuse the Prototype application. Open the Finder and navigate to the location where you saved the *Prototype* project. Right-click on the folder containing the project files and select Duplicate; a folder called *Prototype copy* will be created containing a duplicate of the project. Rename the folder *PrototypePlayer*, and just as we did in Chapter 7, prune the application down to the stub with the Go! button and associated `pushedGo:` method that we'll use to trigger the display of our media player.

 To prune the Prototype application down to the stub, you will need to:

1. Delete the *WebViewController.h*, *WebViewController.m*, and *Web-View.xib* files from your project.
2. Remove the `#import "WebViewController.h"` line from *Prototype-ViewController.m*.
3. Delete the current body of the `pushedGo:` method.

Next, open the *PrototypeViewController.h* interface file, import the Media Player framework into the interface (*.h*) files, and declare your class as an `MPMediaPickerCon trollerDelegate`:

```
#import <UIKit/UIKit.h>
#import <MediaPlayer/MediaPlayer.h>
```

```
@interface PrototypeViewController : UIViewController
  <MPMediaPickerControllerDelegate> {
    IBOutlet UIButton *goButton;
}

-(IBAction) pushedGo:(id)sender;

@end
```

Save your changes, and open the *PrototypeViewController.m* implementation file. In the `pushedGo:` method, instantiate an `MPMediaPickerController` object and present its view modally to the user:

```
-(IBAction) pushedGo:(id)sender {
    MPMediaPickerController *mediaPicker =
      [[MPMediaPickerController alloc]
        initWithMediaTypes: MPMediaTypeAnyAudio];
    mediaPicker.delegate = self;
    mediaPicker.allowsPickingMultipleItems = YES;
    [self presentModalViewController:mediaPicker animated:YES];
    [mediaPicker release];
}
```

Now implement the following two delegate methods:

```
- (void) mediaPicker:(MPMediaPickerController *) mediaPicker
  didPickMediaItems:(MPMediaItemCollection *) userMediaItemCollection
{
    [self dismissModalViewControllerAnimated: YES];

    MPMusicPlayerController *musicPlayer =
      [MPMusicPlayerController applicationMusicPlayer];
    [musicPlayer setQueueWithItemCollection: userMediaItemCollection];
    [musicPlayer play];❶
}

- (void) mediaPickerDidCancel: (MPMediaPickerController *) mediaPicker {
    [self dismissModalViewControllerAnimated: YES];
}
```

❶ The `MPMusicPlayerController` responds to all the messages you might expect (e.g., play, pause, stop, volume). You can link these directly to buttons in your user interface if you want to give users direct control over these functions.

Like the `UIImagePickerControllerDelegate` methods we met earlier in the book, these two methods are used to dismiss the view controller and handle the returned items.

Save your changes, and click on the Build and Run button in the Xcode toolbar to build and deploy your code. Remember that you'll need to configure your project (see "Putting the Application on Your iPhone" on page 37 in Chapter 3) to allow you to deploy the application onto your iPhone or iPod touch so that you can test the application on your device.

Once your application loads, tap the Go! button to bring up the `MPMediaPickerControl ler`, select some songs, and tap the Done button in the navigation bar (see Figure 12-11). Your music should start playing.

Figure 12-11. The initial main view (left) and MPMediaPickerController (right)

Once playback has begun, you need to keep track of the currently playing item and display that to the user, or at the very least provide some way for the user to pause (or stop) playback, or perhaps to change her selection. The `MPMusicPlayerController` class provides two methods: the `beginGeneratingPlaybackNotifications:` method and a corresponding `endGeneratingPlaybackNotifications:` method. Add this line to the `did PickMediaItems:` method:

```
- (void) mediaPicker:(MPMediaPickerController *) mediaPicker
  didPickMediaItems:(MPMediaItemCollection *) userMediaItemCollection {
    [self dismissModalViewControllerAnimated: YES];

    MPMusicPlayerController *musicPlayer =
      [MPMusicPlayerController applicationMusicPlayer];
    [musicPlayer setQueueWithItemCollection: userMediaItemCollection];
    [musicPlayer beginGeneratingPlaybackNotifications];
    [musicPlayer play];
}
```

When the begin method is invoked, the class will start to generate notifications of when the player state changes and when the current playback item changes, which your application can register to handle by adding itself as an observer using the NSNotifica tionCenter class:

```
- (void) mediaPicker:(MPMediaPickerController *) mediaPicker
   didPickMediaItems:(MPMediaItemCollection *) userMediaItemCollection {
     [self dismissModalViewControllerAnimated: YES];

     MPMusicPlayerController *musicPlayer =
     [MPMusicPlayerController applicationMusicPlayer];
     [musicPlayer setQueueWithItemCollection: userMediaItemCollection];
     [musicPlayer beginGeneratingPlaybackNotifications];

     NSNotificationCenter *notificationCenter =
       [NSNotificationCenter defaultCenter];
     [notificationCenter addObserver:self
         selector:@selector(handleNowPlayingItemChanged:)
         name:@"MPMusicPlayerControllerNowPlayingItemDidChangeNotification"
         object:musicPlayer];

     [notificationCenter addObserver:self
         selector:@selector(handlePlaybackStateChanged:)
         name:@"MPMusicPlayerControllerPlaybackStateDidChangeNotification"
         object:musicPlayer];

     [musicPlayer play];

}
```

This will invoke the selector methods in our class when the appropriate notification arrives. (You could, for example, use the first to update a UILabel in your view telling the user the name of the currently playing song.)

However, for now let's just implement these methods to print messages to the console log. In the *PrototypeViewController.h* interface file, declare the selector methods:

```
@interface PrototypeViewController : UIViewController
   <MPMediaPickerControllerDelegate>
{
     IBOutlet UIButton *goButton;
}

-(IBAction) pushedGo:(id)sender;
- (void)handleNowPlayingItemChanged:(id)notification;
- (void)handlePlaybackStateChanged:(id)notification;

@end
```

Then, in the *PrototypeViewController.m* implementation file, add the following method. This will be called when the current item being played changes:

```
- (void)handleNowPlayingItemChanged:(id)notification {
   MPMusicPlayerController *musicPlayer =
     [MPMusicPlayerController applicationMusicPlayer];
```

```
MPMediaItem *currentItem = [musicPlayer nowPlayingItem];❶
NSLog(@"%@", currentItem);
}
```

❶ Unusually, the `MPMediaItem` class has only one instance method: `valueForProp` `erty:`. This is because the class can wrap a number of media types, and each type can have a fairly wide range of metadata associated with it. You can find a full list of possible keys in the `MPMediaItem` class reference, but keys include `MPMediaItemPro` `pertyTitle` and `MPMediaItemPropertyArtwork`, among others.

While the second method handles changes in state, we can use this to update our user interface (e.g., changing the state of the Play and Stop buttons when the music ends):

```
- (void)handlePlaybackStateChanged:(id)notification {
    MPMusicPlayerController *musicPlayer =
      [MPMusicPlayerController applicationMusicPlayer];
    MPMusicPlaybackState playbackState = [musicPlayer playbackState];
    if (playbackState == MPMusicPlaybackStatePaused) {
        NSLog(@"Paused");

    } else if (playbackState == MPMusicPlaybackStatePlaying) {
        NSLog(@"Playing");

    } else if (playbackState == MPMusicPlaybackStateStopped) {
        NSLog(@"Stopped");

    }
}
```

Save your changes, and click on the Build and Run button in the Xcode toolbar to build and deploy your code onto your device. Once your application loads, tap the Go! button to bring up the `MPMediaPickerController` again, select some songs, and tap the Done button in the navigation bar. Your music should start playing, but this time you should see something similar to the following log messages in the Debugger Console:

```
2009-12-11 00:29:42.535 Prototype[447:207] <MPMediaItem 0x1373e0>
 persistentID: 6817778870160863775
2009-12-11 00:29:42.685 Prototype[447:207] Playing
```

Using the Address Book

Just like the `MPMediaPickerController` class in the preceding section, and the other classes we met earlier in the book, Apple has provided an `ABPeoplePickerNavigation` `Controller` and associated delegate protocol to allow you to both prompt the user for contact information and display contact information to the user. However, in this case the framework it provides also allows your application to interact with person and group records directly.

Once you reach the lower levels of the Address Book framework—for instance, dealing with individual person records—the interface presented by the framework is in C rather than Objective-C. This is especially obvious when dealing with the address book programmatically rather than interactively using the navigation controller.

Interactive People Picking

To illustrate how to use the `ABPeoplePickerNavigationController`, we're going to reuse the Prototype application code yet again. So, open the Finder and navigate to the location where you saved the *Prototype* project. Right-click on the folder containing the project files and select Duplicate; a folder called *Prototype copy* will be created containing a duplicate of the project. Rename the folder *Prototype4*, and just as we did before, prune the application down to the stub (as we did in the previous section for the media player example) with the Go! button and associated `pushedGo:` method that we'll use to trigger the display of our address book picker.

Click on the *PrototypeViewController.h* interface file to open it in the Xcode editor. We need to declare the class as both an `ABPeoplePickerNavigationControllerDelegate` and a `UINavigationControllerDelegate`. Both declarations are necessary for the class to interact with the `ABPeoplePickerNavigationController`:

```
#import <UIKit/UIKit.h>
#import <AddressBook/AddressBook.h>
#import <AddressBookUI/AddressBookUI.h>

@interface PrototypeViewController : UIViewController
  <UINavigationControllerDelegate,
   ABPeoplePickerNavigationControllerDelegate>
{
    IBOutlet UIButton *goButton;
}

-(IBAction) pushedGo:(id)sender;

@end
```

Now modify the `pushedGo:` method in the corresponding *PrototypeViewController.m* implementation file:

```
-(IBAction) pushedGo:(id)sender {
    ABPeoplePickerNavigationController *peoplePicker =
     [[ABPeoplePickerNavigationController alloc] init];
    peoplePicker.peoplePickerDelegate = self;❶
    [self presentModalViewController:peoplePicker animated:YES];
    [peoplePicker release];
}
```

❶ Unlike most Objective-C classes, the `ABPeoplePickerNavigationController` uses the `peoplePickerDelegate` property to specify its delegate rather than the more common `delegate` property.

Next, add the three mandatory `ABPeoplePickerNavigationControllerDelegate` methods specified by the delegate protocol:

```
- (BOOL)peoplePickerNavigationController:
  (ABPeoplePickerNavigationController *)picker
  shouldContinueAfterSelectingPerson:(ABRecordRef)person❶
{
    [self dismissModalViewControllerAnimated:YES];
    return NO;
}

- (BOOL)peoplePickerNavigationController:
  (ABPeoplePickerNavigationController *)picker
  shouldContinueAfterSelectingPerson:(ABRecordRef)person
  property:(ABPropertyID)property
  identifier:(ABMultiValueIdentifier)identifier❷
{
    return NO;
}

- (void)peoplePickerNavigationControllerDidCancel:
  (ABPeoplePickerNavigationController *)picker❸
{
    [self dismissModalViewControllerAnimated:YES];
}
```

❶ If this method returns YES, the picker will continue after the user selects a name from the address book, displaying the person's details. If the method returns NO, the picker will not continue. If you intend to return NO, you should also dismiss the view controller.

❷ This method is called only if you want the picker to continue after the user selects a name from the address book. The address record is then displayed to the user. If this method returns YES, the picker will continue after the user selects a property (e.g., a mobile phone number, fax number). If the method returns NO, the picker will not continue. If you intend to return NO, you should also dismiss the view controller.

❸ This method is called when the user taps the Cancel button in the navigation bar of the picker interface.

We've reached a point where you can compile and check the code, but remember that you should also add the AddressBook and AddressBookUI frameworks to the project before clicking the Build and Run button in the Xcode toolbar. When you do so, you should see the familiar gray screen with the Go! button as shown in Figure 12-12; click it and you'll be presented with a view of the address book. Selecting a name in the address book will dismiss the picker view and return you directly to the main gray screen.

Figure 12-12. The initial main view (left) and the ABPeoplePickerNavigationController (right)

The picker is displayed, but even if the user selects a name from the list, we don't do anything with the returned record. Let's add some additional code to the `peoplePick erNavigationController:shouldContinueAfterSelectingPerson:` method to fix that omission:

```
- (BOOL)peoplePickerNavigationController:
  (ABPeoplePickerNavigationController *)picker
  shouldContinueAfterSelectingPerson:(ABRecordRef)person
{

    NSString *name = (NSString *)ABRecordCopyCompositeName(person);❶

    ABMutableMultiValueRef phones =
      ABRecordCopyValue(person, kABPersonPhoneProperty);
    NSArray *numbers =
      (NSArray *)ABMultiValueCopyArrayOfAllValues(phones);

    ABMutableMultiValueRef emails =
      ABRecordCopyValue(person, kABPersonEmailProperty);
    NSString *addresses =
      (NSString *)ABMultiValueCopyArrayOfAllValues(emails);

    NSString *note = (NSString *)
      ABRecordCopyValue(person, kABPersonNoteProperty );
```

```
NSLog( @"name = %@, numbers = %@, email = %@, note = %@",
     name, numbers, addresses, note );

[self dismissModalViewControllerAnimated:YES];
return NO;
}
```

❶ The `ABRecordCopyCompositeName()` method returns a human-readable name for the record.

There are two basic types of properties: single-value and multivalue. Single-value properties contain data that can have only a single value, such as a person's name. Multivalue properties contain data that can have multiple values, such as a person's phone number. You can see from the preceding code that single-value and multivalue properties are handled slightly differently.

> You can find a full list of the different properties available in an address book record in the `ABPerson` class documentation.

Make sure you've saved your changes and click the Build and Run button in the Xcode toolbar to compile and deploy your application into iPhone Simulator. When the application launches, click the Go! button and then select a name from the list. You should see something similar to Figure 12-13 logged to the Console (select Run→Console from the Xcode menu bar to display the Debugger Console).

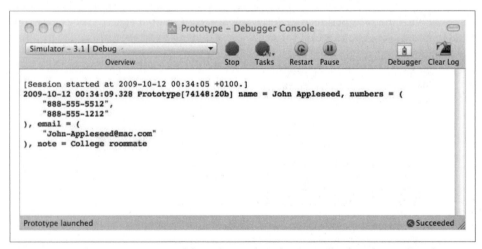

Figure 12-13. The properties returned from the people picker controller for John Appleseed

What if we want to retrieve a specific phone number from the list? It's easier to let the user select the phone number he needs, and that's where the `peoplePickerNavigation Controller:shouldContinueAfterSelectingPerson:property:identifier:` method would come into play (we returned `NO` from this earlier in this section, so this example does not allow the user to select a number).

A multivalue property is a list of values, but each value also has a text label and an identifier associated with it. This second delegate method provides you with both the property and the identifier for the value (i.e., a specific phone number) that is of interest to the user.

However, if you know which property value you're looking for inside the multivalue property, you can programmatically retrieve the identifier for that value. For example, here's how you'd select the mobile phone number from the list of returned phone numbers:

```
ABMultiValueRef phones = ABRecordCopyValue(person, kABPersonPhoneProperty);

ABMultiValueIdentifier identifier;
for( int i = 0; i < numbers.count; i++ ) {
    if( CFStringCompare( ABMultiValueCopyLabelAtIndex(phones, i),
        kABPersonPhoneMobileLabel, 1 ) == 0 ) {
        identifier = ABMultiValueGetIdentifierAtIndex(phones, i);
    }
}
```

You can then retrieve the mobile phone number at any time by using the identifier:

```
NSString *mobile =
  (NSString *) ABMultiValueCopyValueAtIndex(phones,
    ABMultiValueGetIndexForIdentifier(phones, identifier));
NSLog(@"Mobile = %@", mobile);
```

Programmatic People Picking

You do not have to use the `ABPeoplePickerNavigationController` to access the address book; you can access it directly, as shown here:

```
ABAddressBookRef addressBook = ABAddressBookCreate();
CFArrayRef allPeople = ABAddressBookCopyArrayOfAllPeople(addressBook);

for (int i = 0; i < ABAddressBookGetPersonCount(addressBook); i++) {
    ABRecordRef ref = CFArrayGetValueAtIndex(allPeople, i);
    NSString *contact = (NSString *)ABRecordCopyCompositeName(ref);
     NSLog( @"%@", contact );
}
```

The preceding code will instantiate a copy of the address book, retrieve references to all of the records, and then iterate through the array of records. Then, in the same way we dealt with records after interactively retrieving them with the picker controller, we print the full name of each contact to the Debug Console.

CHAPTER 13

Other Native Platforms

If you want to build applications for the iPhone and the iPod touch that will be sold on the App Store, alternatives are available to the traditional Objective-C and Cocoa Touch route. Development platforms now exist allowing JavaScript and C# developers to get direct access to the iPhone's hardware features, such as the accelerometer.

PhoneGap

PhoneGap (*http://www.phonegap.com/*), developed by Nitobi, is an open source development platform for building cross-platform mobile applications with JavaScript.

On the iPhone, it works by providing a prebuilt library containing Objective-C classes that wrap the iPhone's native capabilities (e.g., vibration and accelerometer support) and exposes these capabilities to JavaScript along with an Xcode project template that makes use of the library. You can then compile your application as a hybrid of native Objective-C and JavaScript inside Xcode.

The platform is device-agnostic, allowing you to build an application for the iPhone, Android, and BlackBerry devices simultaneously. Developing applications using the PhoneGap framework is a reasonable alternative to building all-native applications in Objective-C.

In the past, submitting to the App Store applications built around the PhoneGap platform was problematic. However, since the 0.8.0 release, this has been resolved and Apple has approved PhoneGap for building applications intended for the store.

 Since the 0.8.0 release, the PhoneGap platform has embedded a version tag into the compiled iPhone application bundle to allow Apple to identify the version used in your application build during the application review process.

If you're a web developer who wants to build mobile applications in HTML and Java-Script while still taking advantage of the hardware features on the iPhone, Android, and BlackBerry devices, you may want to take a look at the PhoneGap platform.

 If you're interested in developing native iPhone applications using HTML and JavaScript, at least two alternatives to PhoneGap are now available: Appcelerator (*http://www.appcelerator.com/*) and Rhomo-bile (*http://rhomobile.com/*). However, anecdotally at least, PhoneGap is the most well known of the three platforms.

Download and Installation

The easiest way to make use of the PhoneGap platform on the iPhone is to build the *PhoneGapLib* static library for iPhone. This will allow you to create PhoneGap-based iPhone application projects directly using an Xcode project template file.

You can download the latest version of the PhoneGap code, which includes *PhoneGapLib*, either from the project's Git repository (*http://github.com/phonegap/phonegap/*) or from the main PhoneGap website (*http://phonegap.com/download/*). If you're down-loading the code from the project website, you should download version 0.8.2 or later, as earlier versions do not include the *PhoneGapLib* library.

 The PhoneGap platform, and especially the *PhoneGapLib* library, is under active development and installation instructions are therefore subject to change.

After downloading the source, open a terminal window, navigate to the source direc-tory, and type **make** to build the PhoneGap platform. You should see something very much like the following scroll by in your terminal window:

```
$ cd Downloads/phonegap-phonegap-27e998e/
$ ls
total 48
drwxr-xr-x  13 aa   staff    442 16 Nov 18:03 ./
drwx------+ 10 aa   staff    340 18 Nov 15:27 ../
-rwxr-xr-x@  1 aa   staff    132 16 Nov 18:03 .gitignore*
-rwxr-xr-x@  1 aa   staff   3743 16 Nov 18:03 README.md*
-rwxr-xr-x@  1 aa   staff   2742 16 Nov 18:03 Rakefile*
drwxr-xr-x@ 12 aa   staff    408 16 Nov 18:03 android/
drwxr-xr-x@ 10 aa   staff    340 16 Nov 18:03 blackberry/
-rwxr-xr-x@  1 aa   staff   2795 16 Nov 18:03 configure*
drwxr-xr-x@  7 aa   staff    238 16 Nov 18:03 iphone/
drwxr-xr-x@ 25 aa   staff    850 16 Nov 18:03 javascripts/
drwxr-xr-x@  4 aa   staff    136 16 Nov 18:03 util/
drwxr-xr-x@ 11 aa   staff    374 16 Nov 18:03 winmo/
$ cd iphone
$ make
    .
```

```
    .
    .
    .
$
```

If everything looks OK at this point, you can close the terminal window. Now open the Finder and navigate to the *iphone/* directory inside your PhoneGap source code folder. Inside the folder you should see a *PhoneGapLibInstaller.pkg* file.

 If you don't see the *PhoneGapLibInstaller.pkg* file, you can create it manually. In the Finder, open the *iphone/PhoneGapLibInstaller* directory under the PhoneGap source directory. Look for the *PhoneGapLibInstaller.pmdoc* PackageMaker document. Double-click on this file to open it inside the package maker and click the Build and Run button in the PackageMaker toolbar.

Doing this will build the *PhoneGapLib* installer bundle, and save it (at least by default) in your Documents folder. If you return to your Finder window and navigate to your Documents folder, you should see a *PhoneGapLib* installer package file.

If you double-click on the *PhoneGapLibInstaller.pkg* file, you'll start the installer application, as shown in Figure 13-1. Accept all of the defaults.

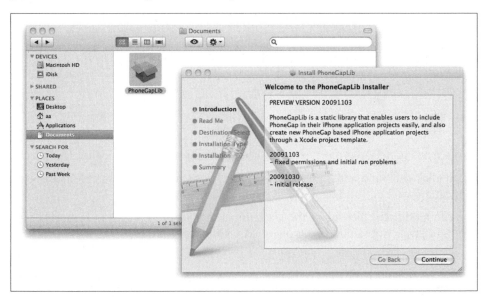

Figure 13-1. The PhoneGapLib Installer

Building a PhoneGap Project

Start Xcode and create a new project. If PhoneGap has been successfully installed, you should now see a PhoneGap project template entry under the User Templates header, as shown in Figure 13-2.

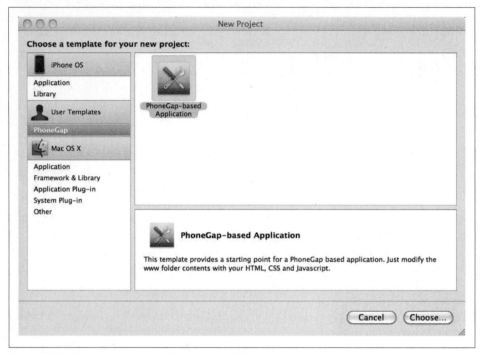

Figure 13-2. Starting a new PhoneGap project in Xcode

Start a new PhoneGap project, and you'll see something much like Figure 13-3.

If you click the Build and Run button on the Xcode toolbar, the sample PhoneGap application will build and deploy into iPhone Simulator.

You can modify the files inside the *www* folder in your project and add your HTML, CSS, and JavaScript to build your own AJAX-based application.

> Since PhoneGap uses the *file://* protocol to load your HTML into a normal UIWebView, you can load and execute JavaScript from other websites, without problems.

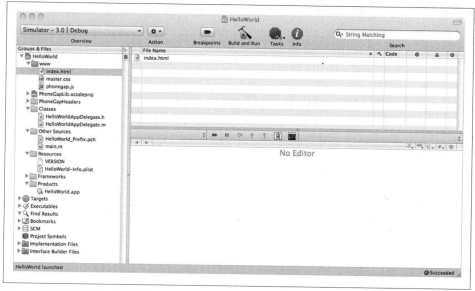

Figure 13-3. The HelloWorld PhoneGap application in Xcode

If you're interested in exploring further the possibility of building iPhone applications using HTML and JavaScript, you might want to look at *Building iPhone Apps with HTML, CSS, and JavaScript (http://oreilly.com/catalog/9780596805791/)* by Jonathan Stark (O'Reilly).

MonoTouch

The MonoTouch platform (*http://monotouch.net/*) from Novell allows you to build C#- and .NET-based applications on the iPhone and iPod touch. It comes in two editions: Professional and Enterprise.

A license for the Professional Edition, intended for individual use, costs $399 per year. The Enterprise Edition, intended for corporate use, costs $999 per year (although you can buy a five-developer pack for $3,999 per year). Alternatively, you can download an evaluation version that enables development and testing against iPhone Simulator only.

Download and Installation

Before downloading and installing MonoTouch, you must download the latest release of Mono, the open source development platform based on the .NET Framework that allows developers to build cross-platform applications in C#. You can obtain it from *http://www.mono-project.com/*.

The Mono framework downloads as a disk image file containing a package installer file. Double-click on this package file to start the Mono installer, as shown in Figure 13-4.

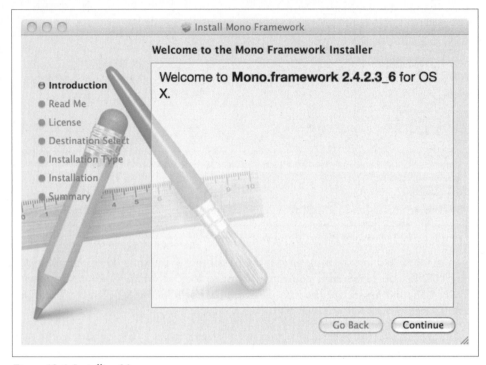

Figure 13-4. Installing Mono

After installing the Mono framework, you need to install the MonoDevelop environment before you can install MonoTouch itself. MonoDevelop is an IDE primarily designed for C# and other .NET languages and you can download it from *http://monodevelop.com/*; it comes as a disk image, and installation is simply a matter of dragging and dropping the *MonoDevelop.app* application from the disk image to your Applications folder.

 You need to use the latest MonoTouch version of MonoDevelop for Mac OS X, as it contains several fixes that are not in the mainstream version of the application. This version is linked from the MonoTouch website.

After installing Mono and MonoDevelop, you can download the trial version of the MonoTouch SDK from *http://monotouch.net/DownloadTrial*. MonoTouch is distributed as a package file that will automatically start the Installer when it downloads, as shown in Figure 13-5.

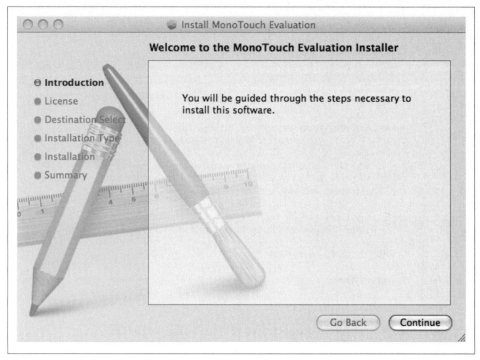

Figure 13-5. Installing MonoTouch

Building a MonoTouch Project

Double-click on the MonoDevelop application that you installed in your Applications folder, and you will be presented with something similar to Figure 13-6. Select File→New Solution from the MonoDevelop menu to open the New Solution window (Figure 13-7). From there, choose a new C#→iPhone→iPhone MonoTouch Project.

After entering the solution name, click the Forward button and then the Okay button to complete the setup process. You do not need to choose any of the optional project features (e.g., Packaging or Unix Integration). In the Solution pane, click the disclosure triangle next to the solution name to expand it, and then expand each subfolder in the same way, and you'll be presented with something that looks a lot like Figure 13-8.

The default template generated by the MonoTouch SDK produces a *Main.cs* file that is used to start your application event loop:

```
using System;
using System.Collections.Generic;
using System.Linq;
using MonoTouch.Foundation;
using MonoTouch.UIKit;

namespace HelloWorld
```

```
{
    public class Application
    {
        static void Main (string[] args)
        {
            UIApplication.Main (args);
        }
    }

    // The name AppDelegate is referenced in the MainWindow.xib file.
    public partial class AppDelegate : UIApplicationDelegate
    {
        // This method is invoked when the application has loaded its UI
        // and its ready to run public override bool FinishedLaunching
        // (UIApplication app, NSDictionary options)
        {
            // If you have defined a view, add it here:
            // window.AddSubview (navigationController.View);

            window.MakeKeyAndVisible ();

            return true;
        }

        // This method is required in iPhoneOS 3.0
        public override void OnActivated (UIApplication application)
        {
        }
    }
}
```

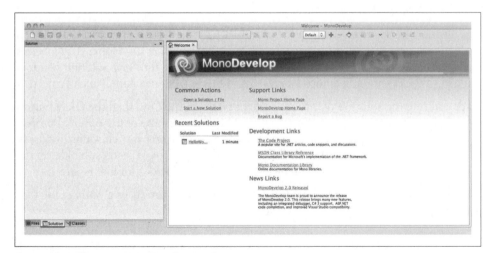

Figure 13-6. The main MonoDevelop window

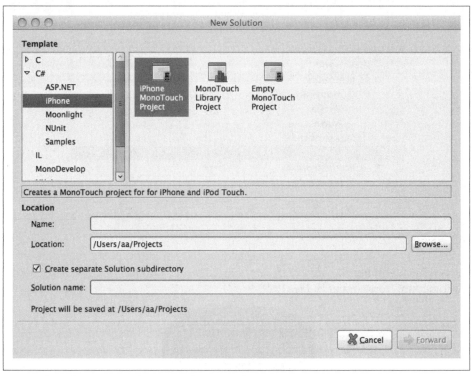

Figure 13-7. The MonoDevelop New Solution window

The default template also creates a *MainWindow.xib.designer.cs* file that MonoTouch will update each time you edit the *MainWindow.xib* file inside Interface Builder. This file will mirror all of the views, controllers, outlets, and actions that you add to your UI and then map those elements to C# properties that you can access from your own code. Here's the default *MainWindow.xib.designer.cs*:

```
namespace HelloWorld
{
    // Base type probably should be MonoTouch.Foundation.NSObject or subclass
    [MonoTouch.Foundation.Register("AppDelegate")]
    public partial class AppDelegate
    {

        [MonoTouch.Foundation.Connect("window")]
        private MonoTouch.UIKit.UIWindow window {
          get {
            return ((MonoTouch.UIKit.UIWindow)(this.GetNativeField ("window")));
          }
          set { this.SetNativeField ("window", value); }
        }
    }
}
```

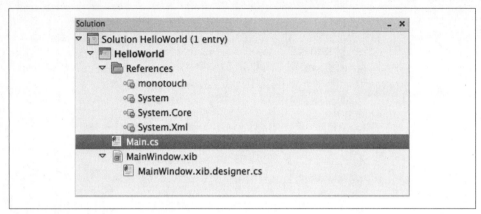

Figure 13-8. The Hello World application in the MonoDevelop Solution Pad

If you select Run→Run from the MonoDevelop menu bar at this point, the application will be built, compiled to native code, and started inside iPhone Simulator. You should see something very similar to Figure 13-9.

Figure 13-9. The default MonoTouch template running in iPhone Simulator

Quit from iPhone Simulator and return to the MonoDevelop environment. Double-click on the *MainWindow.xib* file to open the NIB file in Interface Builder. Drag a button (`UIButton`) and a label (`UILabel`) into the main view window.

Next, click on the app delegate in the *MainWindow.xib* file and go to the Classes segment of the multisegmented control at the top of the Library window. Click on AppDelegate in the list of objects, and then click on the Outlets segment of the multisegmented control underneath the AppDelegate object. Click on the plus sign button below the outlets list to add a new outlet. Add two new outlets, calling them "button" and "label", respectively; see Figure 13-10.

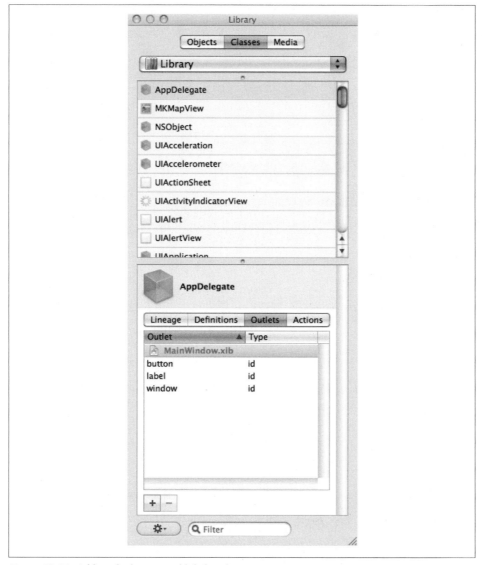

Figure 13-10. Adding the button and label outlets

In the Connections Inspector (⌘-2), connect the button and label outlets to the button and label elements as you've done in other projects. Figure 13-11 shows what the finished NIB should look like (you can use the Attributes Inspector to change the appearance of the button and label).

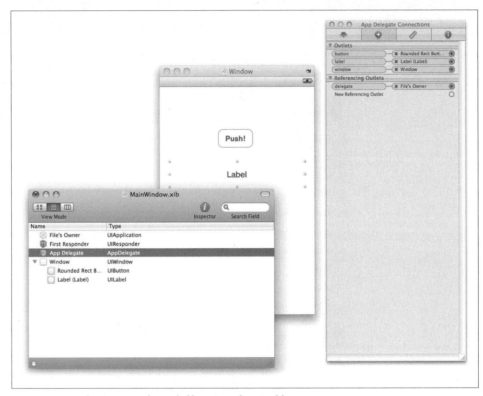

Figure 13-11. The MainWindow.xib file in Interface Builder

Save your changes and return to the MonoDevelop environment. If you look again at the *MainWindow.xib.designer.cs* file, you should see that it reflects the changes you made to the view inside Interface Builder. The changes that MonoDevelop made are shown in bold:

```
namespace HelloWorld {


    // Base type probably should be MonoTouch.Foundation.NSObject or subclass
    [MonoTouch.Foundation.Register("AppDelegate")]
    public partial class AppDelegate {

        #pragma warning disable 0169
        [MonoTouch.Foundation.Connect("window")]
        private MonoTouch.UIKit.UIWindow window {
          get {
```

```
      return ((MonoTouch.UIKit.UIWindow)(this.GetNativeField("window")));
    }
    set {
      this.SetNativeField("window", value);
    }
  }

  [MonoTouch.Foundation.Connect("button")]
  private MonoTouch.UIKit.UIButton button {
    get {
      return ((MonoTouch.UIKit.UIButton)(this.GetNativeField("button")));
    }
    set {
      this.SetNativeField("button", value);
    }
  }

  [MonoTouch.Foundation.Connect("label")]
  private MonoTouch.UIKit.UILabel label {
    get {
      return ((MonoTouch.UIKit.UILabel)(this.GetNativeField("label")));
    }
    set {
      this.SetNativeField("label", value);
    }
  }
}
}
```

 You should not make any changes to the *MainWindow.xib.designer.cs* file, as the MonoTouch framework updates it automatically each time you edit your NIB file in Interface Builder.

Double-click on the *Main.cs* file to open it in the MonoTouch editor and add the following code directly before the line where the window is made visible (`window.Make KeyAndVisible ();`):

```
button.TouchDown += delegate {
    label.Text = "Pushed Button";
};
```

Save your modifications and select Run→Run from the MonoDevelop menu bar. Once the application has been built and been deployed into iPhone Simulator, tap the Push! button. You should see something like Figure 13-12.

Figure 13-12. The MonoTouch Hello World application

You've just built your first iPhone application with MonoTouch.

CHAPTER 14

Going Further

We've managed to cover a lot of ground over the preceding 13 chapters, but there is still a lot more ground to go. While you should by now be confidently building solid applications for the iPhone and iPod touch, there is still a lot to learn.

Cocoa and Objective-C

The Objective-C language has a number of powerful features, and the Cocoa framework that is layered on top of the language is extensive. I've obviously not had the time or space in this book to cover either one in the depth it really deserves.

If you intend to continue developing for the iPhone, you should consider reading further on Objective-C, especially if you're having difficulties with memory management or the Model-View-Controller pattern around which most iPhone application development revolves.

Apple provides some excellent tutorial material on its developer website and that should certainly be your first port of call. I also recommend *Programming in Objective-C* by Stephen G. Kochan (Addison-Wesley) and *Cocoa and Objective-C: Up and Running (http://oreilly.com/catalog/9780596804817/)* by Scott Stevenson (O'Reilly), for a more detailed look at the language. See also *Cocoa Design Patterns* by Erik M. Buck and Donald A. Yacktman (Addison-Wesley) for a detailed look at design patterns in Cocoa.

The iPhone SDK

Predictably, I've focused on the parts of Cocoa and Objective-C that will be most helpful in allowing you to write your own applications for the iPhone. But even there I've left out a lot in an attempt to simplify and get you started quickly. A more in-depth look at the iPhone SDK is available in *iPhone SDK Application Development, First Edition* by Jonathan Zdziarski (O'Reilly).

A good cookbook to help you solve specific problems is *The iPhone Developer's Cookbook: Building Applications with the iPhone SDK* by Erica Sadun (Addison-Wesley). Erica's book consists of an excellent collection of recipes that solve the vexing question: "How do I make my application do X, Y, or Z?" She provides some solid example code that you can lift off the page and use yourself, often without any modification, in your own applications.

Web Applications

This book looked at how to build native applications. As I mentioned in Chapter 1, there is an alternative: you can build your application as a web application, taking it entirely online and doing away with the native SDK altogether. However, many native iPhone applications sit on a blurry line between the native and web worlds, wrapping custom content in a `UIWebView` inside the application, with much of the backend processing done "in the cloud." For instance, I know of several developers who are using Google App Engine to power their applications and store user data, with little or no number crunching actually going on in the iPhone device. Knowing how to build web applications is a useful skill, even for a hardened Objective-C programmer building a native application.

If you're interested in building web applications for the iPhone, you should look at *Building iPhone Apps with HTML, CSS, and JavaScript (http://oreilly.com/catalog/9780596805791/)* by Jonathan Stark (O'Reilly) and *Professional iPhone and iPod touch Programming: Building Applications for Mobile Safari* by Richard Wagner (Wiley).

If you're thinking about using Google App Engine as a scalable backend for your iPhone application, you should look at *Using Google App Engine (http://oreilly.com/catalog/9780596801601/)* by Charles Severance and *Programming Google App Engine (http://oreilly.com/catalog/9780596522735/)* by Dan Sanderson (both published by O'Reilly).

Core Data

One of the most important additions to the iPhone SDK, at least from the perspective of the developer community, was Core Data. It is a powerful and efficient framework for data management and persistence, and while it was new to the iPhone at the time it was added, it had been available to developers on the Mac since the release of Mac OS X 10.4 (Tiger).

Core Data allows you to easily define your application's data model, creating a managed object model that allows you to specify an abstract definition of your model objects. In a similar fashion to how Interface Builder takes much of the heavy lifting out of building complicated user interfaces (the view), Core Data takes the heavy lifting out of building the model.

We didn't even touch on Core Data in this book; if you're interested in this framework, I recommend that you look at *Core Data: Apple's API for Persisting Data on Mac OS X* by Marcus S. Zarra (Pragmatic Programmers). I also recommend that you look at *Core Data for iPhone: Building Data-Driven Applications for the iPhone and iPod Touch* by Tim Isted (Addison-Wesley Professional).

Push Notifications

The Apple Push Notification Service (APNS) APNSallows applications to notify their users of remote events. If the user has turned on Notifications from the Settings application, her device will maintain a persistent IP connection to the APNS. Only one connection is maintained and all third-party notifications are forwarded (by providers) through Apple's own servers (see Figure 14-1).

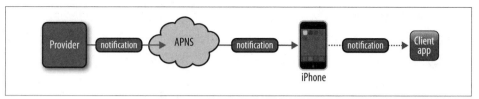

Figure 14-1. A push notification from a provider to a client application

When a device receives a notification for an application and that application isn't running, it notifies the user through an alert message or a sound, or by adding a numbered badge to the application. The APNS does not provide any feedback as to whether the message was successfully delivered to the user.

 Apple argues, "Push notifications serve the same purpose that a background application would on a desktop computer" and that running applications in the background really isn't necessary on a mobile platform outside of core services that the platform provides, such as phone calls and push email. It is not possible to run your own third-party applications in the background on the iPhone or iPod touch. Apple says, "...on a device such as the iPhone, background applications are, for performance and security reasons, prohibited. Only one application may be executing at a time."

However, while Apple has provided detailed documentation regarding how to implement push notifications on the client (device) side, it provides only a high-level overview for implementing the provider (server) side.

Details of the APNS are given in the Apple Push Notification Service Programming Guide available via the iPhone Dev Center (*http://devel oper.apple.com/iphone/*).

Unfortunately, there is also little in the way of third-party documentation at the time of this writing as to how to communicate with the APNS to send the messages that are then pushed to the phone. However, some off-the-shelf third-party implementations are available. If you intend to implement push notifications in your application, these are probably the best places to start:

AnyEvent::APNS
> Perl wrapper code implementation that acts as a provider allowing you to send push notifications using the APNS. See *http://github.com/typester/anyevent-apns -perl* and *http://search.cpan.org/~typester/AnyEvent-APNS/* for more details.

python-apns-wrapper
> Python wrapper code for the APNS. See *http://code.google.com/p/apns-python -wrapper/* and *http://pypi.python.org/pypi/APNSWrapper/* for more details.

php-apns
> A set of PHP scripts which you must run as services and which allow you to send push notifications using the APNS. See *http://code.google.com/p/php-apns/* for more details.

ruby-apns-daemon
> A daemon written in Ruby that acts as a provider to the APNS. The daemon maintains a persistent connection to the APNS for best performance. See *http://code .google.com/p/ruby-apns-daemon/* for more details.

javaapns and apns-provider
> Two independent Java implementations of the APNS. See *http://code.google.com/ p/javapns/* and *http://code.google.com/p/apns-provider/* for more details.

In-App Purchase

The Store Kit Framework is an in-application payment engine for paid applications allowing you to request payment from your users (e.g., for accessing additional content).

You can also simplify your development by creating a single version of your application that uses In-App Purchase to unlock additional functionality, eliminating the need to create two versions of your application: a paid "pro" version and a free "lite" version. You can distribute your application for free, and then ask users to upgrade using In-App Purchase.

Only digital items may be sold using In-App Purchase, not physical goods or services, and these digital goods must be delivered to the application from which they were purchased (and in addition be available on all devices that the user may own). The framework leverages the App Store to collect payment, even sending the user the familiar App Store receipt email she would normally receive after purchasing.

 Details of the Store Kit Framework and the In-App Purchase service are given in the Apple Store Kit Programming Guide available via the iPhone Dev Center (*http://developer.apple.com/iphone/*).

Core Animation

Built on top of the OpenGL libraries, Core Animation was designed from the ground up to allow developers to build lightweight but graphically rich UIs, and is the framework that underlies both Apple's Front Row application and the now almost ubiquitous Cover Flow effects.

If you want to learn more about the Core Animation framework, I recommend *Core Animation for Mac OS X and the iPhone: Creating Compelling Dynamic User Interfaces* by Bill Dudley (Pragmatic Programmers) and *Core Animation* by Marcus Zarra and Matt Long (Addison-Wesley).

Game Kit

Despite the name, the Game Kit framework is not just for games, as it offers two important technologies to developers: peer-to-peer networking using Bonjour over Bluetooth, and in-application voice chat. Interestingly, the voice chat features included in Game Kit work over any network connection, not just the peer-to-peer Bluetooth connections established by the Game Kit framework.

A good general book on peer-to-peer networking with Bonjour, Apple's name for zero configuration networking, is *Zero Configuration Networking: The Definitive Guide* (*http://oreilly.com/catalog/9780596101008/*) by Daniel Steinberg and Stuart Cheshire (O'Reilly). You can find some good iPhone-specific examples using Game Kit in *iPhone SDK Development* by Bill Dudley and Chris Adamson (Pragmatic Programmers).

Writing Games

Apple has advertised the iPod touch as "the funnest iPod ever" and is pushing it heavily as a game platform competing directly with the Nintendo DS and Sony PSP platforms.

However, writing good games is a lot harder than most people would imagine, and is certainly not within the scope of a book such as this. If you're interested in developing games for the iPhone platform, I recommend you look at *iPhone Game Development* (*http://oreilly.com/catalog/9780596159863/*) by Paul Zirkle and Joe Hogue (O'Reilly).

You'll find that this book is a solid guide to the basics of game development, with good coverage of both graphics and audio topics as well as coverage of in-game physics engines.

Look and Feel

Apple has become almost infamous for its strict adherence to its Human Interface Guidelines. Designed to present users with "a consistent visual and behavioral experience across applications and the operating system," the interface guidelines mean that (most) applications running on the Mac OS X desktop have a consistent look and feel, and behave in the same way. Long-time users of the platform generally view applications that don't adhere to the guidelines with some suspicion, and even novice users sometimes get the feeling that there is something "not quite right" about applications that break them.

Even for developers who are skeptical about whether they really need to strictly adhere to the guidelines, especially when Apple periodically steps outside them, the Human Interface Guidelines have remained a benchmark against which the user experience can be measured.

With the introduction of the iPhone and iPod touch, Apple had to draw up a radically different set of guidelines describing how user interactions should be managed on a platform radically unlike the traditional desktop environment.

I heavily recommend that you read the mobile Human Interface Guidelines carefully, if only because violating them could lead to your application being rejected by the review team during the App Store approval process.

> A copy of the iPhone Human Interface Guidelines is available for download from the App Store Resource Center in the "App Store Approval Process" section at *http://developer.apple.com/iphone/appstore*.

However, if you'd like to read more about how these guidelines are interpreted, and how to design engaging and effective user interfaces, I recommend that you read *Programming the iPhone User Experience*, First Edition (*http://oreilly.com/catalog/9780596155476/*) by Toby Boudreaux (O'Reilly).

Hardware Accessories

If you're interested in using the External Accessory framework to work with third-party hardware, you need to consider becoming a member of the Made for iPod/Works with iPhone Developer Program. Licensed developers gain access to technical documentation, hardware components, and technical support so that they can develop their own hardware and software in parallel. More information about this program is available at *http://developer.apple.com/ipod/*.

However, if the thought of yet another set of NDAs is off-putting, you might want to look at *iPhone Hacks (http://oreilly.com/catalog/9780596516642/)* by David Jurick, Adam Stolarz, and Damien Stolarz (O'Reilly). Among other things, this book discusses the pinout for the dock and headphone jack connectors, allowing you to connect external devices to your iPhone without having to join the Made for iPod/Works with iPhone Program.

Index

We'd like to hear your suggestions for improving our indexes. Send email to *index@oreilly.com*.

application version numbers, 243, 245
applicationDidFinishLaunching: method, 30, 77
applications
    deploying (example), 118
    distribution of (see distributing applications)
    putting on iPhone, 37–40
applications, integrating with device, 295–319
    address book, using, 314–319
    application preferences, 295–305
        accessing global preferences, 305
    custom URL schemes, 305–310
        registering, 306–310
        tel: and sms:, 306
    media playback, 310–314
assign attribute (properties), 44
asterisk (*)
    in regular expressions, 213
    as wildcard in bundle identifiers, 16
asynchronous reachability, 148–149
asynchronous requests for data, 167–168
attaching images to email messages, 165
Attribute Inspector, 33, 172
audio input support, 249, 250
AudioToolbox framework, 275
autorelease pools, 48
autoreleased objects, 48, 49
availability date, 244
availability of device for development, 17–18
availability of network, detecting, 145–150
    asynchronous reachability, 148–149
    synchronous reachability, 147–148
AVAudioSession class, 250
AVAudioSessionDelegate protocol, 251

B

backslash (\) in regular expressions, 213, 215
bandwidth limitations, 246
base URL, specifying, 160
battery monitoring application (example), 108–118
    building interface, 110–111
    wiring in Interface Builder, 117–118
    writing code, 112–116
battery power, determining user location and, 254
becoming a developer, 5–18

enrolling in iPhone Developer Program, 7, 19
installing iPhone SDK, 8–11
joining Apple Developer Connection (ADC), 8
preparing device for, 11–18
registration, 5–6
beginGeneratingDeviceOrientationNotificatio ns method, 232
beginGeneratingPlaybackNotifications: method, 312
beta versions, iPhone SDK, 8
BLOB data type, 219
Bluetooth support (hardware), 249
Bonjour over Bluetooth, 339
Boolean variables, 112
Briefs application, 40
browser, embedding in app, 150–160
    displaying static HTML files, 159–160
Build and Run button (Xcode), 25
building applications, 233–241
    ad hoc distribution, 233–239
    for App Store distribution, 240–241
    developer-to-developer distribution, 240
bundle identifiers, 15
buttons, using for images, 283
buzz (see vibration capability)

C

calling methods, 46
calls, making from applications, 306
camera, 253
    hardware support for, 250
canSendMail: method, 162
Capitalize attribute (text fields), 94
caret (^) in regular expressions, 213
casting, 22
categories, App Store, 243
cellForRowAtIndexPath: method, 60, 63, 74
cellular network bandwidth, 246
cellular support, availability of, 249
certificate-signing requests (CSRs), 234
certificates for development, 11, 12–14, 233
certificates for distribution, 234
City Guide application (see guidebook application)
@class declaration, 69
class methods, 21
    declaring, 46

class variables, 20
classes, 19, 20
    declaring and defining, 28, 41–47
        object typing, 43
        properties, synthesizing, 45
        property declarations, 44
    declaring with interface, 41
    delegate classes (see delegates)
    documentation on, obtaining, 29
    frameworks and libraries, defined, 21
    implementations of, 20, 28, 42
    methods, declaring and calling, 45–47
    singleton classes, 109
    template classes, simplifying, 55–58
    view controller classes (see view controllers)
    Xcode template classes, simplifying, 55–58
Classes group (Xcode), 26
CLLocationManager class, 255, 257, 272
CLLocationManagerDelegate protocol, 255,
    258, 273, 280
Cocoa framework, 335
Cocoa Touch framework, 50
code refactoring, 55
compass (magnetometer), 272–274
    hardware support for, 249
compiling applications in Xcode, 25
connecting outlets, 36–37, 62–65
connection:didFailWithError: method, 189
connectionDidFinishLoading: method, 182,
    209
Connections Inspector, 36, 62
connectivity (see network connectivity)
contact information, 243
controller (in MVC pattern), 51
    for table-view-based applications
        connecting to model, 73–75
        creating, 57, 59
copy attribute (properties), 44
copy: method, 48
copyright issues, 243, 245
Core Animation framework, 339
Core Data framework, 224, 336
Core Location framework, 254–266
    Weather program with (example), 256–
        266
Correction attribute (text fields), 94
creating Xcode projects, 23–24
crippled functionality, 246
CSRs (certificate-signing requests), 234

custom URL schemes, 305–310
    registering, 306–310
    tel: and sms:, 306
customer support URL, 243

D

\d, for numeric characters, 213
\D, for nonnumeric characters, 213
data, 191–224
    data entry, 191–195
        UITextField class, about, 191–193
        UITextView class, about, 193–195
    parsing JSON, 199–213
        example of, 201–213
    parsing XML, 182–183, 195–199
        using libxml2, 196–197
        using NSXMLParser, 197–199
    regular expressions, 213–217
        NSPredicate class for, 216
        RegexKitLite library, 214–216
    retrieving from Internet, 166–189
        asynchronous requests, 167–168
        Google Weather Service, 168–170
        synchronous requests, 166–167
        web services, 168–189
    storing, 217–224
        Core Data framework, 224, 336
        in flat files, 217–218
        in SQL databases, 218–224
data persistence, 220–224
data sources, 52
databases, adding to projects, 219–220
DataSource pattern, 52
DataSource protocol, 52
dealloc: method, 50
debugging with NSLog(), 34
declaring classes, 28
    with interface, 41
declaring methods, 45
declaring properties, 44
defining classes with implementation, 20, 42
degree latitude, in miles, 282
degree longitude, in miles, 282
delegates, 21, 23, 52
deleteRowsAtIndexPaths:withRowAnimation:
    method, 89
demo account information, 243
deploying applications (example), 118

Enterprise iPhone Developer Program, 5
error handling with JSON parsing, 211
escaping characters (regular expressions), 213,
    215
event-based parsing, 182
    (see also parsing data)
event loops, 21
events, 21
existing functionality, duplication of, 245
exposure through App Store, 4
External Accessory framework, 341

F
fetchContent: method, 183
files, writing and reading (see storing data)
FindNearbyPlace class, 263
first impressions, 170
first responders, 141
    data entry, 191, 193
FirstViewController class, 120
flat files, 217–218
flipside view (see utility applications)
FlipsideView.xib file (utility applications), 111,
    260
frameworks, 21
Frameworks group (Xcode), 26
free apps with crippled functionality, 246
freeze-dried (see serialization)

G
game development, 339
Game Kit framework, 339
garbage collection, 22
geolocation, 277–293
    (see also user location)
    annotating maps, 285–293
    Where Am I? application, 277–285
GeoNames reverse geocoding service, 256
get-task-allow property, 237
getter attribute (properties), 44
getters (see accessor methods)
global device preferences, 305
global find and replace, 127
Google Weather Service, 168–170
    location-specific (example), 256–266
GPS hardware support, 250
Graham, Paul, 3
graphics belonging to Apple, 245

greedy, regular expressions as, 213
guidebook application (example), 55
    (see also table-view-based applications)
    Add New City interface, 93–100
        Save button, 100–105
    adding city view, 79–85
    adding database to, 219–220
    adding image picker to, 133–143
    adding navigation controls, 75–77
    building model for, 65–71
    connecting controller to model, 73–75
    creating table view for, 58–65
        connecting outlets, 62–65
        organizing and navigating code, 61
    edit mode, 85–105
        adding city entries, 90
        deleting city entries, 89
    as modal view, 126–132

H
handlerMethod: method, 233
hardware, 249–275
    accelerometer, 266–270
    ambient light sensor, 274
    camera, 253
    Core Location framework, 254–266
        example, 256–266
    determining available support for, 249–251
    digital compass (magnetometer), 272–274
    integration with (see integrating application
        with device)
    proximity sensor, 274–275
    setting required capabilities, 251–252
    vibration capability, 275
hardware accessories, 341
heightForRowAtIndexPath: method, 98
help on classes and methods, getting, 29
HIG (see Human Interface Guidelines)
home screen icon (see icons, for applications)
HTML files, displaying, 159
Human Interface Guidelines (HIG), 245, 340

I
IBOutlet, declaring properties as, 44
Icon-Settings.png file, 297
icons
    for applications, 225–227, 245
    Refresh button (example), 173

J

javaapns implementation, 338
JSON, parsing, 199–213
  regular expressions for, 213–217
    NSPredicate class for, 216
    RegexKitLite library, 214–216
  with Twitter search services (example), 201–213
json-framework library, 199
  with Twitter search service, 201–213

K

kCLErrorDenied error, 256
kCLErrorLocationUnknown error, 255
kCLHeadingFilterNone value, 273
keyboard type, 246
keychain, installing development certificates in, 12–14
Keychain Access application, 12, 234
keywords, application, 243
kReachabilityChangedNotification event, 148
kUTTypeMovie media type, 250

L

landscape mode (see rotation of application, enabling)
latitude, detecting (see Core Location framework; geolocation)
latitude degree, in miles, 282
launch images, 227–231
libicucore.dylib library, 214
libraries, 21
Library folder, 17
Library window, 33
libxml2 library, 182
  parsing XML with, 196–197
license, developer, 6
life cycle, iPhone application, 27
light sensor, 274
linear acceleration (see accelerometer)
lite apps with crippled functionality, 246
loadingActivityIndicator property, 261
loadView: method, 52
localization of application, 244
location of device (see geolocation; user location)
location services, disabled, 273
locationManager property, 280
locationManager:didUpdateToLocation:fromLocation: method, 281, 284, 304
locationManagerShouldDisplayHeadingCalibration: method, 273
longitude, detecting (see Core Location framework; geolocation)
longitude degree, in miles, 282
look-and-feel requirements, 340

M

magnetometer (digital compass), 272–274
  hardware support for, 249
mail (see email, sending)
mailComposeController:didFinishWithResult:error: method, 163
main() function, 27
main event loop, 21, 27
main.m file, 26
  creating autorelease pool, 48
MainView.xib file (utility applications), 110
MainWindow.xib file (tab bar applications), 119
making phone calls from applications, 306
MapKit framework, 256, 277–293
  annotating maps, 285–293
  defining user location, 277–285
mapping (see MapKit framework)
maps, annotating, 285–293
MapViewController class, 288, 289
marketing, 4
media playback, 310–314
Media Player framework, 310
media types for video capture, 253
memory management, 22, 47–50
  alloc-retain-copy-release cycle, 48
  object creation, 47
  responding to memory warnings, 50
messages, 21, 30
  calling methods with, 46
MessageUI.framework framework, 161
messaging, from application, 306
methods, 20
  accessor methods, 20
    customizing, 44
  calling, 46
  class (static) methods, 21
  declaring, 45
  documentation on, obtaining, 29
MFMailComposeResult constant, 163

MFMailComposeViewController class, 161–165

attaching images to messages, 165

MFMailComposeViewControllerDelegate protocol, 162

miles, longitude and latitude in, 282

minimal user functionality, 247

minus sign (-) in method declarations, 46

MKAnnotation protocol, 290

mobile provisioning profiles, 11, 16–17, 233

modal view controllers, 125–132

model (in MVC pattern), 51

for table-view-based applications

connecting controller to, 73–75

creating, 65–71

Model-View-Controller (MVC) pattern, 23, 50, 51

Mono framework, 326

MonoDevelop environment, 326

MonoTouch platform, 325–334

movement, device (see accelerometer; digital compass)

MPMediaItem class, 314

MPMediaItemCollection class, 310

MPMediaItemPropertyArtwork key, 314

MPMediaItemPropertyTitle key, 314

MPMediaPickerController class, 310, 311, 312

MPMediaPickerControllerDelegate protocol, 310

MPMusicPlayerController class, 310, 311, 312

multiline text entry (see UITextView class)

multivalue properties, 318

MVC (see Model-View-Controller pattern)

N

names

for applications, 231, 242

for methods, 46

for provisioning profiles, 16

for Xcode template classes, 55

namespace collision, 56

native development platforms

iPhone SDK (see iPhone SDK)

MonoTouch platform, 325–334

PhoneGap platform, 321–325

native vs. web applications, 336

navigation bar, 132

(see also UINavigationBar class)

navigation bar button items, 132

navigation controls, in table-view-based applications, 75–77

network connectivity, 145–189

bandwidth limitations, 246

Bonjour over Bluetooth, 339

detecting network status, 145–150

asynchronous reachability, 148–149

reachability checks, 189, 246

synchronous reachability, 147–148

embedding browser in app, 150–160

displaying static HTML files, 159–160

hardware support for, 249

retrieving data from Internet, 166–189

asynchronous requests, 167–168

populating UI with parsed data, 187–188

synchronous requests, 166–167

web services, 168–189

as XML (see XML, parsing)

sending email, 161–165

attaching images to messages, 165

network performance, 3

NetworkMonitor project (example), 147

new projects, creating, 23–24

NIB files, 31, 32

(see also .xib files)

nibBundle property, 52

nibName property, 52

nil object, calling methods on, 47

nonatomic attribute (properties), 44

NSDictionary class, 209

NSFileManager class, 217

NSIndexPath class, 82

NSLog() function, 34

NSMutableData objects, 168

NSMutableString class, 67

NSNotificationCenter class, 232, 313

NSObject subclasses, creating, 65

NSPredicate class, 9, 216

NSString vs. NSMutableString class, 67

NSTemporaryDirectory method, 218

NSUrlConnection class, 166–189

asynchronous requests, 167–168

synchronous requests, 166–167

web services, 168–189

Google Weather Service, 168–170

parsing XML (see XML, parsing)

UIRequiredDeviceCapabilities key, 252
UISwitch class, 112
    wiring toggle switch in Interface Builder, 117
UITableView applications, 55–105
    adding navigation controls, 75–77
    building model for, 65–71
    creating table view, 58–65
    UITableViewController edit mode, 85–105
    view controller, connecting to model, 73–75
    view controller, creating, 79–85
UITableView class, improper handling of, 246
UITableViewCell class
    allowing metadata input, 93–100
    saving data input, 100–105
UITableViewCellEditingStyleDelete class, 87
UITableViewCellEditingStyleInsert class, 88
UITableViewCellSelectionStyleNone class, 92
UITableViewController edit mode, 85–105
    adding table view cells, 90
    deleting table view cells, 89
UITableViewDataSource protocol, 59
UITableViewDelegate protocol, 59, 60, 208
UITextField class, 94, 191–193
    as first responder, 141
UITextFieldDelegate protocol, 192
UITextView class, 191, 193–195
    dismissing UITextView, 193
    as first responder, 141
    resizing view, 84
UITextViewDelegate protocol, 193
UIView class, Tag attribute, 95
UIViewController class, 20
    viewDidLoad: method, 73
UIWebView class, 150–160
    displaying static HTML files, 159–160
    getting data out of, 160
UIWebViewDelegate protocol, 156
unique device identifier (see UDID of device, getting)
University iPhone Developer Program, 7
updateView: method, using with parsed data, 187
URLs
    for application and support, 243
    custom schemes for, 305–310
        registering, 306–310
        tel: and sms:, 306

    loading inside application (see UIWebView class)
Use for Development option (Organizer window), 17
User Interaction Enabled box, 283
user interface
    enabling rotation, 232–233
    entering data, 191–195
    Human Interface Guidelines (HIG), 245
    importance of (to users), 170
    look-and-feel guidelines, 340
user location
    annotating maps, 285–293
    compass (see digital compass)
    Core Location framework for (see Core Location framework)
    MapKit framework for (see MapKit framework)
    Where Am I? application, 277–285
utility applications, 107–118
    using web services (example), 170–189

V

variables, 20
    casting (see casting)
version numbers, 243, 245
vibration capability, 250, 275
video capture, 250, 253
video selection (see image picker view controllers)
view controllers, 27, 30–31, 51
    class name for, changing, 57
    edit mode, 85–105
        adding table view cells, 90
        deleting table view cells, 89
    FirstViewController class, 120
    image pickers, 133–143
    loadView: method, 52
    modal, 125–132
    navigation (see navigation controllers)
    in table-view-based applications
        adding, 79–85
        connecting to model, 73–75
    for tables (see table views)
view property (view controller), 52
viewDidLoad: method, 73, 83, 100
    utility applications, 114
views, 51
    main and flipside (see utility applications)

W

Y

X

About the Author

Alasdair Allan is a senior research fellow in astronomy at the University of Exeter. As part of his work there, he is building a distributed peer-to-peer network of telescopes that, acting autonomously, will reactively schedule observations of time-critical events. On the side, Alasdair runs a small technology consulting business writing bespoke software and building open hardware, and he is currently developing a series of iPhone applications to monitor and manage cloud-based services and distributed sensor networks.

Colophon

The animal on the cover of *Learning iPhone Programming* is a lapwing (*Vanellus vanellus*), also known as a northern lapwing, a peewit, or a green plover. This wading bird is 11–13 inches long with a 26–28 inch wingspan, a black crest, and rounded wings. Although its plumage is predominantly black and white, the upperparts are metallic green or bronze. The name *lapwing* may refer to the sound its wings make in flight, to its erratic flight pattern, or to its practice of pretending to have a broken wing in order to fool predators. The name *peewit* mimics the sound of its call. One of the lapwing's unique habits is the tumbling flight performed by the male during breeding season: it flies up, wheels, darts down, and climbs again, all while making its shrill cry.

The lapwing is common throughout the United Kingdom, Europe, and Asia, and occasionally makes its way to Alaska and Canada. It has an extensive range and may winter as far south as Africa, India, and China. The lapwing migrates in large flocks, which can be found on farmland, pastures, and wetlands searching for worms and insects.

Lapwing populations have declined since the 1980s, as the species has been affected by intensive agricultural practices, increases in grazing density, and climate change. It is now protected in the European Union, although parts of the Netherlands still enjoy the traditional hunt for the first lapwing egg of the year, thought to be a herald of spring. This hunt is allowed only from March 1 to April 9, and the actual collection of eggs is prohibited by law.

The cover image is from *The Riverside Natural History*. The cover font is Adobe ITC Garamond. The text font is Linotype Birka; the heading font is Adobe Myriad Condensed; and the code font is LucasFont's TheSansMonoCondensed.

Related Titles from O'Reilly

Macintosh

AppleScript: The Definitive Guide, *2nd Edition*
AppleScript: The Missing Manual
Appleworks 6: The Missing Manual
The Best of the Joy of Tech
FileMaker Pro 8: The Missing Manual
FileMaker Pro 9: The Missing Manual
GarageBand 2: The Missing Manual
iBook Fan Book
iMovie 6 & iDVD: The Missing Manual
iPhone Forensics
iPhone Hacks
iPhone: The Missing Manual, *3rd Edition*
iPhoto '08: The Missing Manual
iPod: The Missing Manual, *8th Edition*
iWork '09: The Missing Manual
Mac Annoyances
Mac OS X Tiger Pocket Guide
Mac OS X Leopard Pocket Guide
Mac OS X Snow Leopard Pocket Guide
Mac OS X: The Missing Manual, *Tiger Edition*
Mac OS X Leopard: The Missing Manual
Mac OS X Power Hound, *2nd Edition*
Mac OS X Snow Leopard: The Missing Manual

Mac OS X Unwired
Modding Mac OS X
Office 2008 for the Macintosh: The Missing Manual
Revolution in The Valley
Switching to the Mac: The Missing Manual,
  Snow Leopard Edition

Mac Developers

Building Cocoa Applications: A Step-By-Step Guide
Cocoa in a Nutshell
Essential Mac OS X Panther Server Administration
Learning Carbon
Learning Cocoa with Objective-C, *2nd Edition*
Learning Unix for Mac OS X Tiger
Mac OS X for Java Geeks
Mac OS X for Unix Geeks, *4th Edition*
Mac OS X Panther Hacks
Mac OS X Tiger in a Nutshell
Objective-C Pocket Reference
Running Mac OS X Tiger

Our books are available at most retail and online bookstores.
To order direct: 1-800-998-9938 • *order@oreilly.com* • *www.oreilly.com*
Online editions of most O'Reilly titles are available by subscription at *safari.oreilly.com*